32.

Urban Management

URBAN STUDIES INFORMATION GUIDE SERIES

Series Editor: Thomas P. Murphy, Director, Institute for Urban Studies at the University of Maryland, College Park (on leave) and Director of the Federal Executive Institute, Charlottesville, Virginia

Also in this series:

SUBURBIA—*Edited by Joseph Zikmund II and Deborah Ellis Dennis*

URBAN COMMUNITY—*Edited by Anthony J. Filipovitch and Earl J. Reeves*

URBAN DECISION MAKING: THE BASIS FOR ANALYSIS—*Edited by Mark Drucker**

URBAN EDUCATION—*Edited by George E. Spear and Donald W. Mocker*

URBAN FISCAL POLICY AND ADMINISTRATION—*Edited by John L. Mikesell and Jerry L. McCaffery**

URBAN HOUSING: PUBLIC AND PRIVATE—*Edited by John E. Rouse, Jr.*

URBAN INDICATORS—*Edited by Thomas P. Murphy**

URBAN LAW—*Edited by Thomas P. Murphy**

URBAN PLANNING—*Edited by Ernest R. Alexander, Anthony J. Catanese, and David S. Sawicki*

URBAN POLICY—*Edited by Dennis J. Palumbo and George Taylor*

URBAN POLITICS—*Edited by Thomas P. Murphy*

WOMEN AND URBAN SOCIETY—*Edited by Hasia R. Diner*

*in preparation

The above series is part of the
GALE INFORMATION GUIDE LIBRARY

The Library consists of a number of separate series of guides covering major areas in the social sciences, humanities, and current affairs.

General Editor: Paul Wasserman, Professor and former Dean, School of Library and Information Services, University of Maryland

Managing Editor: Denise Allard Adzigian, Gale Research Company

Urban Management

A GUIDE TO INFORMATION SOURCES

Volume 8 in the Urban Studies Information Guide Series

Bernard H. Ross

Professor of Government and Public Administration

and

Director, Urban Affairs Program

American University
Washington, D.C.

Gale Research Company
Book Tower, Detroit, Michigan 48226

Library of Congress Cataloging in Publication Data

Ross, Bernard H   1934-
    Urban management : a guide to information sources.

    (Urban studies information guide series ; v. 8)
    Includes bibliographies and index.
    1. Municipal government—United States—Bibliography.
2. Metropolitan government—United States—Bibliography.
I. Title. II. Series.
Z7164.L8R67 [JS356]   016.352'008'0973   78-10310
ISBN 0-8103-1430-4

For Marlene who is not always right,
but who is never wrong

VITA

Bernard H. Ross earned a B.S. in economics from the Wharton School, University of Pennsylvania and an M.A. and Ph.D. in government from New York University. He is currently a professor of government and public administration and director of the Urban Affairs Program at The American University. From September 1974-76 he was the director of the University's Center for Local and State Government which developed and administered training and research programs. In 1977, Ross was named codirector of the Center for Urban Public Policy Analysis at the university. The Center serves as a link between the U.S. Department of Housing and Urban Development and the urban affairs academic community.

Ross has written extensively on urban politics and metropolitan problems, with particular emphasis on the governance of Washington, D.C. Recent publications include: "Washington" with Royce Hanson in HOW FEDERAL CAPITALS ARE GOVERNED, edited by Don Rowat (Toronto: University of Toronto Press). In 1973 he published a monograph entitled UNIVERSITY-CITY RELATIONS: FROM COEXISTENCE TO COOPERATION (Washington, D.C.: American Association of Higher Education). He is coauthor of "The Urban Involvement of Higher Education: An Analysis of Selected Trends and Issues," JOURNAL OF HIGHER EDUCATION (July-August 1975), and "Curriculum Reform and Organizational Culture: Public Administration at The American University," URBAN ANALYSIS, 1976.

CONTENTS

Contents

PREFACE

This volume on urban management is a systematic guide to the prominent literature in this field. The literature search covers the period from 1965–76 with
particular emphasis on the 1970–76 period. Any author who undertakes to com-
pile an annotated bibliography of this size must use discretion concerning the
literature selected. The citations chosen for this volume have been based upon
their relevance to the field of urban affairs and their treatment of some aspect
of urban management. Many functional areas have been omitted because they
are the subject of other volumes in the series. The functional area citations
in this book have been included only because they deal directly with management issues.

Most of the articles cited are from scholarly journals or periodicals published
by national associations. Reports, studies, and monographs important to the
field have been included only when there is a high probability the reader can
locate these documents. All books cited are published by national companies
and are available in most college libraries. Readers and textbooks also have
been excluded. Doctoral dissertations, papers delivered at professional meetings,
and intrauniversity publications have been intentionally omitted.

Four students at the American University provided research and editorial assis-
tance in the preparation of this volume. Dan Logan, David Nieto, Marc
Shugoll, and Howard Stone labored long hours on different parts of the book.
I hope they view their time spent as a valuable learning experience.

Lee Fritschler, dean of the School of Government and Public Administration at
The American University, relieved me of several administrative responsibilities
so I could devote my time to the book. Thomas Murphy, the series editor,
assisted in the development of the working outline for the volume and performed
other editorial functions which greatly aided in the development of this volume.
The manuscript was expertly typed by Mary Kay Almy.

My wife Marlene, to whom the book is dedicated, assisted in the development
of the final outline for the volume. Her most heroic efforts, however, included

the management task of convincing our three children that, if Daddy had to work, it was certainly better to have him work at home than in the office. Ultimately, their desire for better performance ratings resulted in my being able to complete my task.

Bernard H. Ross
Kensington, Maryland

INTRODUCTION

In recent years, cost-cutting efforts, employee layoffs, increased taxes, higher bond rates, and service cutbacks have brought the field of urban management to the attention of Americans from the President of the United States to the welfare recipient in the ghetto. The financial crisis in New York City and the potential revenue shortfalls in other large American cities have dramatized the need for experienced and competent urban managers.

In the past, we have tended to view large urban areas as parents occasionally view adolescent children--disobedient, but lovable, and essential parts of the family. Past remedies have included huge infusions of federal and state funds and reorganization of local governments so they would be better able to perform their primary function: providing services to their residents. These efforts, while not viewed as total failures, are being examined with renewed skepticism. More and more people are coming to believe that the most important ingredient in local government may not be either money or organizational structure, but rather the managerial competence of the elected and appointed officials. In short, improving the tools and techniques of urban managers in the long run may have the greatest impact on alleviating urban problems.

The tasks performed by urban managers number in the hundreds, but at a minimum they include the following: assessing needs, establishing priorities, allocating resources, involving citizens, staffing agencies, delivering services, evaluating programs, and interacting with officials from other levels of government. Many of these management functions, such as personnel actions, environmental protection, and budgeting, are routine and mandated by laws. However, management tasks increasingly are becoming unplanned, hurried, and reactive, particularly in the area of bureaucracy-client relations. As public officials move further away from their routine functions and begin to interact more with citizens, they find few rules and regulations to guide them. These tasks require long and careful deliberations which often result in stalemates, legal controversies, and occasionally in open conflict.

Added to these concerns of the urban manager are the twin pressures of time and information which differentiate his/her job from that of state, county, and federal officials. The accelerated pace of urban life places increasing pressure on decision makers to not only act quickly but also wisely. These decision makers are placed in a difficult situation because they have neither the quantity nor the quality of information they need to respond in the allotted time. Techniques to improve productivity, data processing, communication channels, information systems, and records management are only beginning to be used extensively in local government. The inability of managers to obtain accurate and complete information and have it readily accessible slows down the decision-making process and often exacerbates urban problems.

The increased amount of federal aid and technical assistance going to local governments has also had negative impacts. As this aid increased, so too did the regulations and guidelines which hampered the flexibility of the recipient governments and markedly reduced their decision-making authority as well as their ability to respond to constituent needs.

The introduction of general revenue sharing and the increase in block grants in several functional areas have given added administrative and political authority to local government officials. However, these programs have created problems of their own. Some local officials have traditionally used federal and state grant-in-aid monies to launch programs knowing that if they failed to meet their objectives, the federal government could be blamed for restrictive regulations and guidelines. Furthermore, many local administrators and elected officials reason (and probably accurately) that citizens will hold them less accountable for program deficiencies if the funding source is the state or federal government rather than locally collected taxes. Federal funding assistance (and regulations) have, at times, increased the dependency of urban managers on federal programs to the point where it has stifled some of their initiative.

The proliferation of the grant-in-aid system has also clouded many of the relationships in the intergovernmental system. As the three levels of government have begun to interact more frequently, it has become increasingly difficult to determine where managerial accountability resides. The funding, technical assistance, and administrative processes have become so intertwined that plural accountability now best describes the system.

Not everything that goes wrong in urban areas today can be traced to poor management. In addition to inadequate funds for running cities and badly conceived programs, politics is another issue which impacts heavily upon urban management. How many of the problems facing urban areas today are the result of bad management or merely the result of the interaction of political forces is impossible to say. Observers of large urban areas have concluded that many urban problems result from bad politics as often as from bad management. A good program may be difficult to implement in any large, complex urban environment. A bad program created through political expediency can be impossible to implement. The continuous interrelationship of politics and management precludes the possibility of separating the two for accountability purposes.

The problems confronting urban managers are serious and complex. The more we learn from research published in this area, the greater the management problems appear. Still, it is virtually impossible to define a body of literature or a select group of journals which adequately cover the field of urban management.

Much is published in the field of urban affairs, but only a fraction pertains to urban management and this is often case study material. There is a great deal published on the subject of management, a small percentage of which relates to the urban area. There are also many journals in functional areas—housing, health, and law enforcement—which publish articles examining urban management problems and issues from a departmental focus. In short, to adequately cover the field one has to read an enormous amount of literature produced by a diverse array of organizations, associations, institutes, centers, publishers, universities, and government agencies.

This volume, divided into nine chapters, is designed to make the task of understanding urban management a little less chaotic and a little more systematic. Chapter 1 focuses on the conceptual approaches, examining the literature in management and organization theory and organization development.

Chapter 2 looks at administrative leadership including general administrative literature and that dealing with mayors and city managers.

Chapters 3 and 4 concentrate on strategies and techniques used by urban managers. Subject areas reviewed are evaluation data and information systems, productivity, unions and labor-management relations, personnel issues, and recent innovative efforts such as MBO and PPBS.

Chapter 5 examines some of the major writings on forms of urban decentralization. Increased efforts by urban managers to develop new approaches to urban problem solving have led to a great deal of literature, much of which is reviewed in this chapter. After presenting works on both the theoretical and the structural alternatives available to urban managers, the literature on citizen participation, community organization, and neighborhood government is reviewed from a management perspective.

As local government is called upon to provide more services to citizens, the role of the bureaucracy becomes more important. Chapter 6 looks at the literature on service delivery systems and agency-client relations. Several specific services not covered by other volumes in the series are reviewed here.

Chapter 7, concerning budgeting and financial management, focuses on the management rather than the political or fiscal aspects of the subject.

Chapters 8 and 9 are linked by their common concern for the external factors

Introduction

that impact upon cities and the people who try to govern them. Chapter 8 looks at the intergovernmental system in a vertical sense as it impacts upon urban managers. Chapter 9 views the problems of urban management from a metropolitan perspective, with special emphasis on the organization and services of the metropolitan governance mechanism.

From a review of the literature, it is apparent that urban managers react to situations and problems as opposed to controlling or at least directing their agencies, bureaus, organizations, or cities. The citations in this volume clearly delineate the problems confronting urban managers today: lack of funds, limited access to technological advances, short lead times, proximity to clients, poor communication links with many parts of the city, limited and occasionally misleading information, heterogeneous populations, and increasing demands for service.

Given these obstacles, it is amazing that American cities have survived. How much longer urban managers can continue to administer our cities under these conditions is not known. But, without some major changes in our outlook and commitment towards cities, more effective management is a goal not to be achieved in the immediate future.

LIST OF ABBREVIATIONS

CDC	Community Development Corporation
CPL	Council of Planning Librarians
ICMA	International City Management Association
MAPS	Multivariate analysis, participation, and structure
MBO	Management-by-objective
MIS	Management Information System(s)
NTL	National Training Laboratory
OD	Organization Development
OEO	Office of Economic Opportunity
PERT	Program evaluation and review technique
PPBS	Planning-programming-budgeting system(s)
SDS	Students for a Democratic Society
SMSA	Standard metropolitan statistical area(s)
USAC	Urban Information Systems Inter-agency Committee

Chapter 1

CONCEPTUAL APPROACHES

A. MANAGEMENT AND ORGANIZATION THEORY

Brown, F. Gerald. "Management Styles and Working With People." In DE-VELOPING THE MUNICIPAL ORGANIZATION, edited by Stanley Powers, F. Gerald Brown, and David S. Arnold, pp. 69-83. Washington, D.C.: International City Management Association, 1974.

Knowledge of management style is one of a supervisor's greatest assets in dealing with people within the organization. Management styles can be characterized by the degree of active involvement in four areas affecting the achievement of work objectives: initiation of or concern for tasks, concern for people, concern for interfaces, and concern for things. Using a diagram, the author discusses a typology of management styles which includes strategic planner, taskmaster, good shepherd, and ambassador. The ideal would be a manager who could bring these styles together. Several managerial styles are discussed including the managerial grid, the tridimensional grid, and a leadership scale. The author also stresses the ability of managers to listen, to interview, and to solve problems.

_____. "The Municipal Organization as a System." In DEVELOPING THE MUNICIPAL ORGANIZATION, edited by Stanley Powers, F. Gerald Brown, and David S. Arnold, pp. 51-64. Washington, D.C.: International City Management Association, 1974.

The author views local government as a system which receives inputs, produces services aimed at achieving goals, and receives feedback on how well the services are meeting the stated goals. Goals of local government are often defined by the input of citizens suggesting all line departments of government should develop special working re-lationships with their client groups. Another component of the system is developing the technology to provide the services and understanding the available alternative technologies. Coupled with the technological process is the social process of the organization. Between these two components lies the task of defining the jobs to be done. The communications process not only links the components

1

together but is the essence of most work. A discussion is also presented on employee objectives, change, and the role of administrators and supervisors.

Carroll, James D. "Service, Knowledge, and Choice: The Future as Post-Industrial Administration." PUBLIC ADMINISTRATION REVIEW 35 (November-December 1975): 578-81.

Three major characteristics will highlight postindustrial administration--service, knowledge, and choice. The future will see fewer people producing and regulating products and programs and more people providing services to one another in fields such as health, education, public safety, and other social services. Knowledge is becoming increasingly important in the definition of values and in the design, development, and implementation of programs and organizations. The choice characteristic reflects the growing demand for access to public bureaucracy by citizens and the need for greater knowledge parity between experts and the public.

Coleman, Charles, and Rich, Joseph. "Line, Staff and the Systems Perspective." HUMAN RESOURCE MANAGEMENT 12 (Fall 1973): 20-27.

Traditional organizational theory has always espoused the concept that line officers possess command authority in core areas of the organization and that staff officers provide them with specialized assistance. The line-staff concept has led to many areas of conflict which have produced a number of prescriptions for altering line-staff relationships. This article examines and evaluates the traditional ideas on line-staff relations and uses systems theory to suggest new directions for dealing with this problem.

Drucker, Peter F. MANAGEMENT: TASKS, RESPONSIBILITIES AND PRACTICES. New York: Harper and Row, 1973. 839 p.

This is a comprehensive study of management as an organized body of knowledge. Asserting that we have become a society of institutions, the author believes management is applicable in all avenues of public and private life. Making our institutions perform responsibly, autonomously, and at a high level of achievement is our guarantee of improving our quality of life and safeguarding the future. The book tries to prepare managers for their tasks and responsibilities. It is divided into three main sections: the tasks, the manager, and top management. The tasks concentrate on the dimensions of management, productive work, and social impacts and responsibilities. The section on the manager examines managerial skills and organization and the manager's work and jobs. The section on top management focuses on tasks, organization, and strategics.

_____. "On Managing the Public Service Institution." PUBLIC INTEREST

33 (Fall 1973): 43-60.

> Public service institutions are growing at a rapid rate and citizens
> in all developed countries are dependent upon them for the delivery
> of services. These institutions are now under attack for a lack of
> performance and have begun to emulate business organizations in
> order to improve their management capabilities. The author dis-
> counts the popular myths of inadequate performance being caused
> by a lack of good managers, intangible objectives, and nonbusiness-
> oriented managers. Several illustrations of successful public service
> institutions are presented including public monopolies, American
> universities, schools, and hospitals. The requirements for success
> of the institution are: clear objectives and goals, priorities, mea-
> surement of performance, feedback, and an audit of objectives and
> results. The key to success is more likely to be a good system
> rather than good managers.

Dvorin, Eugene P., and Simmons, Robert H. FROM AMORAL TO HUMANE
BUREAUCRACY. San Francisco: Canfield Press, 1972. 88 p.

> The approach of this book is radical-humanistic. The authors argue
> that bureaucracy has traditionally ignored the dignity of individuals
> and has failed to respond to the needs of the people. Administra-
> tive responsibility based on the premise of impeding administrative
> power by competing centers of power is outmoded. Bureaucracy is
> too immersed in the concepts of efficiency, survival, and neutrality
> to genuinely and forcefully promote the public interest. Bureaucrats
> have enormous power at their disposal but they have failed to accept
> the humanistic responsibilities that go with this power because they
> have placed a higher value on efficiency than on human dignity.

Dworak, Robert J. "Economizing in Public Organizations." PUBLIC ADMINIS-
TRATION REVIEW 35 (March-April 1975): 158-65.

> Economizing in public organizations is desired by many, but de-
> fining the concept and determining how economizing can be imple-
> mented are difficult problems. Most public officials stress the
> values of efficiency, effectiveness, and economy as part of their
> administration, but rarely achieve them. The author suggests that
> economizing is a way of maximizing the three values by developing
> a decision process which allows public officials to select the alter-
> native which best mixes these values. Four alternative mechanisms
> are presented: flexibility, delegation of authority, cost assignment
> techniques, and task acquisition systems. Three organizational
> forms are presented which have the potential for implementing the
> alternative systems: true revolving funds, project management
> systems, and decentralized decision making.

Dynes, Russell R. "Organizational Involvement and Changes in Community
Structure in Disaster." AMERICAN BEHAVIORAL SCIENTIST 13 (January-

February 1970): 430–39.

> Every community is composed of organizations, public and private, which maintain the ongoing activities in community life. Once a disaster strikes, the nature, scope, and tasks of organizational involvement become unclear or are unknown. Organizations begin to allocate resources to visible problems and to mobilize other resources, such as additional manpower. The major activities can be conceptualized as creating task subsystems, coordinating task subsystems, and mobilizing manpower, economic resources, and loyalties. Since many of these activities require individuals to work together for the first time, preplanning is essential.

Fitch, Lyle C. "Governing Megacentropolis: The People." PUBLIC ADMINISTRATION REVIEW 30 (September–October 1970): 481–88.

> The author analyzes urban government by focusing on the people who inhabit the central city. He presents a demographic picture and discusses income and jobs, and the impact each has on local government. The changing nature of urban populations has produced large numbers of unskilled workers who require more and better public services. Local governments which had been expanding their social service delivery systems in health, welfare, housing, and education found they could not keep up with the rising costs of these services. The author believes cities will continue to be a major component of our society, but is pessimistic about the increasing demands being placed upon cities and their apparent inability to meet them.

Forrester, Jay W. "Urban Goals and National Objectives." STUDIES IN COMPARATIVE LOCAL GOVERNMENT 6 (September 1972): 18–26.

> Two assumptions underlie this article: We should try to improve the conditions in cities, and improvement can be accomplished through technology to relieve the pressures and strains of urban life. Each of the urban symptoms is caused from within, the environment of the city influences migration to and from the city, and cities exist within a fixed environment where necessities are limited. There are no utopian cities which can be copied, only alternatives which include reexamination of present goals, values, and morality.

Frederickson, H. George. RECOVERY OF STRUCTURE IN PUBLIC ADMINISTRATION. Center for Governmental Studies, Pamphlet no. 5. Washington, D.C., November 1970. 17 p. Paperbound.

> The author begins with a brief review of the evolution of organizations and the way we view them. Recently we have begun to experiment with new techniques to try and improve the effectiveness of organizations. This has occurred for three reasons: first, organization theorists now seek to induce change, not merely study

organizations; second, the hierarchical model no longer seems capable of dealing with our complex society; and third, organizations have become isolated and indifferent to their clients.

In an effort to make organizations more responsive to clients, the author discusses five structural models: the administrative decentralization model, the neighborhood control model, the matrix model, the federated model, and the bargaining model. Many of the models have been implemented with varying degrees of success and are often used at the same time by local administrators. The author suggests that public administrators view organizational structure as being dynamic rather than static, thus accommodating the major problems of client responsiveness and societal complexity.

Grundstein, Nathan D. "The Quality of Urban Management." In THE QUALITY OF URBAN LIFE, edited by Henry J. Schmandt and Warner Bloomberg, Jr., pp. 395-419. Beverly Hills, Calif.: Sage Publications, 1969.

This article attempts to link the urban environment to urban management and discusses how the former creates certain problems for the latter. These problems are indications of the quality of the urban environment as urban management confronts it. The author develops criteria for the quality of urban management and tests its relevance by an equilibrium model developed in a study of New York City. Three possibilities exist: zero capability, negative capability, and a positive capability. At one time, urban management was capable of existing without urban planning. The author discusses some of the forces which have linked these two functions in contemporary urban America. Two other factors which have become coupled to urban management are general management and program operations. The former focuses on the internal environment and the latter on the external environment.

Harmon, Michael Mont. "Administrative Policy Formulation and the Public Interest." PUBLIC ADMINISTRATION REVIEW 29 (September-October 1969): 483-91.

This article seeks to redefine the concept of public interest and to relate this to the role of administrators in formulating public policy. The author reviews several dimensions of public interest theory, including unitary versus individualistic, prescriptive versus descriptive, substantive versus procedural, and static versus dynamic, and concludes with a redefinition favoring individualistic, descriptive, procedural, and dynamic. In relating the public interest to the techniques used by administrators in the policy arena, a typology of administrative styles is presented which is similar to the two-dimensional grid of Blake and Mouton. Administrative styles discussed are survival, prescriptive, rationalist, reactive, and proactive. While no hard conclusions are drawn about the public interest and administrative style, the proactive administration appears best able to function in the public interest.

Hart, David K. "Social Equity, Justice and the Equitable Administrator."
PUBLIC ADMINISTRATION REVIEW 34 (January–February 1974): 3–11.

Public officials are being urged to use social equity as a guideline
in the administration of programs and in the delivery of services.
Proponents of the social equity cause have to define it precisely
so ambiguity and disagreement do not become its major characteristics. The author suggests that the theory of justice developed
by John Rawls can become the ethical foundation for a theory of
social equity. The two major principles of the theory of justice
are reviewed with relation to altruism and the basic nature of
organizations in society. The article concludes with a discussion
of the concept of justice as it relates to the public administrator
in developing an ethical consensus, constraining complex organizations, resolving ethical questions, and establishing a professional
code for public administrators built upon the principle of social
equity.

Hawley, Willis D. "The Possibilities of Nonbureaucratic Organizations."
In IMPROVING URBAN MANAGEMENT, edited by Willis D. Hawley and
David Rogers, pp. 209–63. Beverly Hills, Calif.: Sage Publications, 1974.

The author focuses on the potential benefits of nonbureaucratic
organizations, the difficulties involved in implementing and maintaining such structures, and some techniques for minimizing the
problems of nonbureaucratic organizations. A nonbureaucratic
organization would be characterized by collegial decision making,
lack of status divisions, and organizational autonomy. Conditions
in which nonbureaucratic organizations could improve service delivery are described. These include enhancing technological efficiency and contributions to the motivation of workers. Some of
the major problems confronting nonbureaucratic organizations in the
public sector are: psychological stress, leadership, group cohesion,
and evaluation. The success of nonbureaucratic organizations will
eventually depend upon effective organizational communication
patterns.

Henning, Kenneth K. "Organizing America's Cities." In MANAGING THE
MODERN CITY, edited by James M. Banovetz, pp. 153–87. Washington,
D.C.: International City Management Association, 1971.

This chapter focuses on four topics: the nature of organizations,
the development of modern organizations, the elements of complex
modern organizations, and the organization of the future. Organizations are defined and discussed in the context of modern society,
as well as the classical, human relations and analytic-integrative
approaches to organizations. Complex organizations are discussed
in terms of hierarchy, leadership, and authority and these are related to different forms of organization such as the line form, the
line and staff form, and the functional form.

Kirlin, John J. "The Impact of Increasing Lower-Status Clientele Upon City Governmental Structures: A Model From Organization Theory." URBAN AF-FAIRS QUARTERLY 8 (March 1973): 317-43.

This paper presents a model of how governments react to the emer-gence of unwelcome demands for change. The model draws upon organization theory and is developed through consideration of the impact of population migrations upon city governments. Three ideas are developed: the phenomenon of cities experiencing a growth of lower-status clienteles; factors relevant to the city's governmental organizations are initially the controlling factors in the city's response to the service demands of the new, lower-status clients; and political action will normally be required to ensure an adequate response to lower-status clienteles.

Lithwick, N.H. "Urban Policy-Making: Shortcomings in Political Technology." CANADIAN PUBLIC ADMINISTRATION 15 (Winter 1972): 571-84.

Urban political structures have inherent limitations which create irrelevant policies incapable of satisfying the public needs. Col-lective public needs are measured against a deviation from the norm and the intensity of the need is determined by the degree of deviation and the political clout of the actors involved. Norms and values undergo constant change while governmental political and administrative machinery concentrates on efficiency instead of effectiveness. This emphasis on efficiency makes goal setting and power the chief characteristics of policy making.

Lund, Donald A. "Confrontation Management." POLICE 16 (March 1972): 56-62.

Confrontation management is a theory of intervention in civil dis-order designed to restore order while minimizing the danger of over-reaction from law enforcement officers. Types of disorder, the intensity of effect upon the community, factors which hinder control of disorders, and actions which can reduce the intensity of a disorder are described. Also examined are questions of threat awareness, projection of a professional law enforcement image, confrontation management, supervisory unity, functional responsive-ness, neutral attitudes of police, and the minimum use of force. An outline for evaluating departmental preparedness in confrontation management is presented.

Miller, David W., and Starr, Martin K. THE STRUCTURE OF HUMAN DE-CISIONS. Englewood Cliffs, N.J.: Prentice-Hall, 1967. 192 p.

Using the perspective of an integrated theory of decisions, this book examines the structure of decision problems. Decision prob-lems are divided into different classes and, using mathematical approaches, the authors show how managers can recognize the appropriate classification and how they can approach each class and relate it to contemporary administrative theory. Theories are reduced to mathematical formulations enabling complex decision problems to be resolved simply. Managers can use this book to understand and to apply the essential features of logical and statistical decision theory.

Powers, Stanley P. "Management Concepts and Organization Models." In DEVELOPING THE MUNICIPAL ORGANIZATION, edited by Stanley Powers, F. Gerald Brown, and David S. Arnold, pp. 23-35. Washington, D.C.: International City Management Association, 1974.

Most attempts by managers to improve municipal organization result in a more vigorous effort to do the traditional things better. The author suggests that a blend of classical and modern management theory can improve the management system. Traditional management responses are discussed, including management-by-objectives, management team approaches, greater internal participation, and more decentralization. The classical and human relations approaches invariably require a reconciliation of competing ideas. Recently an effort known as organizational development has emerged taking a total organizational point of view. This approach focuses on goals and objectives as well as individuals within the organization. Several obstacles to achieving the total organization approach are discussed along with some alternative approaches, such as simple and complex matrix organizations and the system four model.

Scott, William G. "Management Theory: Dehumanizing Man?" MODERN GOVERNMENT AND NATIONAL DEVELOPMENT 13 (March 1972): 44, 46, 48, 50, and 52.

Despite increasing discussion and attention to questions of participation and democracy, the author contends that administrative theory is evolving towards increased dehumanization in organizations. Industrial humanism programs, utilizing the behavioral sciences, provide a vehicle for directing nonrational behavior into organizationally beneficial channels and improving interpersonal relations among top governmental administrators. By combining scientific management theory with industrial humanism we have increased rationality but also have concentrated power. This impedes the distribution of power among workers and prevents the creation of structures which could guarantee greater participation to employees.

_____. "Organization Government: The Prospects for A Truely Participative System." PUBLIC ADMINISTRATION REVIEW 29 (January-February 1969): 43-53.

Scott reviews some of the major management ideologies and discusses their inconsistencies and shortcomings in dealing with questions of alienation, decentralization, and participation. Two con-

temporary management creeds are examined and assessed: industrial
humanism which focuses on the human condition and the dignity of
man, and management science which focuses on technological de-
terminism and the capability of a technical elite to manage the
organizations of society. The author is quite pessimistic about
either creed and offers a new proposal for organization government
which stresses the need for organizations to have fair and judicial
appeals systems and full participation by organization members in
the formulation of their rights.

Sherwood, Frank P. "Devolution as a Problem of Organization Strategy." In
COMPARATIVE URBAN RESEARCH: THE ADMINISTRATION AND POLITICS OF
CITIES, edited by Robert T. Daland, pp. 60-87. Beverly Hills, Calif.: Sage
Publications, 1969.

Sherwood examines the institutional role of local government in the
pattern of relationships that comprise a national political system.
He reviews the relationship of local government to organization
theory and discusses several basic concepts of organization theory:
hierarchy and the centralization-decentralization continuum, non-
hierarchial concepts, decentralization and devolution, and autonomy.
A set of conditions is presented under which a society might provide for more independent and autonomous behavior by local governments. The author suggests a conceptual framework in the form
of an institution-building model permitting an examination of strategies for strong local response systems. The real problem is to
accord status to local government, thus making it something to be
cherished by all citizens.

Simmons, James. "Interaction Patterns." URBAN AFFAIRS QUARTERLY 6
(December 1970): 213-32.

Much of the literature analyzing urban processes focuses on static
relationships or institutions, such as urban structure, components
of municipal government, social groups, or service delivery agencies. The author suggests a new dynamic, process-oriented approach
that examines the interactions between and among actors and institutions in the urban system. This is done by analyzing the flows
and linkages between spatially separated phenomena in an urban
area. Flow matrices, including a functional flow matrix, are used
to describe problems in studying intraurban interaction. A number
of sources of bias are presented and flow matrices are discussed as
urban indicators.

Smith, Michael P. "Alienation and Bureaucracy: The Role of Participatory
Administration." PUBLIC ADMINISTRATION REVIEW 31 (November-December
1971): 658-64.

The author examines the factors which contribute to the increasing
feeling of bureaucratic alienation in public sector bureaucracies.

Large scale, complex and bureaucratic environments have impeded rather than assisted the individual in finding self-expression, personal efficacy, and human fellowship. Discussing the ideas of Marx, Mill, and Buber, the article focuses on the question of public problem solving and alienation by reviewing bureaucratic problems in urban school systems and welfare departments. The author is apprehensive that token or symbolic efforts for public participation in local bureaucracies will be made to soften community opposition. However, he is encouraged by recent efforts to increase the participation of both lower level administrators and clients.

Stalling, Robert A. "The Community Context of Crisis Management." AMERICAN BEHAVIORAL SCIENTIST 16 (January–February 1973): 312–25.

Comparative analyses of the crisis management process are discussed in an effort to locate disturbances and problems within community activity in situations defined as crises. A number of different conditions encountered by urban communities are examined and the characteristics of threats which contribute to the suspension of conventional modes of group behavior are described. Also discussed is the nature of crisis situations and their relationship to both the process and the consequences of restructuring patterns of community organization.

Thompson, James D. ORGANIZATIONS IN ACTION. New York: McGraw-Hill, 1967. 192 p.

Organizations are expected to produce results. They were created for a purpose and they are expected to show some evidence that they are fulfilling that purpose. To accomplish this, organizations must order priorities, insure predictability, and minimize uncertainty. These tasks are relatively simple in a closed system, but the author argues that organizations are open systems and, contrary to the classical approaches to administration, must be viewed as natural systems. These open systems are still subject to the constraints of program rationality. The two critical factors causing uncertainty for organizations are technology and environment. Both concepts are discussed in the light of how organizations can apply rationality to their tasks.

Vaupel, James W. "Muddling Through Analytically." In IMPROVING URBAN MANAGEMENT, edited by Willis D. Hawley and David Rogers, pp. 124–46. Beverly Hills, Calif.: Sage Publications, 1974.

This chapter focuses on a discussion of some analytical methods which can be used by decision makers, particularly in those situations where time is short and data is not available. Some of the methods discussed are complete analysis, incomplete analysis, habit, and intuition. Decisional analysis is examined through the use of tables and illustrations. Included in this discussion are the advantages of the decision analysis approach, taking additional factors into account, use of data, and the relationship between intuition and decision making. Deciding how to decide is of great importance to public managers. The arguments for an analytical approach versus habit and intuition are presented.

Vogel, Donald B. "Analysis of Informal Organization Patterns: A Training Technique." PUBLIC ADMINISTRATION REVIEW 28 (September-October 1968): 431-36.

This article presents a training technique to enable public managers to get a clearer understanding of the structural patterns in their organizations which impact upon decision making, leadership, control, and communications. The technique compares formal administrative structure and the informal structure based upon order and advice relationships. Participants in the training program answer a questionnaire which focuses on the types of relationships in the advice and order structures. The relationships are then plotted on organization charts. A step-by-step plan is presented for utilizing the technique described. Participants are able to examine their organizational structural arrangements and relate these to their specific situations.

Whitsett, David A. "Making Sense of Management Theories." PERSONNEL 52 (May-June 1975): 44-52.

The author reviews the basic assumptions in the writings of many of the prominent behavioral science theorists on management. Most of the techniques can be categorized in three areas: information gathering, structural orientation, and process orientation. These techniques are not mutually exclusive in practical application situations and should be used together for maximum effectiveness. The need to make more effective use of management theories and change strategies from the behavioral science will become more important in the years to come.

Wolman, Harold. "Organization Theory and Community Action Agencies." PUBLIC ADMINISTRATION REVIEW 32 (January-February 1972): 33-42.

This is an analysis of the United Planning Organization, a Washington-based community action agency, with an emphasis on the politics of the organization. The author examines the evolution of the community action agencies and some of the social science research to study the behavior of this agency. By focusing on the desire of organizations to survive and their need to build environmental support, much of the political behavior of these agencies is explained. A discussion of goal displacement, competition from other community agencies, and the client demands culminate in several conclusions concerning the decision-making process and the role of the poor. This study presents a framework in which further research on community action agencies can be conducted.

B. ORGANIZATION DEVELOPMENT

Aldrich, Howard. "Resource Dependence and Interorganizational Relations: Local Employment Service Offices and Social Services Sector Organizations." ADMINISTRATION AND SOCIETY 7 (February 1976): 419-54.

This is a study of 19 local employment service offices and 249 social service organizations in New York state. Using a resource dependence model, in which organizations seek to manage their environments to reduce dependencies and uncertainties emanating from other organizations, clients, or government agencies, the author proposes a conceptual framework to explain organizational behavior where interorganizational relations are a critical factor. Four patterns of interorganizational transactions are examined: intensity, reciprocity, standardization of interaction, and the degree of perceived cooperation in the relationship. The results indicate the importance of manipulative authority particularly in legislative mandates.

Argyris, Chris. "Leadership, Learning and Changing the Status Quo." ORGANIZATIONAL DYNAMICS 4 (Winter 1976): 29-43.

Society produces individuals knowledgeable about theories of action that are counterproductive to individual growth and organizational effectiveness; yet these theories are used in the design of organizations. The author discusses two models of organizational behavior. The first model emphasizes that individuals should be articulate about their purposes and simultaneously should control others and the environment in order to achieve goals. The second model links articulateness and advocacy to publicize one's views so decisions can be made on the most valid information possible. The result should be increased decision-making effectiveness, better monitoring of programs, and a greater likelihood that errors will be communicated openly. It is very difficult to change managers from the first to the second model.

___. "Organizations of the Future." In IMPROVING URBAN MANAGEMENT, edited by Willis D. Hawley and David Rogers, pp. 175-208. Beverly Hills, Calif.: Sage Publications, 1974.

Organizations in all walks of life are increasingly coming under attack because of the high costs necessary to maintain them and the inadequate level of services they provide. Some of the causes of organizational deterioration are specialization and fractionalization, excessive management control in planning and defining work standards, and a lack of employee input in policies affecting their work. The author summarizes the major characteristics of the managerial world. Strategies used to change public organizations include: employing consulting firms, using consultants with key insiders to insure that recommendations are carried out, creation of new institutions, and community control. The importance of opportunities for change and self-responsibility are discussed in the context of individual growth and organizational design along with guidelines for organizational structures and an analysis of instituting change processes.

Bennis, Warren G. "Changing Organizations." JOURNAL OF APPLIED BE-HAVIORAL SCIENCE 2 (August-September 1966): 247-63.

The rate of change in American society has accelerated greatly in the post-World War II era. Throughout the industrial world, bu-reaucracy is still the social arrangement which is dominant in our organizations. Several factors contribute to change in organiza-tional life including the population and knowledge explosions and man's quest for self-awareness. Managerial behavior has undergone some changes in the 1950s and '60s. These changes can be classi-fied as a new concept of man, a new concept of power, and a new concept of organizational values. Five essential tasks are defined as confronting the manager trying to coordinate the human side of his organization: integration of individual needs and man-agement goals, social influence, the problem of managing and solv-ing conflicts, adaptation, and the problems of growth and decay. The author concludes with a look at organizations of the future by analyzing population characteristics, work values, tasks and goals, motivation, and structure.

Brouillette, John, and Quarantelli, E.L. "Types of Patterned Variation in Bureaucratic Adaptations to Organizational Stress." SOCIOLOGICAL INQUIRY 41 (Winter 1971): 39-45.

The belief that bureaucratic organizations are ill-equipped or slow to respond to crisis is challenged in this article which asserts that organizations respond to crises by changing their work tasks, their work relationships, or both. The study derives from research con-ducted on seventy national disasters and identifies four basic pat-terns of bureaucratic response. The authors identify four internal and five external factors which affect the type of response that can be expected. This model of how organizations adapt to crisis can be used to describe the structure and functioning of organizations during crisis and also to predict the type of adaptations to expect.

Campbell, John P., and Dunnette, Marvin. "Effectiveness of T-Group Experi-ences in Managerial Training and Development." PSYCHOLOGICAL BULLETIN 70 (August 1968): 73-103.

This paper examines the formal nature of T-Group methods, basic assumptions underlying the technique, and some of the problems faced by T-Group researchers. The authors review available empirical literature, external and internal criteria, individual differences, and T-Group techniques. Conclusions suggest there is evidence to support the theory that T-Group training does induce change but more research is needed in several areas before it can be labeled effective. These areas are: specifying expected behavior outcomes; the need for more measures of individual differences in T-Group studies; and greater attention to the interaction between organizational characteristics, leadership climate, organizational goals, and training outcomes.

Chitwood, Stephen R., and Harmon, Michael M. "New Public Administration, Humanism and Organizational Behavior." PUBLIC MANAGEMENT 53 (November 1971): 13-22.

The authors assess the effects of humanism on public administration and students of public administration by reviewing the works of some of the leading humanist scholars in the field. Also discussed are the concepts of interpersonal trust and effectiveness. Advocates of the new public administration school suggest that organizational development technology should be utilized to develop an effective capacity for change in organizations. The new humanist approach marks a radical departure from the traditional approach. It details the implications for administrative action which result from humanistic actions and can markedly change the discipline of public administration as well as the behavior patterns in public organizations.

Culbert, Samuel A., and Reisel, Jerome. "Organization Development: An Applied Philosophy For Managers of Public Enterprise." PUBLIC ADMINISTRATION REVIEW 31 (March-April 1971): 159-69.

Organization development is a process of planned change which, when used as a management tool, seeks to preserve the viability of the public organization. When used properly by managers, organization development assists the organization in adapting to the internal and external realities of the environment, making the organization more responsive, flexible, and innovative. The authors identify the major characteristics of organization development and discuss their relevance for contemporary managers by illustrating situations in which OD can be effectively used. A demonstration of OD in practice is presented by using a case study of OD processes in an initial application.

Eddy, William B. "The Management of Change." In DEVELOPING THE MUNICIPAL ORGANIZATION, edited by Stanley Powers, F. Gerald Brown, and David S. Arnold, pp. 147-59. Washington, D.C.: International City Management Association, 1974.

Municipal managers are integral to the process of change. They need to realize that resistance to change will be present in many instances. Managers must also be alert to constructive elements that exist in employee resistance to change. Some of the major factors underlying resistance to change are: threats to jobs, wages, security, coping with new situations, status, social relationships, employee trust and confidence in the organization, uncertainty, reaction against authority and general resistance to change. Several strategies for overcoming resistance to change include: communication, participation, dealing with economic issues and working conditions, working through feelings, sensitivity to human relationships, and developing organizational trust and respect. The author also reviews and discusses voluntary change, redeveloping and reviewing organizations, organizational development, and developing an organization climate.

Eddy, William B., and Murphy, Thomas P. "Applied Behavioral Science in Local Governments." In THE HUMAN RESOURCES OF CITY GOVERNMENTS, edited by Charles H. Levine, pp. 201-24. Beverly Hills, Calif.: Sage Publications, 1977.

Attempts by urban managers to solve the problems of communities have been thwarted by a variety of contextual factors--including shortages of resources, political forces, and the sheer complexity and multiplicity of the problems. Over the past decade, however, there has been a growing consensus that traditional managerial approaches may not be adequate for effective problem solving.

OD is catching on in urban management but will not reach full bloom until urban managers have a clearer understanding of how OD can help meet strongly felt needs. The kinds of behavioral science approaches present in the OD movement, as well as those in the PPBS and MBO experiments, should equip urban managers with tools for making effective use of such strategies. The forces that make OD and the applied sciences work or fail are not unique to urban governance.

Eddy, William B., and Saunders, Robert J. "Applied Behavioral Science in Urban Administrative Political Systems." PUBLIC ADMINISTRATION REVIEW 32 (January-February 1972): 11-16.

The purpose of this article is to identify and discuss some issues concerning the application of the behavioral sciences change model to urban agencies, particularly where political-administrative characteristics are different from those in private agencies. Several norms and values of a new model are presented including trust, openness, development of people, shared participation, confrontation, change, and renewal. The authors examine a dozen problem areas where organization development has had difficulty in being implemented in local governments. Most of these problem areas are related to the local political environment. The final section of the paper offers suggestions for coping with the resistance of local government to change and asserts that behavioral scientists and public officials must begin developing new ways to cooperate.

Golembiewski, Robert T. "The 'Laboratory Approach' to Organization Change: Schema of a Method." PUBLIC ADMINISTRATION REVIEW 27 (September 1967): 211-21.

Both public and private agencies and businesses have begun to use the laboratory approach as a vehicle for organization change. This approach utilizes two techniques: the basic T-Group and the variant T-Group. The author discusses both approaches outlining the strengths, weaknesses, and the goals of each and relating these to the concept of facilitating action as opposed to blueprinting an ideal. Values underlying methods and uses are presented in a chart stressing metavalues, proximate goals, desirable means, and organization values. The article concludes with a discussion of values guiding organization change and a guide to the application of the laboratory approach through agreements linking individual change and organizational change.

_____. "Organization Development in Public Agencies: Perspectives on Theory and Practice." PUBLIC ADMINISTRATION REVIEW 29 (July-August 1969): 367-77.

This article examines some of the characteristics of organization development and summarizes the experience with OD in a number of public agencies at the federal and local levels. The author presents a model of findings and hypotheses underlying the typical OD program and discusses its objectives. The constraints in approaching OD objectives are discussed. They are: multiple access points, great variety of individuals and groups, and the chain of command linkages. Also examined as constraints are some of the habit background factors, such as: patterns of delegation, legal habits, need for security, procedural regularity and caution, and the professional manager.

Golembiewski, Robert T., and Kiepper, Alan. "MARTA: Toward an Effective Open Giant." PUBLIC ADMINISTRATION REVIEW 36 (January-February 1976): 46-60.

This article is a case study of the Metropolitan Atlanta Rapid Transit Authority's (MARTA) effort to use a laboratory approach to speed the development of a management team and to build a climate for interpersonal and intergroup relationships. The authors discuss the major tasks facing the Authority, in terms of their target dates and a management concept that could assist the top administrators in achieving different goals at different times. Initially, the project required learning designs directed at a collaborative-consensual system. A team-building approach is discussed along with its rationale for the system. Another approach used was to establish different levels of interfaces with departmental directors, but the results are difficult to evaluate without further studies of how managers feel and work in their organizational environment.

Harmon, Michael M. "Social Equity and Organizational Man: Motivation and Organizational Democracy." PUBLIC ADMINISTRATION REVIEW 34 (January-February 1974): 11-18.

Using Rawls's theory of justice as a starting point, the author contrasts the theory with three utilitarian concepts of organizational man in public administration and proposes that internal organizational democracy must be unequivocal, rather than based upon principles of efficiency, productivity, and loyalty. Research on organizational man is reviewed with attention to the professional-technocratic man who emerged from management science and the politico-administrative man who emerged from the acknowledgment of the inherently-political role of the public administrator. The author concludes that the principle of social equity does not relate to either the research or practice of contemporary public administration, and that major changes will have to be made in the structure, the allocation of power, and the choices made by public officials.

Kilmann, Ralph H. "An Organic-Adaptive Organization: The MAPS Method." PERSONNEL 51 (May-June 1974): 35-47.

Most contemporary organizations are designed according to bureaucratic principles. The author feels new developments call for an organic-adaptive organization staffed by resourceful and self-motivated personnel. Its characteristics are: participative management, management by objectives, management of interdependencies, and organization development. The article discusses the MAPS method of organization (multivariate analysis, participation, and structure) which uses the following procedures: the participation of the members of the organization in defining the tasks they believe would best accomplish the organizational objectives; the use of multivariate analysis to separate the total set of tasks into task clusters; and the use of multivariate analysis to place members into subunit structures where they share similar preferences about their tasks.

Kirkhart, Larry, and White, Orion F., Jr. "The Future of Organization Development." PUBLIC ADMINISTRATION REVIEW 34 (March-April 1974): 129-40.

The authors assess the future direction of organization development by examining grid OD and situational-emergent OD as contrasting approaches which require clarification. The problems facing OD are: What knowledge and methodologies are appropriate to OD and how can these be communicated? How can OD deal with the cult of efficiency? How can OD deal with existing reward structures in organizations? How can OD relate the organization to its environment? After reviewing many theories of organization development and comparing situational-emergent to grid theories, the authors conclude that part of the problems confronting the future of OD may be beyond conscious intervention and rooted in history. OD must emphasize the situational-emergent approaches if it seeks to become a force for social evolution.

Knowles, Malcolm S. "Human Resources Development in OD." PUBLIC ADMINISTRATION REVIEW 34 (March-April 1974): 115-23.

Organizations exist to perform work, but they also serve a human-development purpose where people seek to meet their needs and to achieve certain goals. The key to understanding the role of organization development is educational strategy which, unlike other intervention strategies, is concerned with theories of learning and teaching. The author reviews some OD theories and shows how different models might be applied to human resource development in organizations. Special attention is placed on mechanisms of mutual planning, diagnosing learning needs, formulating program objectives, designing a pattern of learning experiences and operating, and then evaluating the program. Human resources development involves viewing the organization as dynamic, complex, and comprising interacting subsystems of people, processes, and ideas.

Marcus, Philip M., and House, James S. "Exchange Between Supervisors and Subordinates in Large Organizations." ADMINISTRATIVE SCIENCE QUARTERLY 18 (June 1973): 209-22.

Social exchange theory is used to formulate hypotheses about superior-subordinate relations in large, complex organizations. From a self-administered questionnaire, the collected data support the hypotheses derived from the model and suggest further research using social exchange theory. The behavior of supervisors is characterized as expressive and instrumental which increases loyalty to the superior, promotes greater compliance with demands, and reduces conflict between the two organizational levels.

Mohr, Lawrence B. "The Concept of Organizational Goal." AMERICAN POLITICAL SCIENCE REVIEW 62 (June 1973): 470-81.

This article reviews major contributions to the organizational goal concept and synthesizes many of its components into a more comprehensive conceptualization. The main goal concepts are discussed. They include the importance of viewing organizational goals as multiple and empirically determined, a dual conceptualization so goals are dichotomized into those with internal referents and external referents, and subsetting the goals of organizations into program goals and differentiating goals from subgoals and activities. This goal concept can be used by managers to evaluate organizational effectiveness, conduct research on organizational behavior, and view the role of the organization in society.

Palumbo, Dennis J. "Power and Role Specificity in Organization Theory." PUBLIC ADMINISTRATION REVIEW 29 (May-June 1969): 237-48.

Using data from a sample of fourteen local public health departments, the author examines the way control is achieved in an organization. The major dimension is the distribution of power in the organization, defined as the degree of specificity of role prescription. Variables are classified as organizational or output of performance. The former include: formalization, centralization, span of control, role conflict, goal agreement, professionalization, management style, and specialization. The latter include: innovation, productivity, per unit costs, self-evaluation, and scope of programs. The author concludes that as organizations become more centralized, formalized, and less participatory, morale, innovation, and productivity decrease. When subgroups, instead of individuals, within the organization are examined, the same negative consequences do not materialize.

Patti, Rino J. "Organizational Resistance and Change: The View From Below." SOCIAL SERVICE REVIEW 48 (September 1974): 367-83.

The article presents an analytical framework for assessing certain elements of resistance to organizational change proposals emanating from low-power practitioners in social agencies where the changes sought must be approved by an administrative superior. The paper assumes that resistance to practitioner-initiated proposals is not a constant phenomenon but varies with the nature of the change suggested, the personal goals of the decision maker, the administrative distance between the practitioner and the decision maker, and the previous investment the organization has made in the arrangements to be altered. Each variation is discussed along with implications for goal selection and organizational change strategies.

Powers, Stanley P. "The Human Side of Organization." In DEVELOPING THE MUNICIPAL ORGANIZATION, edited by Stanley Powers, F. Gerald Brown, and David S. Arnold, pp. 36-50. Washington, D.C.: International City Management Association, 1974.

To meet their goals and objectives, organizations must control some aspects of employee behavior; the range of control will vary from organization to organization. Early efforts at control focused on objectives: more recently, organizations are focusing on objectives as well as on the satisfaction levels of the people involved. The author reviews the scientific management concept and outlines its strengths and weaknesses. A similar discussion is presented for the human relations approach to management, the concept of man as being basically good, and the hierarchy of human needs. The two latter concepts are viewed as positive and realistic approaches to

achieving organizational goals and objectives while maintaining the
dignity of the individual.

Schein, Edgar H. "In Defense of Theory Y." ORGANIZATIONAL DYNAMICS
4 (Summer 1975): 17-30.

Theory Y assumes that workers are capable of integrating their own
needs and goals with those of the organization. The theory further
states that workers are not indolent, they can exercise self-control
and self-direction, and can direct their efforts towards organizational goals. Theory Y does not imply that human and organizational needs are congruent and integratable, nor does it suggest
that management should be participative. It states what workers
are like and what behavior they are capable of if organizational
conditions are appropriate. We must learn to separate managers'
assumptions about human nature from their actual managerial behavior. Theory Y managers will recognize that groups are a fact
of life, and they will accept the reality of dual loyalties and the
fact that conflict is not inevitable but rather the consequence of
how groups and individuals are managed.

Segal, Morley. "Organization and Environment: A Typology of Adaptability
and Structure." PUBLIC ADMINISTRATION REVIEW 34 (May-June 1974):
212-20.

Citing several studies of organizational typology, the author asserts
that organizational structure often is a defense against an uncertain
environment, and organizations selectively perceive their environment as static so as not to have to adapt continuously. A typology
of organizations is presented--chain structured, meditatively structured, and adaptively structured--which analyzes the perceptions,
interrelationships, decision bases, support strategies, and extent of
decentralization. The problems encountered by an organization
with multiple structures trying to respond to its environment are
also discussed.

Tichy, Noel. "An Analysis of Clique Formation and Structure in Organizations."
ADMINISTRATIVE SCIENCE QUARTERLY 18 (June 1973): 194-208.

Organizational development literature has acknowledged the effects
of various formal organizational variables on informal structure.
However, very few systematic and empirically testable propositions
have been formulated specifying relationships in this area. This
article develops several propositions which relate the variables of
compliance, mobility, and size to motivation for clique formation
and to constraints within which cliques form. A typology of five
cliques is discussed; they are: coercive cliques, normative cliques,
high-mobility utilitarian cliques, seniority-utilitarian cliques, and
no-mobility utilitarian cliques.

Warner, W. Keith, and Havens, A. Eugene. "Goal Displacement and the Intangibility of Organizational Goals." ADMINISTRATIVE SCIENCE QUARTERLY 12 (March 1968): 540-55.

> A common characteristic of organization behavior is the preoccupation of groups at the operating level with style and methods of activity. Often the way things are done is a presumption of job competence and a guarantee of meeting organization objectives. Goal inversion occurs with the means becoming the operating values and the announced goals serving to justify and support the means. The authors develop a theoretical framework for empirical research into this problem. They examine goal succession and goal change, and they develop an axiom and five working hypotheses to test.

Wessman, Fred. "The Group Construct: A Model for OD Interventions." PERSONNEL 50 (September-October 1973): 19-29.

> The author suggests that the greater the consensus of individual interpretations of a group's functioning and purpose, the greater will be the group construct. The health and effectiveness of a group can be assessed by the size of the group construct. The objective of organizational development should be to develop a congruence of constructs. Eight steps are discussed which translate the group construct into a consultative activity: entry, relationship structuring, selection of work setting and methods, individual construct analysis, data feedback and construct sharing, priority selling and action planning, interpretation and follow-up, and evaluation.

White, Orion F. [Jr.]. "The Dialectical Organization: An Alternative to Bureaucracy." PUBLIC ADMINISTRATION REVIEW 29 (January-February 1969): 32-42.

> One of the factors contributing to a demand for change in bureaucratic organizations is the way people are being treated by administrative systems. Two models of client relations are discussed. One model treats the client as a child by perceiving the client as powerless, personally oriented and dependent upon the agency. The other model treats the client as an adult who is not afraid of the agency, can rationalize impersonal behavior, and understands the costs of his relationship with the agency. Two traditional concepts of administration are discussed: policy rationality, and the efficiency criterion. A case study is presented of a church-related social service agency. It highlights client relations, client interaction, administrative structure, organizational ideology, and organizational mentality.

_____. "The Problem of Urban Administration and Environmental Turbulence." In NEIGHBORHOOD CONTROL IN THE 1970S: POLITICS, ADMINISTRATION AND CITIZEN PARTICIPATION, edited by George Frederickson, pp. 117-37. New York: Chandler, 1973.

Complete solutions to our urban problems will probably require radically revised governmental structures and processes on all levels of government. Since this is not likely to happen, the author discusses change processes brought about by degrees of environmental threat to the organization. Three categories of variables are defined to see if environmental threat conditions impacting upon organization structure and process would produce change at the agency-client interaction level. The three groups of variables are: external system factors, internal system factors, and relevant conditions stemming from individuals. The balance of the paper is a case study of an agency, which discusses the sources of role stress, the organizational dynamics, flexibility and rigidity under conditions of role stress, and flexibility and rigidity in the agency staff.

Whyte, William F. "Models for Building and Changing Organizations." HUMAN ORGANIZATION 26 (Spring-Summer 1967): 22-31.

Theoretical assumptions usually guide efforts to create or change organizations. Models used often are incompatible with the environmental realities of the groups which interact with the organization. A clear understanding of the model and its assumptions is imperative and this must be coupled with greater versatility and inventiveness in organization design. Several models are examined, including the community democracy model, the town meeting style, and the war relocation camp. In complex organizations harmony should not be the goal; rather, the objective should be to create an organization capable of assessing its problems and developing ways of coping with them. Organizational design should begin from the bottom up and not from the top down. Several potential areas of research are listed.

Wilcox, Herbert G. "Hierarchy, Human Nature, and the Participative Panacea." PUBLIC ADMINISTRATION REVIEW 29 (January-February 1969): 53-63.

The 1960s have been marked by a great deal of social and cultural change culminating in conflict. Much of this conflict has centered on public institutions and, in particular, the hierarchical arrangement by which large numbers of people are controlled and coordinated. The works of several organization theorists favoring participative management are reviewed as arguments against hierarchy. Particular attention is focused on the different approaches to the concept of self-actualization. Several concepts of the participative management school are discussed as positive alternatives to hierarchical arrangements. The author is pessimistic about the claims of the participative-management theorists, claiming they rely too much on faith and trust and not enough on economy, efficiency, and effectiveness.

Chapter 2

ADMINISTRATIVE LEADERSHIP

A. GENERAL ADMINISTRATION

Adrian, Charles R. "The Quality of Urban Leadership." In THE QUALITY OF URBAN LIFE, edited by Henry J. Schmandt and Warner Bloomberg, Jr., pp. 375-93. Beverly Hills, Calif.: Sage Publications, 1969.

The quality of urban leadership is difficult to assess and often is left to intuition. It requires a willingness to grapple with the difficult issues and an ability to coordinate activities with other leaders in the complex intergovernmental system. The types of people who become political leaders, either elected or appointed, can be categorized as professionals, hobbyists, advertisers, status-seekers, or ideologues. Two new types of leadership categories are also discussed: ethnic and minority leadership, and youth leadership. The source and quality of leadership in a community depends upon the image the community leaders have of their community and of the purposes of local government. These images are defined as: booster, amenities, caretaker, and brokerage functions. The pool from which urban political leaders are drawn is widening, but so are the problems confronting that leadership.

Albers, Henry H. PRINCIPLES OF MANAGEMENT: A MODERN APPROACH. 4th ed. New York: Wiley, 1974. 579 p.

This book discusses the current understanding of the practice of management in formal organizations. The author believes that basic principles of management can be applied in different kinds of organizations, in various functional issues, and at different levels of hierarchy. Three basic elements of management are highlighted: planning, communication, and motivation, and these are related to the themes of managerial structure, relation of organization to functions, relation of knowledge and techniques to organization, and the problem of limited resources.

Alford, Robert. "The Bureaucratization of Urban Government." In SOCIAL

CHANGE AND URBAN POLITICS: READINGS, edited by Daniel N. Gordon, pp. 263-78. Englewood Cliffs, N.J.: Prentice-Hall, 1973.

This is a study of bureaucratization and professionalization of urban government agencies. Bureaucratization refers to specialization of work tasks, separate organizational units, and supervisors assigned to monitor and evaluate the performance of the employees. Professionalization relates to employee competence and membership in a peer group which sets standards of performance. Six indicators of bureaucratization are presented: form of government, civil service system, chief personnel officer, planning department planning expenditures, and a capital budget. Highly bureaucratized cities are likely to have removed many decisions from the public arena and vested these in technicians. Also found in this type of system are public hearings and internal procedures for settling interdepartmental disputes over budgets, jurisdiction, and areas of responsibility.

Ayres, Douglas W. "Municipal Interfaces in the Third Sector: A Negative View." PUBLIC ADMINISTRATION REVIEW 35 (September-October 1975): 459-63.

The major contention of this essay is that unprofitable functions ultimately become governmental functions and conversely profitable operations will ultimately be transferred from public to private control. Briefly recounted is the changing nature of certain functions which caused them to be shifted from one sector to the other. The major contacts between the private and public sector occur in the areas of consulting services, leasing space, public boards and commissions, and the purchasing of public equipment. The private sector is increasingly becoming more visible and accountable to shareholders at the same time the public sector is being urged to become more efficient. As lines of demarcation between the two sectors become blurred, fewer and fewer functions will be considered solely public or private in the future.

Banfield, Edward. "Why Government Cannot Solve the Urban Problem." DAEDALUS 97 (Fall 1968): 1231-41.

The author feels that government cannot solve the problems of the cities and probably has made things worse. Serious problems--unemployment, race, poverty, and crime--are separated from others, such as urban sprawl and commuting time. Serious problems are in the inner city and government seems incapable of dealing with these. Solutions might include elementary impediments to a free labor market, such as monopolistic unions and minimum wage laws, and permission of only skilled workers to immigrate and expand the economy in the South and Puerto Rico. It is difficult to implement these programs because there are no payoffs for the affluent.

Banovetz, James M. "The City and Change: Programming for Control." In his MANAGING THE MODERN CITY, pp. 44-73. Washington, D.C.: International City Management Association, 1971.

More city administrators are becoming aware of the need to change their focus from a traditional caretaker approach to one of a people-oriented approach. A community urban development scheme is presented which includes goal formulation, continuous data collection and analysis, anticipation of problems, and goal-centered policy development. The role of the city administrator in goal-centered programming is outlined. Programming urban services requires administrative planning, employee training and development, management staff development, and intergovernmental cooperation. Reorienting local government to deal with human needs involves development of alternative organizational arrangements. New areas of change for administrators to deal with are likely to include communications, intergovernmental relations, employee relations, and participatory politics.

Baron, Harold M. "Institutional Racism in the Modern Metropolis." In ON THE URBAN SCENE, edited by Morton Levitt and Ben Rubenstein, pp. 99-114. Detroit: Wayne State University Press, 1973.

The subjugation of black people has often been hidden behind myths. In some circumstances, notably the Kerner Commission Report, the existence of institutional racism has been cited but has not been analyzed in depth. The major components of institutional racism are the organizations that develop and define black subsectors in housing, employment, and public services, the accepted institutional patterns that reinforce these subsectors and the controls that dominate black people. The institutions--public and private--that allocate resources have become so racist that improving the quality of life for blacks almost implies a restructuring of our major institutions and organizations.

Botein, Bernard. OUR CITIES BURN WHILE WE PLAY COPS AND ROBBERS. New York: Simon and Schuster, 1972. 192 p.

This book critiques the criminal justice system and suggests new ways of administering the system, primarily by increasing the involvement of society in the criminal justice system. The system as presently structured is virtually unmanageable because it is called upon to deal with many crimes that are either societal problems or could be better handled by other agencies of government. Such crimes--intoxication, housing-code violations, traffic violations, drug addiction, and morals offenses--should be redefined. In examining the system, the author argues for better educated policemen who are control-oriented instead of arrest-oriented; that probation agencies should be based in local neighborhoods; and that our prison system should be modernized and humanized.

Brewer, Garry D. POLITICIANS, BUREAUCRATS AND THE CONSULTANT: A CRITIQUE OF URBAN PROBLEM SOLVING. New York: Basic Books, 1973. 291 p.

This is a study of the experiences of Pittsburgh and San Francisco when each contracted with consultants to design urban renewal programs using the latest theoretical techniques. In each case, the team of consultants used extremely sophisticated problem-solving techniques, such as simulation and systems analysis. These techniques were applied to the urban problems of housing, pollution, and transportation, but the results hardly resembled what the consultants promised to deliver. The author conducted interviews with all the actors involved and reviewed the computer models in light of the political and administrative realities in each city to see what went wrong.

Brown, David S. "Making Decisions." In MANAGING THE MODERN CITY, edited by James M. Banovetz, pp. 134-50. Washington, D.C.: International City Management Association, 1971.

Many local public officials never have the opportunity to analyze how they make decisions. However, almost all decisions involve some of the following: recognition of the problem, identification of factors, identification of alternatives, weighing and testing of alternatives, choice, and implementation of choice. Individual decisions are affected by timing, the form of the question, skills and habits, custom, group approval, passion, prejudice, and personal needs. Standards for evaluating managerial decisions are offered, such as quantity, quality, cost, improved relations with clients, and the methods used in the decision-making process. Several guidelines are provided for improving both individual and organizational decisions.

Buchanan, Bruce. "Government Managers, Business Executives, and Organizational Commitment." PUBLIC ADMINISTRATION REVIEW 34 (July-August 1974): 339-47.

Several studies have concluded that business organizations are more successful in stimulating commitment to their purposes than government agencies. Public sector executives do not have the same positive attitudes toward their organizations that business executives have. The author reviews several studies and then discusses his own survey of 280 managers in eight public and private organizations seeking to determine which organizational experiences have the greatest impact on organizational commitment and whether there are significant differences between public and private managers on both experience and commitment. Testing such factors as personal significance, stability of expectations, first-year job challenge, reference group cohesion, and perceived commitment expectations, the author concludes that business managers have more positive attitudes than government managers in areas of experience, satisfaction, and commitment.

Cantine, Robert R. "How Practicing Urban Administrators View Themselves: An Analysis of the Workshop Deliberations." In EDUCATION FOR URBAN ADMINISTRATION, edited by Frederic N. Cleveland and Thomas J. Davy, pp. 1-19. Philadelphia: American Academy of Political and Social Science, 1973.

Data was collected from seventy urban administrators attending a workshop. Most of the participating administrators felt there were enough substantive differences in knowledge and skill requirements, outlook, and processes among different careers in urban administration so that no single educational program would be appropriate for all administrators. Today's urban managers must make effective use of their time by building and maintaining a sensitive information system. Managers must also set objectives, build consensus among different interests, promote values they believe, arbitrate conflicts, oversee financial management, and manipulate the system to achieve certain tasks. Urban administrators are people of action who are constantly responding to problems which require decisions. Their real challenge is to learn how to wisely invest time and energy.

Caro, Robert A. THE POWER BROKER: ROBERT MOSES AND THE FALL OF NEW YORK. New York: Vintage Books, 1974. 1,368 p.

This is a study of politics, planning, and administration in both New York City and state and the one man who has done most to shape the development patterns for the past fifty years--Robert Moses. The author blames much of New York's current problems on the policies initiated by Moses. Caro discusses how Moses achieved his position of influence and how he developed his power base so it could be mobilized to coerce mayors and governors to follow his position. Moses, who never held elected office, wielded more power than any other political figure in New York, enabling him to build public works projects almost at will throughout most of his career. This book provides a comprehensive look at power relationships in urban and state politics and the impact these relationships have had on the politics and administration of New York city and state.

Cohen, Henry. "Governing Megacentropolis: The Constraints." PUBLIC ADMINISTRATION REVIEW 30 (September-October 1970): 488-97.

Large metropolitan cities are becoming increasingly difficult to govern because of the inability to respond to demands for changes in programs and services, the problems involved in maintaining service levels, and the struggles encountered by mayors. The major problems confronting urban managers are: city size, bureaucratization and professionalization of services, rising citizen expectations, complexities in intergovernmental relations, nature of migration to cities, metropolitan context of many urban problems, inability to renew older sections of the city, and the prevailing feelings of alienation and powerlessness. The author discusses each of these problems and concludes that big-city problems are more sociological and political than managerial and administrative. Additional funds, strengthened mayoral powers, and improved mechanisms for resolving conflict are some of the suggestions offered to improve urban governance.

_____. "Urban Disgovernance." CITY 5 (March-April 1971): 65-69.

At a time when local governments have expanded their responsibilities, increased their responsiveness in areas of human welfare, and tried to increase the quality of the services they offer, the difficulties of governing large urban areas have also increased. Twelve factors are cited as causes for "urban disgovernance," ranging from political and sociological issues to managerial and administrative problems. For cities to correct these deficiencies, they must begin to provide services more efficiently so citizens receive the services they want.

Costello, Timothy W. "Change in Municipal Government: A View From the Inside." JOURNAL OF APPLIED BEHAVIORAL SCIENCE 7 (March-April 1971): 131-45.

The rules of political activity as they affect change are discussed briefly, including the need to be reelected, the importance of power, and the need for reciprocity if things are to be accomplished. Several types of change implemented in New York city are identified. The author outlines and discusses the differences in management between the public and private sectors. The major differences are: periodic changes in top leadership, techniques for quantifying goals, heterogeneous nature of the clients in the public sector, visibility of public sector activities, and constraints on decision making. The balance of the article focuses on the dynamics of municipal change by examining planned-change, a confluence of force, event-dominated change, accidental innovation and external intervention. The role of the behavioral scientist in this process is briefly outlined.

Cunningham, Luvern. "Educational Governance and Policy Making in Large Cities." PUBLIC ADMINISTRATION REVIEW 30 (July-August 1970): 333-39.

This article discusses some popular misconceptions about schools and school problems. Several studies are cited showing citizen satisfaction levels with teachers, schools, and school boards. The author also presents data on the numbers, structure, composition, and turnover of school boards in large cities. The major issues facing school systems and their administrators are: community control, decentralization, the use of ombudsmen, performance measurement, teacher strikes, finances, and the relationship of school system bureaucracies to citizens. Many reforms have been proposed, but obtaining consensus on these reforms is difficult; so the author suggests that the mass media be used in a nationwide public educational effort to inform citizens of the scope of public problems.

Derr, C. Brooklyn. "Conflict Resolution in Organizations: Views From the Field of Educational Administration." PUBLIC ADMINISTRATION REVIEW 32 (September-October 1972): 495-501.

> This article discusses the subject of resolving conflicts in organizations from an administrator's point of view with particular reference to administrators who daily face crises and confrontations. The most difficult task of the administrator is to identify the type of conflict occurring. Conflict situations are categorized as: intrapersonal, interpersonal, organizational, interorganizational, or revolutionary. Three conflict-resolution methods are discussed: training administrators to cope with various conflicts, to use organization development consultants, and to resolve substantive and procedural problems that cause conflict. An organizational conflict resolution grid is presented, relating the types of conflict to the proposed methods showing the potential implication for each method with each conflict.

Doig, Jameson W. "Police Problems, Proposals, and Strategies for Change." PUBLIC ADMINISTRATION REVIEW 28 (September-October 1968): 393-406.

> For most of the post-World War II era, political science studies of the police were very sparse. Only after riots erupted, crime increased, and tensions between police and the community escalated, did studies of police power and administration emerge. The author suggests that the field of criminal justice and police requires a number of small, semiautonomous organizations which can implement change. Small pilot projects need to be developed and tested and careful evaluations need to be conducted in order to determine the advantages and disadvantages of each project tested. One organization which operates in this manner is the Vera Institute of Justice in New York City. The approach used by the institute is examined in a bail reform project and a police summons project.

Donabedian, Avedis. ASPECTS OF MEDICAL CARE ADMINISTRATION. Cambridge, Mass.: Harvard University Press, 1974. 649 p.

> The author provides health care administrators--planners, researchers, and managers--with a set of guidelines for determining medical care requirements. The major questions posed are: How do we measure the need for health services? What health services are needed? And what resources are needed to provide these services? An initial discussion focuses on the values and the problems involved in setting overall objectives. A model is then presented to assist practitioners in planning for health care services.

Drucker, Meyer. "The Importance of Internal Review for Local Governments." GOVERNMENTAL FINANCE 2 (February 1973): 25-28.

> The intelligent management of available resources has become even more important now that revenue sources for local government are

tighter than ever. Internal review within local governments is necessary, but in some states audits are not required. Citing a study of cities and counties with populations over 100,000, the author finds that local governments are far behind both private industry and the federal government in using internal auditing as a tool for controlling operations. In the local governments where it is used, internal auditing is not sufficiently independent of the activities being reviewed.

Filley, A.C. "Committee Management: Guidelines from Social Science Research." CALIFORNIA MANAGEMENT 13 (Fall 1970): 13-21.

This article examines committee management and focuses on purposes, size, leadership, and membership. The major functions of committees are exchanging information, generating ideas, recommending action, and making decisions. Research is presented showing the problems inherent in large and small committees and the author suggests meetings include only five or six participants. Social homogeneity is an important characteristic for effective committee work; mutual understanding and similar behavioral norms provide a smoother committee process. This summary of the research on committees has great utility for managers.

Fletcher, John E., Jr. "Governing Tomorrow's Cities." NATION'S CITIES 12 (September 1974): 25-32.

This article is a summary of a series of conferences designed to determine city executive management needs and to develop programs to improve local government management capacity. Six management needs identified were: adequate authority, increased planning and management capacity, improved information and communication, qualified personnel, better citizen relations, and improved intergovernmental support. Five types of service activities which can help managers meet these needs are discussed. The conference participants indicated that all parts of the cities' institutional support network must begin to undertake new roles and responsibilities in the future.

Fox, Douglas M. THE POLITICS OF CITY AND STATE BUREAUCRACY. Pacific Palisades, Calif.: Goodyear, 1974. 124 p.

Fox examines what bureaucrats do to affect various policies on different levels of government. Using the bureaucracy as the central focus, the author examines the relationship between bureaucrats and other actors in the policy-making process to determine which actors are most powerful under which sets of circumstances. The limitations and opportunities to influence policy by all actors is discussed by analyzing the roles of executors, legislators, judges, career bureaucrats, public sector unions, interest groups, the media, party officials, and advisory groups. The increasingly important role of the professional bureaucrat is discussed in the context of policy development and policy implementation. One chapter, for example, is devoted to the role of the bureaucracy in budgeting.

Gable, Richard. "Modernizing Court Administration: The Case of the Los Angeles Superior Court." PUBLIC ADMINISTRATION REVIEW 31 (March-April 1971): 133-43.

This is a study of the administration of the Los Angeles County Superior Court, the largest trial court in the country. In attempting to deal with an increasing case load, the California state legislature created the position of executive officer in 1957. The author traces the evolution of the court prior to and since the establishment of the executive officer. The article focuses on the areas of budgeting control, salaries, related agencies doing court work, personnel management, and relations with the county clerk. The executive officer concentrates on implementing sound management practices and eliminating the unnecessary and inefficient functions performed by the court. The executive officer directs his attention toward gaining the support of the sitting judges and separating the court system from the political influence of the county government.

Gordon, Diana R. CITY LIMITS: BARRIERS TO CHANGE IN URBAN GOVERNMENT. New York: Charterhouse, 1973. 329 p.

Written by a former New York City employee, the six case studies in this book highlight the problems encountered in trying to institute changes in urban bureaucracies. The cases center around the conflict between urban reformers and career civil servants, emphasizing the importance of the bureaucracy in urban policy making. Unions are not viewed as major obstacles to reform, except as they represent the views of bureaucrats. The major innovative efforts of the Lindsay administration achieved some change, but not enough to make a difference. Structural change is a necessity, but it will not come from within the government. Only a demand by an aroused public will prompt the necessary bureaucratic response to change.

Grigsby, William, and Rosenburg, Louis. URBAN HOUSING POLICY. New Brunswick, N.J.: Center for Urban Policy Research, Rutgers University, 1975. 331 p.

Focusing on Baltimore, this study examines housing policy in five areas: the definition of low-income housing, the families which are affected, discrepancies between inadequate or inappropriate housing, the impact of the real-estate industry on the problem and, finally, what can and should be done. The authors conducted a series of household surveys and then examined residential structures to determine their quality. They also surveyed owner-investors and then met with members of this group to assess their potential for

management and to try to formulate housing policy. The authors
conclude that, with the assistance of major interest groups, an
effective housing policy can be developed. Housing policy, to
be effective, must become part of an overall program to improve
the quality of the urban environment.

Herbert, Adam W. "The Minority Administrator: Problems, Prospects and Challenges." PUBLIC ADMINISTRATION REVIEW 34 (November-December 1974):
556-63.

In the past few years, there has been a marked increase in the
number of blacks in both elected and administrative posts in small
and large cities. Blacks are now much more involved in urban
policy development and implementation and are becoming much
more aware of their important and unique role in urban management. With this increased importance, a clearer understanding of
the needs, responsibilities, and problems of minority public administrators has developed. A breakdown of minority employment by
functional area in federal, state, and local government is presented.
Six major-role demands on minority administrators are discussed:
system demands, traditional role expectations, colleague pressures,
community accountability, personal commitment to community, and
personal ambition. Recommendations are offered for the public
sector, schools of public affairs, and minority administrators.

Holland, Arthur J. "The Business Administrator--As Seen by the Mayor."
PUBLIC MANAGEMENT 55 (June 1973): 14-15.

Urban mayors spend much of their time lobbying, attracting business
and industry, mediating disputes, and interacting with the community.
With all of these duties, the mayor must count on his top administrative assistant to assume major responsibilities. Unlike a city
manager, the administrator is less dependent upon the administrative
code than he is on the mayor's policies and programs. The administrator is both a professional and a political appointee, and
he is likely to be more politically sensitive than a city manager
but he should try to be above politics.

Jones, Victor. "Representative Local Government: From Neighborhood to
Region." In NEIGHBORHOOD CONTROL IN THE 1970S: POLITICS, AD-
MINISTRATION AND CITIZEN PARTICIPATION, edited by George Frederickson,
pp. 73-84. New York: Chandler, 1973.

The author suggests that the challenges to local government in the
1970s will not be very different from those faced in the 1960s.
Local governments will be called upon to be effective, responsive,
just, and representative. Several issues discussed are: the slow
pace of change, the skepticism concerning local government organization and operation, the changing nature of the intergovernmental system, the growing interdependence of public and private

groups, the movement towards smaller administrative units, and more linkages among governments at the metropolitan and regional level.

Keane, Mark E. "City Hall's Management Challenges." NATION'S CITIES 8 (June 1970): 24-29.

The problems of local government are being discussed by many people, including the media and new national organizations interested in urban affairs. The major problem articulated by the author is the lack of understanding by those who control national resources for the difficulties involved in managing a city government. City officials have been blamed for much that has gone wrong in urban America and have not been praised for many of the things they have accomplished. The major problems confronting local governmental leaders in the future are: regional government, state government responsiveness, citizen participation, neighborhood government, unions, environmental protection, police, revenue sharing, civil conflict, and social and economic concerns. The author concludes with suggestions on how to use professional management talent in order to make the job of local managers more effective.

Kennedy, Will C. "Police Departments: Organization and Tasks in Disaster." AMERICAN BEHAVIORAL SCIENTIST 13 (January-February 1970): 354-61.

The organization of municipal police departments can be viewed in different ways. Three approaches discussed in this article are time, function, and authority. Time is important since demands on the police vary by time periods. Functions can be viewed from the standpoint of field operations, services, or administration. Police departments can also be analyzed on the basis of levels of authority. Each of these three factors is important in understanding the functions of a police department during a disaster. The major tasks performed by police during a disaster are: traffic and crowd control, protection of life and property, search and rescue, and warning and evacuation. Each of these tasks requires careful planning so personnel can be allocated, resources mobilized, and action coordinated.

Kirlin, John J., and Erie, Steven P. "The Study of City Governance and Public Policy Making: A Critical Appraisal." PUBLIC ADMINISTRATION REVIEW 32 (March-April 1972): 173-84.

Studies of urban politics and administration have concentrated on cities as isolated providers of services, emphasizing internal administrative structure and decision-making processes. This traditional approach has not focused attention on either the impact of municipal government actions upon citizens or the external interdependencies of cities which affect their actions. The authors review six contemporary models of urban governance broadly defined as input-oriented approaches, intermediate structural approaches, and output approaches. None of these models is easily transferable to suggestions for public policy for metropolitan America. The authors recommend three new directions for studying local political systems. The first is microoutputs and analyzes policy outputs in terms of actual services rendered to citizens. The second is the impact of local governmental activity on citizens and concentrates on citizen perceptions and evaluations of governmental action and inaction. Third are the external relationships among cities in a metropolitan area and between city, state, and federal agencies.

Kreps, Gary A. "Change in Crisis-Relevant Organizations: Police Departments and Civil Disturbances." AMERICAN BEHAVIORAL SCIENTIST 16 (January-February 1973): 356-67.

Police departments are identified as crisis-relevant organizations. Changes in police department planning, training, and emergency equipment due to civil disturbances are examined. Fifteen cities are analyzed by focusing on organizational change in police departments, the process of change development, and important organizational factors associated with the development of changes.

Lewin, Arie Y., and Blanning, Robert W. "The Urban Government Annual Report." In IMPROVING URBAN MANAGEMENT, edited by Willis D. Hawley and David Rogers, pp. 28-54. Beverly Hills, Calif.: Sage Publications, 1974.

This article discusses the need for and the feasibility of requiring local governments to publish annual reports to their citizens similar to the process used by corporations in reporting to their stockholders. The growth and complexity of urban governments today makes it extremely difficult for citizens to evaluate the performance of their government. Current municipal reporting practices are discussed. Five types of decision makers who could use information in an annual report to help make decisions are identified. They are: citizens, special interest groups, legislators, journalists, and other governments. The contents of an annual report should include statements of revenue and expenses, financial position, cost and performance, and reports of the economic and social states of the city. Examples of annual reports are presented as is a discussion on the implementation and political feasibility of the report.

Lewis, Harold. "Management in the Nonprofit Social Service Organization." CHILD WELFARE 54 (November 1975): 615-23.

Many managers in nonprofit, social service organizations find they are being called upon to manage increasingly complex operations. They lack a set of management principles which can guide their decision making, particularly in the areas of building trust while respecting privacy. Principles are needed to help develop an appropriate mix of optimal unit cost and client satisfaction levels.

Also needed are guiding principles for making political and economic decisions affecting organizational efficiency. Managers require a guide for understanding and using technologies in a fair and just manner so they can respond to requests for accountability.

Lindsay, Franklin A. "Managerial Innovation and the Cities." DAEDALUS 97 (Fall 1968): 1218-30.

The irony of the urban crisis in America is that it has occurred in a country with the greatest resources available to solve its problems. What we are lacking is an understanding and acceptance of what must be done to solve these problems and the commitment necessary to mobilize human, physical, and economic resources. The author suggests that we must greatly increase our technical, economic, managerial, and social research. We must develop the capabilities to view cities as interrelated systems. We must fund large-scale training and education programs to insure a supply of trained managers for our urban organizations. Existing governmental organizations must provide for greater creativity and innovation and more opportunities for effecting change. We must also create new governmental institutions which will specifically focus on major urban problems.

Lineberry, Robert L., and Fowler, Edmund P. "Reformism and Public Policies in American Cities." AMERICAN POLITICAL SCIENCE REVIEW 61 (September 1967): 701-16.

Earlier research on reformism had suggested that socioeconomic cleavages help to determine political forms--type of ballot, methods of electing councilmen, and so forth. The authors expand this causal relationship and argue that political form is one factor that impacts upon political output. Reformed and unreformed governments impact differently on policy making in American cities. They demonstrate this by using two policy outputs: taxation, and expenditure levels of cities, as dependent variables. The independent variables are several socioeconomic characteristics. The findings show that reformed cities spend and tax less than unreformed cities with some expectations. Responsiveness of political systems to class, racial, and religious cleavages depends very much on the local government political structure.

Long, Norton E. "The City as Underdeveloped Country." PUBLIC ADMINISTRATION REVIEW 32 (January-February 1972): 57-62.

This essay asserts that cities in America have begun to lose their viability because being a citizen of a city no longer has the same rewards nor does it extract the same commitments. Several studies are cited which highlight the plight of the city in the areas of transportation, criminal justice, finance, land use, education, and health. The author states that many of our centers have come to resemble Indian reservations. Most mayors seem powerless to cope with the mounting tide of problems confronting them. The author suggests viewing our older cities as underdeveloped countries and concentrating on restoring them to a viable economic position. This can be done by providing more productive employment opportunities for youth and assisting the educational system to work more effectively with young people.

_____. "Have Cities A Future?" PUBLIC ADMINISTRATION REVIEW 33 (November-December 1973): 543-52.

Long contends that most observers fail to look at the city as it truly exists. He views the city as an economic entity which must respond to the daily needs of its citizenry. City books must be balanced and expenditures treated as investments rather than as consumables as is currently done. City powerlessness has resulted from declining revenue bases and the departure of middle-income residents who have settled in suburbia. The city is left with a disproportionate share of the poor who require much more in services than they contribute in taxes. Citing studies in Gary, Indiana and New Haven, Connecticut, Long concludes with a call for more community-based and community-oriented organizations to help overcome the powerlessness of the cities.

_____. THE UNWALLED CITY. New York: Basic Books, 1972. 208 p.

Cities have failed to utilize all of their resources in an effort to improve their local economies. Failure to view cities as local economies by all public officials means cities will continually be linked to the national economy. Cities that have been successful in expanding their boundaries have experienced increased growth. Cities that are stagnating economically have no choice but to ask state and federal levels of government to assist them financially. However, this is not a long-term solution and can only lead to the city becoming a ward of higher levels of government. Cities need to begin a systematic inventory of their assets and liabilities so they can begin meaningful human resource planning and development.

Lowi, Theodore J. "Machine Politics--Old and New." PUBLIC INTEREST 9 (Fall 1967): 83-92.

Political machines which were institutions peculiar to American cities have all but passed from the scene. Only now can they be put in perspective. The author briefly reviews the reasons for the divergent political structures in New York and Chicago, such as population, efficiency, reform and merit systems. The author feels that the new machines are really the city bureaucracies which, instead of becoming neutral, have become independent. New machines are similar in organization to old machines but different in that they are more numerous, they are functional rather than geographic, and rely upon formal authority instead of popular vote. Several examples are cited to show how centralized authority is thwarted in light of the existing fragmentation. The 1961 mayoral election is shown to be similar to past elections where bosses put their tickets together carefully. In the end, the old machines are seen to be not as bad as once depicted.

McCarty, Donald J., and Ramsey, Charles E. THE SCHOOL MANAGERS: POWER AND CONFLICT IN AMERICAN PUBLIC EDUCATION. Westport, Conn.: Greenwood, 1971. 297 p.

This book is a study of power and conflict in American education. Different definitions of power are discussed, with the authors concluding that power involves both a controller and the one being controlled. They suggest that elite and pluralist power structures are not the only ones that exist within a community school board. They show the existence of an inert power structure in which there is no visibly-active group and a factional power structure in which political activity centers on criteria such as: religion, politics, occupation, and economic philosophy. In each case, the superintendent must assume a role of professional adviser, decision-maker, and political strategist. Using data from fifty-one communities in the Northeast and Midwest, the authors conclude that community environment plays an important role in determining how the superintendent and the school board will act.

Marland, Sidney P., Jr. "The Changing Nature of the School Superintendency." PUBLIC ADMINISTRATION REVIEW 30 (July-August 1970): 365-71.

The role of the school superintendent has changed dramatically over the past ten years. The author examines the causes and effects of these changes as they impacted upon public policy in this country. The role of the superintendent is in many ways similar to appointed and elected executives in local government. Recently superintendents are finding increased relationships with both chief executives and community leaders, who are asking for new programs and activities which are often beyond the competence, resources, and readiness of the school system. The changing role of the superintendent is examined in terms of community demands, faculty, students, federal programs, and local political realities.

Mars, David. "Governing Megacentropolis: The Problem." PUBLIC ADMINISTRATION REVIEW 30 (September-October 1970): 474-80.

The five largest cities in the United States--New York, Chicago, Los Angeles, Philadelphia, and Detroit--contain over seventeen million people and are labeled megacentropolises. These cities are newsworthy, the centers of economic, political and cultural activity, centers of political influence, and examples of the isolation and anomie felt by many citizens in our large and complex

society. The author discusses the role of the central city and the
need for changes within it. A statement of goals on what the city
wants to achieve should be the first step in a process of change.
The other two suggested process changes are: advocacy planning,
which would involve citizens directly in one government function,
and citizen councils, which would be established through an elec-
tive process and would involve citizens in a given governmental
area.

Meade, Marvin. "Participative Administration—Emerging Reality or Wishful
Thinking?" In PUBLIC ADMINISTRATION IN A TIME OF TURBULENCE, edited
by Dwight Waldo, pp. 169-87. Scranton, Pa.: Chandler, 1971.

Many people who are disappointed in the performance of our public
bureaucracies have begun to advocate participative administration
as one possible reform. One problem that emerges is a lack of
clarity concerning the term "participation." The author reviews
both the substance and the literature of participative management.
Also discussed is the role of participation as it pertains to the
relationship between clients and bureaucrats. The experience of
the 1960s, when the federal government sought to increase citizen
participation, is used as an illustration to highlight political,
social, and psychological problems. The distribution and redistribution of power is a key element in understanding participation.
The ability to transform conceptual innovations into practical applications remains one of the major obstacles associated with social
science solutions to political and administrative problems.

Miles, Raymond E., and Ritchie, J.B. "Participation Management: Quality
or Quantity." CALIFORNIA MANAGEMENT REVIEW 13 (Summer 1971): 48-
56.

The two major models of participatory management are the human
relations model and the human resources model. The first uses
frequent superior-subordinate consultation as a means of cooperation,
while the latter recognizes untapped potential of the organization's
members and advocates participation as a means of directly improving individual and organizational output. The authors administered
questionnaires to 380 chief executives and department supervisors
to measure the quantity of participation and the quality of participation and satisfaction with immediate supervisors. Quantity of
participation correlated positively with satisfaction. Satisfaction
was also high where supervisors had confidence in the subordinate,
but this was usually coupled with quality of consultation not quantity. Supervisors' attitudes towards subordinates' capabilities and
potential is as important as the amount of consultation. Cooperative and ongoing planning with subordinates produces best results.

Mintzberg, Henry. "The Manager's Job: Folklore and Fact." HARVARD
BUSINESS REVIEW 53 (July-August 1975): 49-61.

Historically, managers have been assumed to be like orchestra leaders coordinating the diverse talents of their subordinates. However, when management studies are analyzed, it is seen that managers are not reflective, regulated workers, informed by scientific and professional management information systems. The evidence indicates that managers play a complex combination of interpersonal and decisional roles. The author's research suggests that managers spend a great deal of their time in the transmission of information. Many management schools have done a good job of training organizational specialists, but for the most part they have not trained managers in skills necessary for effective management.

Murray, Michael A. "Comparing Public and Private Management: An Exploratory Essay." PUBLIC ADMINISTRATION REVIEW 35 (July–August 1975): 364–71.

This article focuses on the similarities and differences in management in the public and private sectors. The major points of comparison are: fact versus value, profits versus politics, objectivity of measurement, attitudes of business and government, accountability, visibility, evaluation methods, personnel systems, planning, and questions of efficiency. The conclusion is that there are many more similarities than differences between the public and private sector management practices. Differences are becoming blurred as each sector begins to absorb characteristics of the other. Myths associated with each sector often disappear with closer scrutiny, particularly in the areas of efficiency and openness.

Nelson, William E., Jr., and Van Horne, Winston. "Black Elected Administrators: The Trials of Office." PUBLIC ADMINISTRATION REVIEW 34 (November–December 1974): 526–33.

The article begins by tracing the increased number of black officials in all levels of government. The authors examine the impact these officials have had on the black community, public policy, and the problems they have faced in the decision-making process. The election of black officials has not automatically improved the quality of life for black residents. Black officials still face the problems of race and, because they have been excluded from public office before, they have to learn more in a shorter period. Problems also are encountered in black officials dealing with white bureaucracies and trying to find political, economic, and technical resources to administer programs. Blacks have begun using political accommodation and community resources mobilization to overcome these problems.

Parker, John K. "Administrative Planning." In MANAGING THE MODERN CITY, edited by James M. Banovetz, pp. 238–54. Washington, D.C.: International City Management Association, 1971.

Administrative planning is one form of planning carried out on an almost continuous basis by different members of local government. It involves deciding in advance what the organization will do in the future, by whom, and how. Planning helps to achieve community goals and improve management. Administrative planning requires decisions to plan, definition of objectives, setting of priorities, developing action programs, implementing action programs, and evaluation and revision of plans. Comprehensive administrative planning includes forecasting, policy planning, programming and scheduling, and budgeting and control. Techniques for making planning more effective are presented.

Penne, R. Leo, and Ryan, Sharon. "Managing Urban Decline: An Urban Conservation Report From Dayton." NATION'S CITIES 14 (March 1976): 17-24.

This is a report on a management strategy being used in Dayton, Ohio which could be of value to managers in other cities. Groups of coordinated responsibilities have been placed under the direction of assistant city managers for administrative services, community services, and development services. Short-term problems are dealt with through team management and interdisciplinary approaches. Citizen participation is implemented through six neighborhood planning councils. The county government works closely with the city on a growth line for public services to insure that extension and overcommitment are prevented.

Phares, Donald, and Greytak, David. MUNICIPAL OUTPUT AND PERFORMANCE IN NEW YORK CITY. Lexington, Mass.: Lexington Books, 1975. 180 p.

This study uses primary source data to examine changes in operations of New York City departments and agencies between 1960 and 1973. The departments of police, fire, sanitation, health, hospitals, and human resources are studied. Each of the departmental expenditure categories is analyzed by output and performance criteria. Using indexes of change, the authors examine each of the functional areas in the study, including shifts in the service areas covered by these departments.

Rich, Wilbur. "Special Role and Role Evaluation of Black Administrators of Neighborhood Mental Health Programs." COMMUNITY MENTAL HEALTH JOURNAL 11 (Winter 1975): 394-401.

Recruitment of black administrators for community mental health programs has been slow and the turnover has been high due to the role conflicts these administrators experience. They are viewed as performing a racial function in addition to their normal administrative functions. White colleagues see them as racial experts, while the black community regards them as mediators and access points. They run great risks in trying not to offend their white superiors or the community they are serving. The special problems of the

black administrators should be recognized; unnecessary demands
should not be placed upon them.

Rogers, David. THE MANAGEMENT OF BIG CITIES: INTEREST GROUPS AND
SOCIAL CHANGE STRATEGIES. Beverly Hills, Calif.: Sage Publications,
1971. 189 p.

This is a study of three large American cities--New York, Philadelphia, and Cleveland--and how their political and organizational
structures affect their ability to respond to economic, demographic,
and technological change. Each of the cities is examined in historical perspective with an analysis of contemporary political, social,
and economic factors affecting the city's ability to deliver necessary
services. The author reviews proposals for new delivery systems, as
well as the tendency for frustrated inner-city residents to blame the
mayor for all of the problems affecting them. The ability of large
cities to adapt to change is affected by the various actions of the
states and federal government which often impose constraints on
action at the local level. All three levels of government exhibit
characteristics that contribute to poor service delivery: fragmentation, lack of coordination, conflict, and low productivity. Cities
have to learn how to produce better services even without an increase in funds.

_____. 110 LIVINGSTON STREET: POLITICS AND BUREAUCRACY IN THE
NEW YORK CITY SCHOOL SYSTEM. New York: Random House, 1968.
584 p.

This is a comprehensive study of New York City's educational administration and how it interacts with other city organizations,
civic groups, teachers, and administrators. Data for the book was
gathered from over 1,200 interviews with school officials and politicians and attendance at numerous public and private meetings.
Additional information was obtained from media coverage, outside
studies of the system, and a review of board actions. The book
begins with a discussion of New York City's failure to desegregate
the schools and it examines the city's housing patterns and the
neighborhood school movement. The author examines the board of
education, its decision-making patterns, and the major decision
makers. An analysis of the professional bureaucracy and the exercise of administrative controls is presented. Some suggestions for
institutional reform are: decentralization, community control, alternative competing school systems, and a coalition of public and
private interests working together to upgrade educational programs.

Rosenthal, Alan. "Administrator-Teacher Relations: Harmony or Conflict?"
PUBLIC ADMINISTRATION REVIEW 27 (June 1967): 154-61.

The relationship between classroom teachers and school administrators
has often been strained over the conflict between classroom autonomy

and hierarchical authority. Outside pressures, such as demands for curriculum changes, integration movements, and problems of disadvantaged students, have caused increased tensions between teachers and administrators. Teacher participation in educational policy making is analyzed from the perspective of both the teacher and the administrator. The changing nature of teacher organizations has also affected educational administrators as they attempt to cope with growing militancy. The resolution of differences is discussed in terms of common interests and the uses of conflict.

Rosner, Martin M. "Administrative Controls and Innovation." BEHAVIORAL SCIENCE 13 (January 1968): 36-43.

Bureaucratic organizations are being attacked because they are not amenable to innovation. Their procedural and regulatory controls are often cited as the reasons why they are unreceptive to changing behavior patterns and environmental concerns. Control procedures and program evaluation are two important functions in organizations, the former inhibiting innovation while the latter should encourage it. The author conducted a study in twenty-four voluntary hospitals in the Chicago area to identify the rate of innovation by using the introduction of new drugs into the hospitals and the frequency and promptness of their introduction. He found the more activity control exercised by the hospital, the less frequently new drugs were introduced, and the more visible the consequences of hospital activities, the more frequently the new drugs were tried.

Rossi, Peter; Berk, Richard A.; and Eidson, Bettye K. THE ROOTS OF URBAN DISCONTENT: PUBLIC POLICY, MUNICIPAL INSTITUTIONS AND THE GHETTO. New York: Wiley-Interscience, 1974. 499 p.

This book is an analysis of some of the problems raised by urban discontent. The authors conducted interviews with public officials and black and white citizens in fifteen large American cities and then compared the local institutions in cities, such as Boston, Chicago, Pittsburgh, and San Francisco. The study shows how local government agencies differ from city to city and how these differences affect citizens and their political activity. Also included are discussions of problem areas, such as police behavior, education, welfare, and discrimination in employment.

Rowe, Lloyd A. "The Coming Crisis of the Urban Administrator." MIDWEST REVIEW OF PUBLIC ADMINISTRATION 5 (August 1971): 105-9.

Local elected officials are finding it increasingly difficult to provide effective leadership in coping with the causes of urban ills. More and more professional administrators have vast amounts of knowledge at their disposal which may result in conflicts between the administrator's traditional role of subordination and responsiveness to locally-elected officials and the community's demand for relevant and responsible decision making. Several participatory decision-making systems in local government are examined for guidelines and suggestions to help urban managers resolve conflict.

Schmandt, Henry J.; Goldbach, John C.; and Vogel, Donald B. MILWAUKEE: A CONTEMPORARY URBAN PROFILE. New York: Praeger, 1971. 237 p.

This book seeks to increase the understanding of the politics and administration of an urban political system. Attention is focused on the governmental structure, decision-making processes, and administrative organization as the community attempts to govern itself. Change is slow and suburban governments resist metropolitan approaches preferring to maintain the status quo. The authors believe that increasing interest and aid on the part of state and federal agencies is the direction of the future. This large-scale administrative and policy direction may be balanced by greater interest in local control over issues of great importance to local residents.

Scott, David C. "Making Decisions." In DEVELOPING THE MUNICIPAL ORGANIZATION, edited by Stanley Powers, F. Gerald Brown, and David S. Arnold, pp. 102–12. Washington, D.C.: International City Management Association, 1974.

Decision making is, in essence, problem solving. It involves choosing among or between alternatives by following a series of steps. Four types of decisions are identified with which local government managers must deal. They are: policy decisions, administrative decisions, management decisions, and individual and organizational decisions. Policy analysis is the tool most often used by managers to make decisions; it involves defining the problem, developing and testing alternatives, and selecting appropriate courses of action. It often utilizes mathematical analysis, computer technology, and the quantification of data. Several factors which affect decisions are discussed: form of the question, views of others, habits and custom, emotions, personal needs, and individual skills. The concluding section discusses the evaluation of decisions and the improvement of supervisory decisions.

Shapek, Raymond A. "Problems and Deficiencies in the Needs Assessment Process." PUBLIC ADMINISTRATION REVIEW 35 (December 1975): 754–58.

The listing of needs by local governments is viewed as being inconsistent, lacking meaning, and of limited utility. Often the goals, problems, or needs which are identified by state or local officials are unachievable, insoluble, or beyond the technological or political capability of government to correct. Consequently, needs assessments are often ignored, or when acted upon, fail to meet the expectations of local public officials. Needs listings have proved to be inaccurate because of internal organizational and political factors, external relations among governments, and economic factors. Other variables which affect this technique include rank ordering of needs, current versus future needs, and citizen participation. One solution proposed is to view needs assessment as a limited technique which can be included in the overall planning process directed at a more comprehensive and accurate listing of local needs.

Shipman, George A. DESIGNING PROGRAM ACTION--AGAINST URBAN POVERTY. University: University of Alabama Press, 1971. 128 p.

Shipman examines the techniques of utilizing available resources in the public, volunteer, and private sectors to eliminate urban poverty. The first step in the process is defining urban poverty, its causes and attributes. Next the trends and capabilities, fiscal and operational, are studied. Finally, the community is examined as a possible framework for intervention. A comprehensive program must flow from the productive efforts of operating agencies, producing major programs. Control is viewed as an essential element in the operation of a systems approach. Operating responsibility is accepted in consideration of the assurance of the supports that are necessary. By contractual linkages, jurisdictional lines are crossed over and a wide range of public, private, and voluntary resources become available.

Spindler, Arthur. "Management By Crisis or Management By Plan?" PUBLIC WELFARE 30 (Spring 1972): 44-47.

Spindler focuses on the capabilities of local public welfare administrators to assume leadership roles in shaping public welfare policy for the next generation. He presents several suggestions to assist the urban welfare administrators in effective planning and evaluation. An analysis is offered of the impact of pending federal and state proposals on state and local income maintenance and service programs and the development of a departmental monitoring program. Also presented is a guide to the preparation of a socioeconomic analysis comparing 1970 census data with 1970 public assistance and service recipient data.

Steiss, Alan W., et al. DYNAMIC CHANGE AND THE URBAN GHETTO. Lexington, Mass.: Lexington Books, 1975. 144 p.

The authors examine the implications of social change for urban ghettos. Using the model city area of Miami, the study utilizes a simulation model over time of individual and aggregate behavior of three social variables--education, income, and health. Key variables are identified which can be manipulated to improve the quality of social programs in the urban ghetto. The authors also discuss the issue of technological change by using other variables to forecast the effect of improved accessibility on overall performance in the model cities area.

Stone, Robert S. "Changing Patterns in Local Environmental Health Administration." JOURNAL OF ENVIRONMENTAL HEALTH 37 (May-June 1975): 544-54.

Stone traces the trends in local government environmental health program administration which have generated rapid changes in organizational structure. He also discusses organizational, societal, and interorganizational pressures responsible for these changes. The author also examines the relationship of the affected professional groups within health departments, namely the medical administrators and environmentalists. He demonstrates how their attitudes and interactions have helped to shape the present situations and evaluates the implications of new organizational patterns for the administrator.

Turem, Jerry S. "The Call for a Management Stance." SOCIAL WORK 19 (September 1974): 615-23.

The rapid increase in funding for social welfare programs in the past decade makes it mandatory that agencies administering these programs become accountable for the public funds received. There has been a great deal of pressure generated for increased accountability in social welfare programs. Social work managers can fulfill certain needs by assembling reliable data, having the means to analyze the data, and developing the skills to use the data in decision making. Managers can then decide which goals they can reasonably expect to attain and begin to allocate resources in an effort to achieve their goals efficiently and effectively.

Van Dersal, William R. THE SUCCESSFUL SUPERVISOR IN GOVERNMENT AND BUSINESS. New York: Harper and Row, 1968. 206 p.

This is a guide for supervisors in both government and industry which proceeds from the assumption that there is a gap between academic theory and managerial practice. Seven principles of supervision are developed, ranging from letting the employee know what is expected of him, to working in a safe and healthy environment. Techniques of criticizing employees and the degree of participation in organizations are also discussed, as are strategies for motivating employees. Communication is assumed to be an easy function, yet it is the cause of many managerial problems. Speaking, writing, and listening are three important characteristics of good managers. Several case studies are presented.

Watt, Graham W.; Parker, John K.; and Cantine, Robert R. "Roles of the Urban Administrator in the 1970s and the Knowledges and Skills Required to Perform These Roles." In EDUCATION FOR URBAN ADMINISTRATION, edited by Frederic M. Cleaveland and Thomas J. Davey, pp. 50-79. Philadelphia: American Academy of Political and Social Science, 1973.

This article summarizes data collected from over 130 urban administrators. Most of the respondents feel that urban administrators are in the center of intense political conflict dealing with the disadvantaged, the disenchanted, and the disenfranchised. The role of the manager as he sees it and as others see him can be assessed in three broad areas: determining the procedural aspects of how the community should be governed, determining the dimensions of governmental responsibility and response, and determining how best to manage public resources. Tables are presented of managers' views of the important service areas and also of the skills that will be needed by future administrators. The authors include a list of twenty real world challenges that urban administrators face constantly. The rapid pace of change, the increasingly complex urban environment, and the need for greater interaction with people sum up the challenge to urban administration in the future.

Weaver, Jerry L. CONFLICT AND CONTROL IN HEALTH CARE ADMINISTRATION. Beverly Hills, Calif.: Sage Publications, 1974. 196 p.

Health administrators face a dilemma between economic, social, and political realities of large organizations and the need to maintain the personal nature of doctor-patient relationships. The author presents a profile of health care administrators, occupational variations, job characteristics, and problems that arise with co-workers. The major problem areas confronting the administrators are financing, budgeting, regulations, and maintaining adequate information flows. The book defines the skills required by health care administrators and discusses the need for in-service and midcareer training and education.

Weiler, Conrad. PHILADELPHIA: NEIGHBORHOOD AUTHORITY AND THE URBAN CRISIS. New York: Praeger, 1974. 210 p.

The author attempts to determine people's attitudes towards the Philadelphia government and their feelings of control over it. He finds most respondents have a negative attitude about the government and feel they have little control over it. The city's attempt to satisfy citizen demands starts from a weak financial base. Little progress in the financial area can be made unless the entire context of Philadelphia politics is understood, including relationships with the state and federal governments. The relationship between reformers, liberals, and the ethnic neighborhoods is discussed. The major problem preventing solutions to the city's problems lies in the fact that the city and its neighborhoods have relatively little power compared to the state, the federal government, and the metropolitan area.

Wilson, James Q. "Dilemmas of Police Administration." PUBLIC ADMINISTRATION REVIEW 28 (September-October 1968): 407-17.

The administration and policy-making functions of large city police departments are hampered by attempts to achieve two goals, one of which produces conflict and the other which is unattainable. The problems center on the inability to obtain agreement on what constitutes satisfactory performance and the difficulty of finding a strategy to reach this objective. The two major objectives of police work are order maintenance and law enforcement. The inability of the police to satisfy citizen requirements in both leads to administrative problems, some of which are: hiring unqualified personnel, manipulating crime reports, over-reaction, use of illegal procedures, and use of patrol techniques that create tension. Changing each of these failures might have only a marginal impact on police performance and administration. It is more likely that the class composition of the community is the critical variable in improving the police function.

Yutzy, Daniel. "Priorities in Community Response." AMERICAN BEHAVIORAL SCIENTIST 13 (January-February 1970): 344-53.

Disasters tend to upset traditional human social arrangements in communities. The impact of a disaster may affect community resources and threaten or impede the delivery of services which are deemed important or essential. The major organization goals in a disaster are identified as: preservation of life, restoration and maintenance of public order, restoration and maintenance of essential services, and maintenance of community morale. Many basic activities around which the community is organized are changed during a disaster. These include: the production-distribution-consumption function, the socialization function, the social control function, social participation, and mutual support activities.

B. MAYORS

Allen, Ivan, Jr. MAYOR: NOTES ON THE SIXTIES. New York: Simon and Schuster, 1971. 241 p.

This is an analysis of the politics and administration of Atlanta in the 1960s as recounted by the two-term mayor of the city. The major programs discussed are school construction, freeways, urban renewal, rapid transit, and the new stadium. Candid views are presented of the problems involved in managing and governing a large city with emphasis on the racial issue. During his second term, the mayor organized the business community to cooperate in making Atlanta a better place to live. Many successful programs were instituted and completed in the second term by this coalition of business and political leaders.

Bancroft, Raymond L. "America's Mayors and Councilmen: Their Problems and Frustrations." NATION'S CITIES 12 (April 1974): 14-22.

This article presents the findings from a nationwide survey of mayors and councilmen conducted by the National League of Cities.

It summarizes the major urban problems confronting these municipal officials. The problem of refuse and solid waste received the most votes from the twenty-eight problems in eight categories. The other major problem areas were: law enforcement, streets and highways, relations with counties, fiscal and tax policies, downtown development, planning and zoning, citizen participation, public transit, and the use of general revenue-sharing funds. Also included in the study are profiles of the average mayor and councilman along with salary data.

Boynton, Robert Paul, and Wright, Deil S. "Mayor-Manager Relationships in Large Council-Manager Cities: A Reinterpretation." PUBLIC ADMINISTRATION REVIEW 31 (January-February 1971): 28-36.

The authors administered a questionnaire to forty-five council-manager cities with populations over 100,000 to determine the interrelationships of mayors and managers and some perceptions of the role of the manager in local government. The questionnaire focused on the electoral process, roles and characteristics of the council, budget processes, the use of boards and commissions, intergovernmental relations, and the administration of public policies. The authors conclude that managers have become more involved in policy initiation and policy making. This is the result of changing community needs more than manager preferences. Managers in large cities appear to be performing more like strong mayors than the traditional stereotype of a city manager.

Cunningham, James V. URBAN LEADERSHIP IN THE SIXTIES. Waltham, Mass.: Lemberg Center for the Study of Violence, Brandeis University, 1970. 93 p.

Cunningham focuses on the mayors of Cleveland, Chicago, Pittsburgh, and New Haven, and compares their performance in mobilizing and utilizing scarce resources to deal with urban problems. The author presents the major socioeconomic characteristics of the four cities and then develops a list of seven traits of mayoral leadership against which the four mayors are compared. These traits are: originality, risk-taking, initiative, energy, openness, organizational ability, and promotional ingenuity. A brief case study of each city and its political leadership in the 1960s is presented. The author concludes that New Haven exhibited the greatest entrepreneurship under its mayor, while Chicago and Cleveland ranked fairly low. The author suggests several characteristics which ought to be considered in the selection of urban mayors other than ethnicity and party loyalty.

Diamond, Ted. "Mr. Urban America: An Evaluation of the Lindsay Mayoralty." MAXWELL REVIEW 9 (Winter 1972-73): 97-106.

This article evaluates the Lindsay administration on the basis of what was accomplished with the resources available rather than what might have been done. Lindsay became a national spokesman for all big-city mayors. He was able to increase the city's taxing power, state aid, flexibility, and he forcefully presented New York's views in Washington. However, New York proved inefficient and indecisive in the use of funds and the job of the mayor on many boards and commissions was not clearly defined. Mediating disputes and participation in confrontation politics had been mishandled, reorganization had been used to cover inefficiency, and resources had not been allocated in an effective manner.

Gleason, Bill. DALEY OF CHICAGO. New York: Simon and Schuster, 1970. 368 p.

Daley is pictured as a politician who served his apprenticeship in Illinois politics during the 1940s and 1950s. In each political office he held, Daley learned a little more about the operation and management of a political organization. Daley had guided the political life of Chicago since 1955. The book discusses Daley's strategy and techniques for getting things done in the city. It examines Daley's policy in the area of civil rights and civil disturbances. His relationship to state and federal officials is also discussed.

Harman, Douglas, and Carter, Steven C. "Currents of Change." PUBLIC MANAGEMENT 55 (June 1973): 7-9.

Mayor-administrator relationships have been affected by related factors: formal powers, local community needs, and individual personalities. The past preoccupation with the separation and balance of powers resulted in an adversary-type description of the political and administrative relationships. Today the mayor-administrator relationship is viewed more as a team approach to community needs and individual personalities. This team approach is directed at maximizing resources to combine strong political leadership with strong administrative leadership.

Kotter, John P., and Lawrence, Paul R. MAYORS IN ACTION: FIVE APPROACHES TO URBAN GOVERNANCE. New York: Wiley-Interscience, 1974. 287 p.

This book challenges some myths about the function and impact of mayors. Using a large-scale comparative research approach, the authors analyze the behavior of twenty mayors and their administrations during the 1960s. The authors conclude that there are five basic approaches that mayors use in performing their job--ceremonial, caretaker, executive, individualist, and entrepreneur. Using this typology and interviews with over 200 citizens and urban experts, the authors develop an empirical model of mayoral behavior. The model helps the reader understand how and why mayors behave as they do and how this affects the administration of local government.

Kuo, Wen H. "Mayoral Influence in Urban Policy Making." AMERICAN JOURNAL OF SOCIOLOGY 79 (November 1973): 620-38.

> Political behavior of big-city mayors was studied to determine their impact upon local decision making. The argument that mayors are weak and act only as brokers among local interests was tested with data collected from ninety-three northern cities. A comparison of community programs that were adopted with those that were rejected revealed the probability of adoption was directly related to how actively the mayor campaigned on behalf of the program. City government plays an important role in initiating community programs, particularly when the city provides a strong organization for the mayor.

Levine, Charles H. RACIAL CONFLICT AND THE AMERICAN MAYOR. Lexington, Mass.: Lexington Books, 1974. 176 p.

> Case studies of the administrations of three mayors--Stokes in Cleveland, Hatcher in Gary, and Seibels in Birmingham--are used to highlight the conflict approach to management in racially troubled cities. Conflict is not always a limitation, it can be used creatively in racially polarized communities. Executive-centered coalitions appear to work more effectively in pluralistic situations where there is a low level of conflict while other models work better in cities characterized by a high degree of conflict. In a pluralistic context, the mayors in this study are not considered successful. However, when the pluralist and the conflict models are compared, different results are found and the management performance of the three mayors becomes more effective.

Lindsay, John V. THE CITY. New York: W.W. Norton, 1969. 233 p.

> The author contends that most Americans harbor negative feelings about cities, believing them to be desolate and undesirable places to live. For most of their history, cities have been unfairly represented in the state legislatures but still were able to support themselves financially. Federal policy in housing and transportation had a negative impact on the cities. Cities experienced a series of financial, management, and citizen involvement problems which prompted the movement toward neighborhood city halls. Coordination and cooperation between government and citizens increased. Welfare problems seriously weaken the ability of the city to respond to citizen needs. Problems of crime and relations with state governments are discussed. The federal government must begin to reorder priorities so greater resources are redirected back to the cities. Cities must take steps to involve more citizens in decision making.

LOCAL CHIEF EXECUTIVES' PERCEPTIONS OF POLICY-MAKING AND MANAGEMENT NEEDS. Vol. 1. Washington, D.C.: U.S. Department of Housing and Urban Development, Office of Policy Development and Research, February 1975. 160 p.

This study focuses on mayors, councilmen, county executives, and county commissioners and how they perceive their policy-making and management needs. Over 400 documents were reviewed and excerpted in order to determine the views of local chief executives. The major problem confronting local chief executives was the need to deal with many problems simultaneously. Policy-making and management priorities are not ranked but several areas of concern are delineated: intergovernmental relations, citizen participation, reorganization, policy-making processes, management techniques, personnel, and technical assistance. A series of recommended actions is proposed.

Miles, C.R. "The Working Relationship Between Mayors and Administrators." PUBLIC MANAGEMENT 55 (June 1973): 18-19.

Charters define the relationship between the mayor and the city administrator in clear and precise terms. However, they do not determine who will provide community leadership, speak for the community, or serve as the legislative liaison person. These issues are often among the most important in the mayor-administrator relationship. The mayor should undertake the community leadership role and the administrator should undertake the organizational leadership role. These two functions are apt to run together and will require a management team approach. If the mayor does not assume a leadership role, this role will be filled by either the administrator, the council, or interest groups.

Pressman, Jeffrey L. "Preconditions of Mayoral Leadership." AMERICAN POLITICAL SCIENCE REVIEW 66 (June 1972): 511-24.

Explores the politics of mayoral leadership in Oakland, California. Seven resources are outlined as essential to mayoral leadership. To pursue his goals, a mayor must have control over the city council and the major departments of government. Nongovernment groups in the community must be activated in support of mayoral programs. Local businesses must be convinced to remain in the city and encouraged to initiate job-training programs for minority groups. Public relations must be used to support the mayor and to further his programs. The mayor must be paid enough to permit him to work full time. The mayor of Oakland faces serious problems in the area of revenue shortages and rising personnel costs. These in turn nullify five of the seven resources he needs to exercise strong political and administrative leadership.

Rakove, Milton. DON'T MAKE NO WAVES--DON'T BACK NO LOSERS: AN INSIDER'S ANALYSIS OF THE DALEY MACHINE. Bloomington: University of Indiana Press, 1974. 296 p.

This study of the Daley political organization in Chicago was written by a participant who, over a period of years of watching, listening, and doing, was able to analyze the political and administrative system of Chicago. Discusses the demographics of Chicago and Daley the man, the mayor, and the politician. The majority of the book is devoted to understanding the structure and dynamics of the Cook County political organization, the ward organizations, and the relationship between the political machine and the Democratic Party. The Republicans, as the loyal opposition, are examined as is the machine's relationship with politicians in the state capital and in Washington. A final analysis in the book analyzes the impact of both suburbs and minorities on the future of the machine. The author concludes with the belief that the machine will survive by making the minor adjustments necessary to contemporary change.

Royko, Mike. BOSS: RICHARD J. DALEY OF CHICAGO. New York: E.P. Dutton, 1971. 215 p.

This critical analysis traces Richard Daley's political career from the early days as a precinct captain through his rise to mayor of Chicago. Daley learned all of the skills of a ward leader by watching the men for whom he worked. In 1955, Daley was elected mayor of Chicago and took control of the political machine which ran the city. The strengths of his political organization were 20-25,000 patronage jobs, the support of organized labor and an ample supply of money at election time. The author recounts many incidents of fraud and abuses of the law during Daley's terms of office. Daley's inability or failure to deal with civil rights problems is documented. The turmoil and violence surrounding the Democratic National Convention of 1968 marked the slow decline of Daley's power in national elections and politics. However, he still maintained strong control over the political and administrative machinery of Chicago.

Stokes, Carl B. PROMISES OF POWER: A POLITICAL AUTOBIOGRAPHY. New York: Simon and Schuster, 1973. 280 p.

This personal account of governing a large American city by the first black man to be elected mayor of a large municipality touches upon many contemporary urban problems. The book follows the educational process that Stokes was exposed to as he dealt with the problems of racism, violence, political patronage, and black voting strength. Even though Stokes became disillusioned with urban politics and decided not to run for reelection, he saw much hope for black politics in the future. This future lies in working within the political process rather than establishing independent or quasisovereign political institutions for blacks. Politics is an important component of American life because through politics one can change the way people live.

Talbot, Allan R. THE MAYOR'S GAME: RICHARD LEE OF NEW HAVEN AND THE POLITICS OF CHANGE. New York: Praeger, 1967. 274 p.

> This is a political and administrative study of efforts to rebuild the city of New Haven, Connecticut. It outlines the program developed by Mayor Lee and analyzes how this program was organized and who were his major allies and opponents. A discussion is presented of how resources were mobilized to attack the physical problems confronting the city. One section is devoted to an examination of improving the human resources of the city by trying to solve the problems of racial injustice and poverty. The focus of the book is on the mayor and his ability to use the political and administrative resources available to bring about change.

C. CITY MANAGERS

Banovetz, James M., et al. "Leadership Styles and Strategies." In MANAGING THE MODERN CITY, edited by James M. Banovetz, pp. 108-33. Washington, D.C.: International City Management Association, 1971.

> City managers are often required to perform a number of leadership roles with respect to their subordinates, the council, neighboring governments, interest groups, and friends and critics. The concept of leadership and its prerequisites are not clearly defined. The authors present a definition of leadership and examine the leadership environment of the administrator focusing on the nature of administrative leadership in both an organizational and political context. Asserting that some leadership styles can be learned, the authors discuss the development of leadership capacities by examining motivation, leadership styles, and the resources of leadership. The strategies and tactics of leadership are also discussed.

Bollens, John C., and Ries, John C. THE CITY MANAGER PROFESSION: MYTHS AND REALITIES. Chicago: Public Administration Service, 1969. 54 p.

> This monograph is part of a series that analyzes the major characteristics, historical developments, acceptance, and growth of the council-manager form of government. It discusses the myths that have historically pursued the role of the manager and the realities of city manager performance. The authors dismiss the myth of the city manager as politically neutral and depict him as a functioning member of the policy process. City managers have many of the resources available to other appointed executives. These include: expertise based on experience and training, budgetary control, and day-to-day supervision of city departments. The political environment of the city also affects the manager's use of political resources. A typology is presented using as its main characteristics the pattern of community organization and the functions the city performs.

Also discussed is the future of the manager profession.

Boynton, Robert Paul, and Wright, Deil S. "The Media, The Masses and Urban Management." JOURNALISM QUARTERLY 47 (Spring 1970): 12-19.

Focuses on communication problems relevant to community conflicts and civil unrest. Citing the civil unrest in our cities, the authors feel one component to reduce alienation of citizens might be better communication between public leaders and ghetto residents. Using data from a survey of city managers in cities over 100,000, the authors test the perceptions of the comparative impact of the press, radio, and television on local politics. Managers were asked to estimate the involvement, quality of coverage, and influence of the three media types. The overwhelming majority felt newspapers were more influential and more interested in local affairs than radio or television. Newspapers are the least frequently used media source of the three by ghetto residents. Strategies are offered by which political officials and the media can better reach the urban poor.

Carrell, Jeptha J. "The City Manager and His Council: Sources of Conflict." PUBLIC ADMINISTRATION REVIEW 22 (December 1962): 203-8.

Examines the strains and conflicts between the city manager and his council. Results are based upon questionnaires and interviews from managers in eight cities and informal discussions with political actors in many other cities. Six types of conflict which limit the effectiveness of the manager form of government are identified. These are: power prerogatives, personality clashes, political setting, policy versus expediency, inflexibility and rectitude, and communication and cognition. Examples and a discussion of each of the conflict types are presented. Some of these conflicts are present the first day the manager takes over. Others develop over time. Managers are constantly being called upon to make decisions keeping political, administrative, and ethical considerations in mind.

————. "The Role of the City Manager: A Survey Report." PUBLIC MANAGEMENT 44 (April 1972): 74-78.

Examines the sources of conflict between city managers and city councilmen. Findings are based on a role study of six council-manager cities in Illinois, Kansas, and Missouri. Councilmen were asked to rate the manager's performance on a series of character-istics. Some of the findings are: managers are seen as untainted by partisan political activity, they are much more rigid than they report themselves to be, and they believe their activities are more comprehensive than the councilmen feel they are. Performance of managers is seen in a very positive light by councilmen while their personal characteristics are not viewed as positively. Also included are self-evaluations by managers of their satisfaction with their jobs.

Charles, Henry T. "Urban Manager Roles in the '70's." PUBLIC ADMINISTRA-
TION REVIEW 31 (January–February 1971): 20–27.

> Several reasons are advanced why urban managers should be in the
> forefront of the effort to solve national problems. First, urban
> managers have a competence and long-term perspective on the
> priority issues of urban areas. Second, their training and experi-
> ence contrasts sharply with that of local elected officials, urban
> faculty members, and specialized urban administrators. Third, city
> managers have had contacts with public officials on all levels of
> government. Fourth, many council-manager cities will be called
> upon to test the impact of various proposed policies. Several rea-
> sons are advanced why city managers are restricted in actively
> solving national problems, including professional ethics, lack of
> managers in large cities, and the constraints of time available to
> work on these problems. There are several ways managers could
> be given more time to participate in these projects.

Cookingham, L.P. "Urban Administration--A New Ball Game." AMERICAN
CITY 85 (January 1970): 63–66.

> This article, written by a former city manager, examines the past
> and raises question for the future of urban administration. The
> author discusses the impact of the automobile, the growth of sub-
> urbs, the Depression, the development of industrial unions, World
> War II, and the jet age as they have affected city management.
> The result has been the evolution of the city manager from an
> engineer concerned with physical needs of the city to a manager
> more and more involved in the policy-making process. Looking
> to the future, the author feels a new type of local government
> executive may be needed. State governments will become more
> involved in city problems and urban administrators will become
> more energetic, better educated, and better trained.

Fletcher, Thomas W. "What is the Future For Our Cities and the City Manager?"
PUBLIC ADMINISTRATION REVIEW 31 (January–February 1971): 14–20.

> In trying to understand what the future holds for the city manager
> and for cities, the author lists major problems that appear to be
> on the horizon and offers possible solutions. The problem areas
> discussed are: environment, citizen participation, law and order,
> service delivery, housing, transportation, labor relations, equal
> opportunity, costs of government, intergovernmental relations,
> budget processes, and the role of the city manager. Change is
> occurring at a rapid rate and, if city managers cannot adapt to
> these changes, it may well be the end of the professional city
> manager in local government. Suggestions offered include:
> strengthened political leadership, retraining of managers, changing
> attitudes and methods of managers, and making the manager a
> socially oriented member of his community.

Ginsburg, Sigmund G. "Managing for Change: The Chief Administrator's Office." MANAGEMENT INFORMATION SERVICE. Washington, D.C.: International City Management Association, February 1970. 15 p.

> Report is based upon responses to a questionnaire received from sixteen cities and counties concerning management practices in their jurisdictions. The beginning of the report focuses on management innovations by discussing questions of department head assistance to the chief administrative officer, number and format of cabinet meetings, number of professional assistants in the administrator's office, governmental reorganization, management research, and future planning. The bulk of the report focuses on management innovations in New York City. Some of the areas discussed are: PPB, labor relations, policy planning, contract compliance, and the use of a management advisory council. The report concludes with a discussion of managing the Chief Administrator's office.

_____. "The New York City Administrator: A Critical Eulogy." NATIONAL CIVIC REVIEW 64 (October 1975): 451-58.

> The city administrator's office in New York City was established in 1954 and consisted of the city administrator, three deputy city administrators, a few senior management consultants, and a clerical staff. During its first twelve years, the vacancy rate of the top officials was very high and the office lacked continuity. The role of the office was constantly down-played by giving it minor functions to perform, bypassing it, or paying no attention to it at all. In 1974, Mayor Beame formally abolished the office and the position of deputy mayor-city administrator.

Hebert, F. Ted, and Bingham, Richard D. "The City Manager's Knowledge of Grants-in-Aid: Some Personal and Environmental Influences." URBAN AFFAIRS QUARTERLY 7 (March 1972): 303-6.

> This article is the result of a study of 148 cities with populations under 100,000 which use a council-manager government. The survey was conducted in Arkansas, Missouri, Kansas, and Oklahoma to determine and measure local officials' knowledge of grants-in-aid. Fifty-seven grants which applied equally to all cities were used in the questionnaire. Some conclusions reached were: HUD programs are better known to the managers than the programs of HEW or OEO. Managers of larger cities exhibited greater knowledge of grants than managers of smaller cities. Cities which employed grantsmen had more knowledgeable managers than cities which didn't. City size appeared to be the most explanatory variable.

Kennedy, David J. "Legal Services and Regulatory Procedures." In MANAGING THE MODERN CITY, edited by James M. Banovetz, pp. 402-23. Washington, D.C.: International City Management Association, 1971.

In carrying out all of the functions of local government, chief administrative officers must be aware of the limited legal authority of the municipal corporation circumscribed by both state statutes and the constitution. Also of importance is a familiarity with the law in giving advice and counsel on legal and administrative questions. This chapter examines the legal framework of municipal government and the implications for the administration of the work of city attorneys. Included are discussions of preparing legal documents, legislative drafting, and hearings and investigations. Organizing and administering the law department are reviewed as is the administration of the regulatory program.

Kline, Robert L., and Blanchard, Paul D. "Professionalism and the City Manager: An Examination of Unanswered Questions." MIDWEST REVIEW OF PUBLIC ADMINISTRATION 7 (July 1973): 163-74.

The recent growth in the number of professionals in local government has been coupled with an increase in the number of adoptions of the council-manager plan of government. Part of this growth is attributed to the status accorded city managers and the aspirations of many to achieve this professional status. Literature on the role of city managers as professionals is reviewed. The authors develop a working definition of the term "professional" and then attempt to determine if city managers, examined in light of the characteristics of professionalism, are in fact professionals.

Loveridge, Ronald O. "The City Manager in Legislative Politics: A Collision of Role Conceptions." POLITY 1 (Winter 1968): 213-36.

Examines the perceived role of the city manager from his own perspective and that of the city council. Focuses on the manager's role in the policy-making process. Survey data was collected from managers and councilmen in the San Francisco Bay area. Managers hold similar and positive attitudes about their role in the policy process. Most managers reject the traditional role dichotomy between politics and administration. Managers show more reluctance to get involved as policy advocates in issues of great community conflict. City councilmen view the manager's role as one of administrator, where he merely implements the policy made by the council. Differences in perception of policy roles between managers and councilmen may be due to socialization, recruitment, or standards of evaluation. To avoid conflict, the author suggests that managers limit their political activity to noncontroversial issues or engage in political activity behind the scenes.

_____. CITY MANAGERS IN LEGISLATIVE POLITICS. Indianapolis: Bobbs-Merrill, 1971. 224 p.

Focuses on the role of the city manager in policy making. Examines the origin of the controversy of what the policy role of the manager should be, by tracing the history, the evolution, and the major features of the council-manager form of government. The author compares the attitudes towards the policy-making process of both city managers and city councilmen. Results indicate that the manager sees himself as a political executive who takes part in formulating policy. City councilmen take a more traditional approach toward the role of the city manager. They see the manager as an administrator and as a source of advice and information for the council. The author examines the reasons for the difference of opinion and offers some possible grounds for resolution. The manager's performance is also discussed in various areas, such as community leader and administrative strategies.

Lyden, Fremont J., and Miller, Ernest G. "Why City Managers Leave the Profession: A Longitudinal Study in the Pacific Northwest." PUBLIC ADMINIS-TRATION REVIEW 36 (March-April 1976): 175-81.

This study is based upon a questionnaire administered to all city managers in the Pacific Northwest in 1966. In 1974, a follow-up questionnaire was sent out revealing that more than 25 percent had left the profession. The survey focused on job responsibilities, career aspirations, and satisfactions. The major variables analyzed included size of city, age, education, job satisfaction, and career-choice satisfaction. The findings indicate that managers who left the profession sought greater challenges, more opportunities, and better working conditions. They also expressed dissatisfaction with salary and their relationship with councils. The managers questioned in 1966 who remained in their profession in 1974 were those who generally expressed satisfaction with their jobs.

Morris, Robert B. "Professional Local Administration in Municipal Government." ANNALS OF THE AMERICAN ACADEMY OF POLITICAL AND SOCIAL SCI-ENCE 405 (January 1973): 145-50.

Cities require more professional leadership to cope with increasing problems from the neighborhood to the metropolitan level. This need is evident in the increasing number of council-manager cities and mayor-council cities which use professional city administrators. Professional managers are employed in half the cities with populations of between 10,000 and 50,000. Local government professional managers are urged to become generalists who have close working relationships with other officials. Managers must develop a better understanding and rapport with the community and learn to use innovative techniques in problem solving.

Mulrooney, Keith F. "Prologue: Can City Managers Deal Effectively with Major Social Problems?" PUBLIC ADMINISTRATION REVIEW 31 (January-February 1971): 6-14.

The focus of this article is on the ability of city managers to effectively deal with social problems and with responsiveness to the needs of minorities. The author reviews some of the literature on city managers and then reports on his interviews with managers, academicians, and consultants concerning city managers and social problems and minority needs. The author concludes that the council-manager plan should be able to deal with major social problems and the manager should, in most cases, be able to communicate with and respond to the needs of minority groups. What is needed are some pioneering efforts by managers which will set positive and successful examples for managers around the country.

Nolting, Orin F. PROGRESS AND IMPACT OF THE COUNCIL-MANAGER PLAN. Chicago: Public Administration Service, 1969. 92 p.

This monograph examines the growth of the council-manager plan. Included are a discussion of the origin of the plan, the need for this form of government, the implementation of the manager form of government in Texas, its support from the advocates of the short-ballot movement, and the early deviations from the plan at the beginning of the century. The growth of the plan is divided into three major periods: post-World War I, the Depression years, and post-World War II. Several reforms associated with the manager plan are discussed: short ballots, at-large elections, and nonpartisanship in council elections. Also included is an examination of the evolvement of the manager as a professional, the creation of the International City Management Association, and the goals and standards of this professional organization.

Scheiber, Walter. "Regionalism: Its Implications for the Urban Manager." PUBLIC ADMINISTRATION REVIEW 31 (January-February 1971): 42-46.

Over the past twenty years, new institutions have emerged to help local governments cope with urban and metropolitan problems. Among these are: city-county consolidations, allocation of services to higher levels of government, and multipurpose regional councils of government. Recounting the evolution of the city-manager plan and the history of federal involvement in encouraging areawide councils, the author builds a case for closer cooperation between council directors and city managers. Many regional council directors are former city managers who understand the complex problems of local government and are in a position to foster greater cooperation among local jurisdictions. By blending the techniques, goals, and philosophies of managers and regional council directors, metropolitan areas may be able to take action against some of their problems.

Stillman, Richard J. THE RISE OF THE CITY MANAGER: A PUBLIC PROFESSIONAL IN LOCAL GOVERNMENT. Albuquerque: University of New Mexico Press, 1974. 170 p.

Examines the creation, development, present contributions, and future role of the city manager form of government. The roots of council-manager government were in the progressive era. The four major factors contributing to the birth of council-manager government were: growth of American cities, the demand for an end to boss rule, the popularity of corporate ideals, and the movement toward scientific management and public administration. The author presents a profile of the city manager using such characteristics as education, age, work habits, background, and professional attitudes. He concludes that city managers are a relatively homogeneous group. Present problems faced by managers are discussed as are the future directions this office might take.

Welborn, David M. "The Environment and Role of the Administrator." In MANAGING THE MODERN CITY, edited by James M. Banovetz, pp. 77-107. Washington, D.C.: International City Management Association, 1971.

Professional administration at the local level has undergone dramatic changes. City managers are now grouped with county managers, mayor-appointed generalists, executive heads of special districts, and directors of councils of governments. The author traces the evolution of the council-manager plan and includes the contemporary view of the changing role of managers. The manager's role in community decision making is analyzed by looking at stages in the decision-making process and questions of participation and influence. Community values have a strong impact upon the role and functions of the manager. These values are manifested in patterns of activity, elections, individual and interest-group activity, and commentary by the media. A discussion of the manager's relationship with the mayor, the council, and the city employees is presented.

Wise, Jeremy A. "The Roles of the City Manager." NATIONAL CIVIC REVIEW 62 (June 1973): 306-10.

The city manager is becoming the administrative head of local government in more and more American cities today. This article examines the different actors the manager must interact with in administering the city. Interactions with the city council, municipal employees, the mass media, the general public, and other governments are discussed. The author also considers the background and qualifications that a city manager needs today. Included are: development of the manager's personal approach, creation of temporary or permanent advisory committees, the ability to deal less and less with specific details and pay more attention to persuading others, and knowing what technological innovations are occurring in other cities.

Woollett, William, Jr. "Governance Promises/Problems in New Towns." PUBLIC ADMINISTRATION REVIEW 35 (May-June 1975): 256-62.

This is a study of new town management from the perspective of
the city manager of Irvine, California. Management of the city
is organized in a team concept with the manager as head of the
team which reports directly to the city council. A discussion of
service, delivery, participative representation, fiscal and economic
management, and planning techniques is presented. Irvine does
not offer answers to all of the urban problems plaguing new towns
but he does indicate that successful problem solving is more likely
to occur if all of the actors are committed, enthusiastic, energetic,
and positive. The major actors are: councilmen, citizen groups,
developers, landowners, universities, and public employees.

Wright, Deil S. "The City Manager as a Development Administrator." In
COMPARATIVE URBAN RESEARCH: THE ADMINISTRATION AND POLITICS
OF CITIES, edited by Robert T. Daland, pp. 203-48. Beverly Hills, Calif.:
Sage Publications, 1969.

Summarizes and analyzes selected data from a survey of forty-five
of the fifty-five council-manager cities with populations in excess
of 100,000. The author discusses three major areas: developmental
politics, developmental roles of the executive, and developmental
policies. In the first area, data is presented on the partisan political patterns in council-manager cities, the participation of selected
groups in these cities, and the role of the mass media. In the
second area, the author discusses the managerial, the political,
and the cognitive role of the managers. In the third area, the
policy orientation of managers is analyzed with respect to physical
facilities, intergroup relations, and industrial and commercial growth.
The manager's role is more than that of a politician; he must be
an administrator, a politician, and a policy maker.

Chapter 3

MANAGEMENT OPERATIONS

A. EVALUATION

Blair, Louis H., and Schwartz, Alfred T. HOW CLEAN IS OUR CITY? A
GUIDE FOR MEASURING THE EFFECTIVENESS OF SOI _ WASTE COLLECTION
ACTIVITIES. Washington, D.C.: Urban Institute, 1^? 67 p.

> The Urban Institute and Washington, D.C. de\ ,ed . ' ested a
> system for measuring the effectiveness of solid ,aste cui: . ion and
> street and alley cleaning operations. The essence of the system 's
> periodic inspections, citizen surveys, and a cleanliness rating system
> that is constructed by using photographs depicting varying degrees
> of litter. The authors also discuss establishment of the measurement
> system, training of inspectors, analyzing citizen complaints, survey
> techniques, interpretation and use of findings, and estimated costs.

Bloch, Peter B., and Specht, David I. EVALUATION OF OPERATION NEIGH-
BORHOOD. Washington, D.C.: Urban Institute, 1973. 148 p.

> This study reports on the neighborhood team policing concept intro-
> duced in New York City in 1971. The evaluation was undertaken
> when 10 percent of the city's police force was working in this de-
> centralized policing system. The authors discuss the program's
> origin and expansion, patrolmen's attitudes, citizen reactions,
> crime statistics, arrest records, and vehicle dispatch data. The
> authors conclude that neighborhood team policing is having a posi-
> tive impact on the community, but it is not a panacea for all cities
> and changes are not likely to be seen for a few years. Recommen-
> dations for improving the program are offered.

Boyce, David E. "Toward a Framework for Defining and Applying Urban Indicators in Plan-Making." URBAN AFFAIRS QUARTERLY 6 (December 1970):
145-71.

> Urban indicators research tries to measure and quantify urban prob-
> lems and trends so social science research can be applied to public
> policy goals. Urban indicators are applied to standards, criteria,

and forecasts in the planning process to develop an interdependent definition of performance characteristics. Standards and criteria are labeled normative while indicators and forecasts are viewed as nonnormative. Indicators concern past and present performance, forecasts are future oriented and standards and criteria can be past, present, or future in character. Six major metropolitan land use and transportation studies are examined.

Caputo, David A. "Evaluating Urban Public Policy: A Developmental Model and Some Reservations." PUBLIC ADMINISTRATION REVIEW 33 (March-April 1973): 113-19.

The problems of policy evaluation are discussed and the author asserts that evaluators should consider the complexity of the program, the need for feedback which will permit periodic adjustments, the political factors which affect the program, and the incorporation of citizen input throughout the evaluation process. A model is presented based upon observation of the Gary, Indiana Model Cities Program. The major components of the model are: program evaluators, group interaction, citizen evaluation, academic and professional evaluation, and the public policy being evaluated. Two hypothetical urban programs are evaluated using the model, and conclusions are presented on the limitations and utility of evaluating urban programs.

Carter, Genevieve W. "How Do We Measure the Outcomes of Our Efforts?" PUBLIC WELFARE 29 (Summer 1971): 267-76.

Evaluation and accountability are potential change agents within public welfare organizations. Evaluations usually have political overtones when mandated by legislative bodies. This in turn may change the objectives of the evaluation. With a clarification of ultimate, intermediate, and proximate objectives, efficiency and effectiveness studies can begin to determine accountability. Evaluation programs which are flexible and provide for redefinition and regrouping are best. Several evaluation techniques are reviewed, including management by objectives, cost-benefit analysis and planning-programming-budgeting systems. Evaluation and accountability programs need sound research methodologies, adequate budgets, and a political climate willing to ask the right questions.

Etzioni, Amitai. "Alternative Conceptions of Accountability: The Example of Health Administration." PUBLIC ADMINISTRATION REVIEW 35 (May-June 1975): 279-86.

The term "accountability" is used by many actors in the political process. However, the term has come to be used symbolically because of its ambiguous interpretation. Four different approaches to the term are presented. The symbolic use of accountability is a gesture. The political aspects of accountability are reflected in the political pressure exerted by groups on decision makers. Formal checks and balances promote accountability. The guidance approach combines all of these factors and includes a moral component. Under the guidance approach, administrators take an active stance in educating, mobilizing, and coalition building.

Friedman, Lewis, and Marlin, John T. "Rating Cities Performance." NATIONAL CIVIC REVIEW 65 (January 1976): 12-19.

Careful monitoring of local government performance is needed. Economy in government is one test of performance but other standards are needed to supplement it. Efficiency is best used to guide the everyday delivery of municipal services, but not to determine what programs should be funded at what levels. Evaluating program effectiveness is a new challenge to the current way of doing things. It is directed at uncovering which programs succeed in obtaining their goals and which do not. An accurate rating performance can help in setting city priorities and in allocating scarce resources to different departments and functions of government.

Garn, Harvey A.; Tevis, Nancy L.; and Snead, Carl E. EVALUATING COMMUNITY DEVELOPMENT CORPORATIONS. Washington, D.C.: Urban Institute, 1976. 148 p.

This is a case study of three community development corporations--the Bedford-Stuyvesant Restoration Corporation in Brooklyn, the Woodlawn CDC in Chicago, and the Zion Investment Associates in Philadelphia. The authors and the CDC managers jointly developed goals which were identifiable and quantifiable and the performance record of the CDCs is evaluated in light of these goals. Two of the goals were: number of housing units rehabilitated and number of trainees finding employment after completing their training programs. The three case studies highlight the advantages and disadvantages of the community development corporations.

Gruber, Alan R. "The High Cost of Delivering Services." SOCIAL WORK 18 (July 1973): 33-40.

One way to improve the delivery of social services is to encourage agency administrators and board members to recognize the importance of knowing how time is being spent by staff members and what are the costs of delivering services. The unit of service rendered by an organization can be equated with a product and service, and cost accounting techniques can be implemented and applied to the system. Service agencies have to become cognizant of accountability to the public and service and cost accounting techniques are shown to facilitate this accountability. A detailed system of services and cost accounting is presented for the purchasing of services.

Hatry, Harry P. "Measuring the Quality of Public Services." In IMPROVING URBAN MANAGEMENT, edited by Willis D. Hawley and David Rogers, pp. 3-27. Beverly Hills, Calif.: Sage Publications, 1974.

Efforts to measure the quality of public services have increased in recent years as new management tools have been developed and have become available to local governments. Benefits derived from public service quality measurement are: problem identification, program information feedback, evaluation of employee and management performance, and increased community involvement. Quality of public service has different meanings. The major components of such a program include: intended purposes, negative effects, adequate quantity, equitable distribution, response time, citizen input, perceived satisfaction, and efficiency. The author discusses different ways quality measurement can be undertaken including how to set quality targets or standards. The people and institutions who should be responsible for measuring public service quality are the local government, citizen groups, universities, and legislatures.

Hatry, Harry P., and Dunn, Diana R. MEASURING THE EFFECTIVENESS OF LOCAL GOVERNMENT SERVICES: RECREATION. Washington, D.C.: Urban Institute, 1971. 47 p.

This guide is designed for local public officials to supplement routine data that they collect about local recreational facilities and activities. Some of the measures used are: accessibility, crowding, participation rates, safety, and perceptions of citizen satisfaction with recreational services. The authors provide estimated costs and techniques for collecting the necessary data.

Hatry, Harry P.; Winnie, Richard E.; and Fisk, Donald M. PRACTICAL PROGRAM EVALUATION FOR STATE AND LOCAL GOVERNMENTS. Washington, D.C.: Urban Institute, 1973. 134 p.

This study is a guide for public officials who wish to assess and evaluate the impact of spending programs. A step-by-step plan for implementing the evaluation system is presented as well as how to define objectives, establish criteria, and identify client groups for the study. Several evaluation designs are discussed, including a variety of techniques to be used. The authors also make suggestions on data collection, cost, and staffing estimates which officials should undertake in the evaluation, and how evaluation results can be translated into public policies.

Hatry, Harry P., et al. MEASURING THE EFFECTIVENESS OF BASIC MUNICIPAL SERVICES: INITIAL REPORT. Washington, D.C.: Urban Institute, 1974. 118 p.

This study is the result of a joint effort between the Urban Institute and the International City Management Association in St. Petersburg, Florida and Nashville, Tennessee. The project developed procedures by which local public officials can receive regular feedback on citizen satisfaction on a range of basic services. Effectiveness criteria have been developed for solid waste collection and disposal, recreation, library services, police and fire protection, local transportation, water supply, and complaint processing. Objectives and data collection methods and sources are provided for each of the services. Citizen surveys and questionnaires are discussed from the perspective of implementation and interpretation.

_____. PROGRAM ANALYSIS FOR STATE AND LOCAL GOVERNMENT. Washington, D.C.: Urban Institute, 1975. 155 p.

This study is a companion volume to the study on program evaluation previously published by the Urban Institute. Focusing on proposals for future implementation, the study develops an approach for estimating costs and effectiveness of both state and local programs. Also discussed are staffing and institutional requirements for analysis of programs as well as other components, defining the problem, identifying the alternate approaches to be analyzed, identifying objectives, selecting evaluation criteria, and delineating client groups served by the program. A framework for implementation feasibility is presented using many program examples.

Havens, Harry S. "MBO and Program Evaluation, or Whatever Happened to PPBS?" PUBLIC ADMINISTRATION REVIEW 36 (January-February 1976): 40-45.

Recent efforts to improve the quality of management, namely to make it more of a science than an art, have been characterized by a simplistic view of public sector decision making, and the nature of those decisions, and the belief that all important public goals are quantifiable. Some management innovations are tried in the private sector and then transferred to the public sector. However, the ambiguity in goals in public policy often doesn't lend itself to precise measurement. More and more federal programs are requiring the application of analytical techniques to evaluate their success. The introduction of MBO will have an impact on government long after it is gone by encouraging more legislative bodies to specify program objectives. Accompanying these objectives must be an analysis of what needs to be done and what is necessary to accomplish the objective.

Levy, Frank; Meltsner, Arnold J.; and Wildavsky, Aaron. URBAN OUTCOMES: SCHOOLS, STREETS AND LIBRARIES. Berkeley and Los Angeles: University of California Press, 1974. 271 p.

This is one of a series of books to emerge from the Oakland Project. It examines the government's distribution of goods and services to local citizens. Agencies concerned with schools, streets, and libraries are examined to see how they allocate services and what makes them allocate these in a particular way. The authors also discuss how organizational decisions lead to particular outputs. School budgets are analyzed, as are the allocations to major traffic routes and the resources allocated to the central library. The final chapter examines the comparative analysis of outcomes by focusing on patterns of resource distribution, redistribution dilemmas, and ways of judging outcomes.

Lovrich, Nicholas P., Jr., and Taylor, G. Thomas, Jr. "Neighborhood Evaluation of Local Government Services: A Citizen Survey Approach." URBAN AFFAIRS QUARTERLY 12 (December 1976): 197-222.

Discusses the major contributors to two different approaches to evaluating programs--technocrats and advocates of local control. The technocrats use a variety of quantitative techniques in policy evaluation and performance measurement while the local control advocates argue their approach will automatically improve bureaucratic responsiveness to neighborhood needs. This study reports the findings of a survey from 800 voters in the city and county of Denver conducted in 1972. The voters selected represented districts that were heavily populated by white, black, or Mexican Americans. The survey sought to determine attitudes of these three communities toward local government services. Variations in the perception of services received were evident among the three groups. The authors feel that the technocrats and the community control proponents should join ranks in the evaluation of local government services with the aim being to improve bureaucratic responsiveness.

Ostrom, Elinor. "On the Meaning and Measurement of Output and Efficiency in the Provision of Urban Police Services." JOURNAL OF CRIMINAL JUSTICE 1 (Summer 1973): 93-111.

Proposals for changing the organization of police departments in metropolitan areas are usually presented with little supporting evidence for the change. It is assumed by many that large-scale police departments are more effective and more efficient. The author defines the concepts of output and efficiency for police agencies, and then develops some potential measures of output and efficiency which can be used in evaluating the comparative output and efficiency of differently organized police departments serving metropolitan areas. Four types of police activities are discussed as are the problems of measurement for each type.

Ostrom, Elinor, and Smith, Dennis C. "On the Fate of 'Lilliputs' in Metropolitan Policing." PUBLIC ADMINISTRATION REVIEW 36 (March-April 1976): 192-200.

Citing three negative assumptions about small police departments, the authors cite several studies which helped to frame these assumptions. This study reports on police performance in a number of jurisdictions in the St. Louis metropolitan area. Data was obtained from 4,000 respondents in 44 neighborhoods served by 29 jurisdictions to assess the performance of small, medium, and large police departments. Some of the findings are: the size of police departments was negatively related to performance on most indicators, small police departments are performing at higher levels than the two largest departments in the St. Louis area, and the size of a department was not associated with years of college education. Some small departments might be consolidated but no recommendation for consolidation of all the area's police departments seems warranted, based upon the data.

Sadacca, Robert, et al. MANAGEMENT PERFORMANCE IN PUBLIC HOUSING. Washington, D.C.: Urban Institute, 1974. 144 p.

This study assesses the quality of management in public housing projects by interviewing 9,000 tenants and staff members, utilizing HUD documents, and other sources. Quality management is determined by examining operation attitudes, procedures, and conditions closely associated with successes and failures in public housing. One interesting finding is that most tenants are satisfied with the services they receive. The authors conclude that some causes of tenant dissatisfaction are beyond the control of housing managers. This is true where the projects are located in deteriorating neighborhoods and where there are inadequate police and sanitation services. Quality management and high tenant satisfaction are usually found where there are low operating costs.

Schaenman, Philip S., and Muller, Thomas. MEASURING IMPACTS OF LAND DEVELOPMENT: AN INITIAL APPROACH. Washington, D.C.: Urban Institute, 1974. 93 p.

This report suggests ways to estimate the impact of land development on local jurisdictions. The techniques are applicable to both proposed and past land developments. The authors recommend specific data collection procedures for evaluating land development impacts on economic, environmental, housing, and public service issues. Use of these techniques will enable local public officials to assess land use decisions in a systematic and comprehensive way. The study outlines the issues to be confronted before the evaluation system can be implemented and illustrates how the measurement system can be used in short-term situations.

Skogan, Wesley G. "Efficiency and Effectiveness in Big-City Police Departments." PUBLIC ADMINISTRATION REVIEW 36 (May-June 1976): 278-86.

The concepts of efficiency and effectiveness are basic to evaluating the activities of organizations. These terms are examined in the context of their relationship between inputs and outputs and their

relative processing costs. Effectiveness is defined as being high
when organizations approach their stated goals. Efficient organizations are those that achieve more using less resources--men,
equipment, or money. Input levels in law enforcement are measured
in terms of the number of crimes committed in eight different categories. Outputs are measured in arrest figures for each of the
categories. In big-city police departments, efficiency and effectiveness appear to go together. The author cautions that exclusive
use of these measures may reduce other police functions in the
quest for higher measurable outputs.

Sparer, Gerald, and Johnson, Joyce. "An Evaluation of OEO Neighborhood
Health Centers." AMERICAN JOURNAL OF PUBLIC HEALTH 61 (May 1971):
931-42.

The Economic Opportunity Act states several objectives when re-
ferring to comprehensive health services. These objectives are
vague and should not confuse evaluation teams. There is a difference between evaluation and research and this relates to the
difference between assessing outputs in health care versus the
effectiveness of preventive medicine. An evaluation of comprehensive health care in local health centers is presented focusing
on quality, continuity with backup hospitals, patient-physician
continuity, training and manpower utilization, and cost. Conclusions find the health centers providing clinical service at costs
comparable to private providers, competitive with many prepayment
groups, and less than many other neighborhood health centers.

Stein, Herman D.; Hougham, George M.; and Zalba, Serapio R. "Assessing
Social Agency Effectiveness, A Goal Model." WELFARE IN REVIEW 6 (March-
April 1968): 13-18.

This article concerns itself with the concept of agency effectiveness and when an agency is justified in investing public resources
based on its program effectiveness. Attention is paid to the social
welfare agency but the main ideas are applicable to other fields
of governmental activity. The idea of effectiveness varies greatly
from agency to agency. Effectiveness can be determined in several
ways. Agencies can be evaluated on the basis of client and problem definition, operating techniques, or economic and efficient
attainment of goals. The authors see these approaches as interdependent and combine service effectiveness and organizational effectiveness into an integrated evaluation of the agency's accomplish-
ment in realizing its stated objectives. This is termed a goal model
and is utilized with four different types of goals.

Winnie, Richard E., and Hatry, Harry P. MEASURING THE EFFECTIVENESS
OF LOCAL GOVERNMENT SERVICES: TRANSPORTATION. Washington, D.C.:
Urban Institute, 1972. 84 p.

This study is citizen oriented in that it tries to help consumers
assess the quality of local transportation. The proposed system
provides local officials with a mechanism for evaluating how well
their transportation services are meeting the needs of citizens.
Twelve measures of effectiveness are analyzed against goals such
as safety, accessibility, convenience, travel time, and environmental quality. Communities are shown how to collect data for
different transportation users. Recommendations and cost estimates
are provided.

Young, Dennis R. "Evaluating Organizational Change in Public Services."
In IMPROVING URBAN MANAGEMENT, edited by Willis D. Hawley and
David Rogers, pp. 55-88. Beverly Hills, Calif.: Sage Publications, 1974.

The effective delivery of public services often requires more than
the creation and implementation of better programs. What is needed
is change in the organizational relationships under which production
and consumption decisions are made. This need is highlighted by
the fact that similar programs administered by different agencies in
different places with different organizational arrangements produce
very different results. The article focuses on the major issues
pertinent to structuring evaluations of organizational change. The
author discusses the implications for evaluating organizational change
including what is to be varied and what is to be controlled, the
time frame for evaluation, and what is to be measured. Two applications of experiments in the field of education are analyzed.
They are performance contracting and the education vouchers program.

Zamoff, Richard B. GUIDE TO THE ASSESSMENT OF DAY CARE SERVICES
AND NEEDS AT THE COMMUNITY LEVEL. Washington, D.C.: Urban Institute,
1971. 100 p.

This guide, developed in Washington, D.C. neighborhoods, is designed to assist local governmental agencies and community groups
to determine the need for day care services in their areas. The
study includes alternative ways in which these services are being
provided, questionnaires, techniques for sampling, data collection
and interviewing, estimates of costs, and suggestions for using
statistical analysis once the data has been collected.

B. TECHNOLOGY, DATA, AND INFORMATION SYSTEMS

Berkman, Herman G. "The Scope of Scientific Technique and Information
Technology in Metropolitan Area Analysis." In GOVERNING URBAN SOCIETY:
NEW SCIENTIFIC APPROACHES, edited by Stephen B. Sweeney and James C.
Charlesworth, pp. 165-80. Philadelphia: American Academy of Political and
Social Science, 1967.

The metropolitan area communication network between science, technology, and social, economic, and political systems has some missing links. Missing are people who should be engaged in information transfer and public systems engineering. Organization and management are critical to the solution of urban problems. Information and communication are vital to urban management. Advances in management information technology and hardware systems can produce more efficient and effective management. Tools for more effective urban administration include: systems analysis, operations research, modeling and computers for sensing, storing, processing, and retrieving data. In order to achieve the advances discussed, local governments must have access to data processing equipment. This in turn may require revision of data flow and adjustments in the decision-making process.

Brewer, Garry D. "Systems Analysis in the Urban Complex: Potential and Limitations." In IMPROVING URBAN MANAGEMENT, edited by Willis D. Hawley and David Rogers, pp. 89-123. Beverly Hills, Calif.: Sage Publications, 1974.

Systems analysis can be an important tool for the urban manager in the decision-making process. It is becoming increasingly important because of the difficult, complex, and urgent problems confronting local public officials. Systems analysis can help a decision maker by investigating the problem, defining objectives and alternatives, assessing them in light of their consequences, providing an analytical framework, and calling forth the best judgment for the problem at hand. Data deficiencies in demographic data, management information systems, and social indicators are discussed. Theoretical limitations and orientations are presented. The selection process for an analytical arrangement requires an understanding of principles, levels of analysis, timing and policy making, creativity, skill, and judgment. Practical problems inherent in the introduction of an analytical system are discussed, including motive, client relations, and the business environment of the analyst who develops the model.

Catanese, Anthony James, and Steiss, Alan Walter. "Programming for Governmental Operations: The Critical Path Approach." PUBLIC ADMINISTRATION REVIEW 28 (March-April 1968): 155-67.

Several techniques successfully used in the private sector, particularly in production scheduling and industrial management, have potential public sector applications. In order to transfer these techniques to the public sector, there must be a clearly stated work program and the ability to attach cost and resource estimates to each work element in this program. The two techniques discussed are Critical Path Method and Hueristic Programming. Each technique is described and the authors show how this transfer was utilized in a state department of housing and urban development. The new approach, they conclude, offers flexibility while using a relatively simple set of analytical tools.

Churchman, C. West. "The Use of Science in Public Affairs." In GOVERN-
ING URBAN SOCIETY: NEW SCIENTIFIC APPROACHES, edited by Stephen B.
Sweeney and James C. Charlesworth, pp. 29-48. Philadelphia: American
Academy of Political and Social Science, 1967.

> Focuses on the question of what role can science play in public
> affairs. Can science, as it is now constituted, serve as an aid
> to the policy maker or can science be constituted to serve as such
> an aid? Presently science can assist us in precisely defining al-
> ternatives, determining goals, predicting policy outcomes, selecting
> optimum alternatives, and collecting unbiased information. Several
> counterarguments to the use of science in public affairs are pre-
> sented. These include: the subjectivity of information used in
> policy making, lost opportunity costs, and the irrational way people
> order their goals. A major problem confronting the scientific com-
> munity is its inability to face its own public policy questions.
> Once science has faced up to its own political and managerial
> problems it may, sometime in the future, become a valuable asset
> to public policy makers.

"City Hall's Approaching Revolution in Service Delivery." NATION'S CITIES
10 (January 1972): 9-40.

> This special report summarizes a federally sponsored, six-city study
> of the development and implementation of an integrated municipal
> information system. The cities are Charlotte, North Carolina;
> Dayton, Ohio; Long Beach, California; Reading, Pennsylvania;
> St. Paul, Minnesota; and Wichita Falls, Texas. They are research-
> ing the various ways an integrated approach to the development of
> information systems can be used to support the operation of munici-
> pal governments. The summary discusses the research efforts, the
> concepts used, and the past experiences, advantages, and planning
> systems used by local officials.

Crecine, John P. "Computer Simulation in Urban Research." PUBLIC ADMIN-
ISTRATION REVIEW 28 (January-February 1968): 66-77.

> Computers are being used more in simulating the processes and pro-
> cedures of urban life. As a research tool to guide urban managers
> and decision makers, the computer holds great promise. Two areas
> where they have been used frequently are urban growth models and
> studies in local government decision making. The author discusses
> a series of computer applications to real urban problems that have
> been recently undertaken. Included in these studies are urban re-
> newal programs, transportation planning, land use models, and edu-
> cational budgeting systems.

Davy, Thomas J. "Determining Priorities and Developing Basic Research on
Urban Problems." In GOVERNING URBAN SOCIETY: NEW SCIENTIFIC AP-
PROACHES, edited by Stephen B. Sweeney and James C. Charlesworth, pp. 229-

39. Philadelphia: American Academy of Political and Social Science, 1967.

The urban observatories concept highlights some basic concerns
about our standard of living, our inability to systematically analyze
urban problems, the separation between scholars and practitioners,
and the need to devise organizational arrangements that bring
scholars and practitioners closer together. Scholars produce three
different types of studies: research studies which test propositions,
developmental studies that apply the results of basic research, and
consensus-building which forms standards. Urban observatories
could become involved in all three types of studies and thus build
their credibility with the practitioners. To become successful, the
urban observatory program must develop integrated information systems, relate scholarly research pursuits to practitioner needs, and
be mindful of the time lag before significant results can be achieved.

Diebold, John. "Impacts on Urban Governmental Functions of Developments in
Science and Technology." In GOVERNING URBAN SOCIETY: NEW SCIEN-
TIFIC APPROACHES, edited by Stephen B. Sweeney and James C. Charlesworth,
pp. 85-100. Philadelphia: American Academy of Political and Social Science,
1967.

Technological change has had a profound impact on the scope and
complexity of the problems facing urban areas. This impact has
been found in the increasingly diverse nature of service demands,
a need for quality education, the ability to cope with crime, increased unemployment, and strained financial resources. Technology
can help solve some of these problems through systems analysis,
sharing of facilities, jurisdictional flexibility, and increased cooperation. In several areas, local governments have not kept pace
with advances in the application of technology to urban problems.
Technology, and computers in particular, can assist in substituting
capital for labor, accurately evaluate public demands, and help to
develop a conceptual framework for comparing public and private
goals. The goal of this application of technology to local governments should be to enable these governments to perform their proper
functions more effectively.

Downs, Anthony. "A Realistic Look at the Final Payoffs From Urban Data Systems." PUBLIC ADMINISTRATION REVIEW 27 (September 1967): 204-10.

This article examines the final payoffs--improvements in government
or private action--resulting from the decision to implement an urban
data bank system. Several reasons are presented for the lack of
detailed analyses on the final payoffs. Technical improvements in
data caused by urban data systems are discussed and these are related to estimates of technical payoffs from these improvements.
Power payoffs are the direct result of changes in organizational
structure or decision-making processes, but these are usually clouded
by discussions of technical improvements. Downs examines the
power shifts caused by automated data systems and how power pay-

offs influence the type of urban data systems used.

Dueker, Kenneth J. "Urban Information Systems and Urban Indicators." URBAN AFFAIRS QUARTERLY 6 (December 1970): 173-78.

Examines the relationship between urban indicators and urban information systems. While the terms are similar, urban indicators are concerned with information requirements or needs and urban information systems focus on the means of providing information--the data processing aspects. The similarity is pertinent in their efforts to use urban data to develop measures which describe specific subsystem relationships. Another model emphasizing cost-effectiveness is introduced and the model depends upon both urban information systems and urban indicators to delineate costs. Both systems are necessary components in developing a planning-effectiveness model.

Duel, Henry J. "Some Manager Problems in the Development of Information Systems." PERSONNEL ADMINISTRATION AND PUBLIC PERSONNEL REVIEW 1 (September-October 1972): 51-55.

This article examines management functions common to the development and implementation of new information systems. Managers tend to overemphasize the contribution of information systems and view them as the essential component in decision making. The basic requirements of a sound information system and the pertinent data for making personnel decisions are presented. The major problems in information systems occur in communications breakdowns between the manager, the systems analyst, and the computer technician.

Evans, James W. "Public Finance and Urban Information Systems." GOVERNMENTAL FINANCE 1 (May 1972): 27-30.

The author discusses the use of computers by cities to automate routine manual tasks in functional areas. Emphasis is placed on public finance. He suggests that using integrated municipal information systems, based on automation of routine operations and a constantly updated integrated data base common to all city functions, would assist city administrators in planning as well as reducing costs and increasing service delivery.

Fowles, Agnes M. "Public Information." In DEVELOPING THE MUNICIPAL ORGANIZATION, edited by Stanley Powers, F. Gerald Brown, and David S. Arnold, pp. 279-87. Washington, D.C.: International City Management Association, 1974.

Public information officers can play a vital role in assisting management officials to communicate and develop positive relations with citizens. They can also open up internal avenues of communication through the use of newsletters, reports, and directories. Since

communication is a two-way process, the more the public information process of local government informs citizens, the more likely
they are to take an active interest in government and communicate
their ideas and opinions. The author outlines the objectives of a
public information program and different types of public that are
interested in what government is doing. The council, the chief
administrator, and the employees are all involved in the public
information process. Their roles should be reviewed periodically
to assure that information going to the public is both fair and
complete.

Giles, Peter B. "Systems Analysis and Urban Information." In DEVELOPING
THE MUNICIPAL ORGANIZATION, edited by Stanley Powers, F. Gerald Brown,
and David S. Arnold, pp. 193-210. Washington, D.C.: International City
Management Association, 1974.

The author examines how data are collected and processed and describes systems project management and operating techniques. This
assists urban administrators in understanding the essentials of information systems analysis, design, implementation, and project evaluation. The six topics discussed are: the systems approach; systems
project organization; project planning, scheduling and control; description and analysis; and design and evaluation. Diagrams and
charts throughout the article illustrate the different techniques discussed. Once the system has been installed, actual costs should
be measured against estimated costs and actual benefits against
anticipated benefits. Users of the system should be involved in a
qualitative identification of problems and reactions.

Goldberg, Edward M. "Urban Information Systems and Invasions of Privacy."
URBAN AFFAIRS QUARTERLY 5 (March 1970): 249-64.

As the capabilities of high-speed computers increase, local governments have begun to use them for storage and retrieval of important
information on people, programs, and policies. This has raised the
problem of access to the stored information and the invasion of
privacy that might result. The author reviews three different urban
information systems--physical data bank, people information system,
and a local government information control system. The concept
of privacy is discussed by citing laws, court cases, and constitutional rights protecting the privacy of citizens. Suggestions are
offered for new legislation to protect the right of privacy. Finally,
it is suggested that the burden be placed on those who wish to in-
vade the privacy of others, not on the individuals whose privacy
is being invaded.

Hearle, Edward F.R. "The Scope of Management Information Systems in Governmental Administration." In GOVERNING URBAN SOCIETY: NEW SCIENTIFIC
APPROACHES, edited by Stephen B. Sweeney and James C. Charlesworth,
pp. 197-208. Philadelphia: American Academy of Political and Social Science,
1967.

Management information systems are rapidly becoming vital tools in the public-sector administrator's arsenal. In the near future, we will be using optical readers; computers that produce output in printed, vocal, or graphic form; unlimited storage; increased processing speed; remote input and output devices linked to central computers; and smaller and cheaper computers. As a result, public-sector managers will be able to: obtain more data on their environment, monitor their agency's internal operations, expand interagency information systems, bypass middle management, utilize national and regional data centers, and share equipment with other agencies. Not all information a manager receives should be systematized. Much of the information he receives through informal and ad hoc channels is important in the decision-making process.

Herzlinger, Regina E., and Moore, Gordon T. "Management Control Systems in Health Care." MEDICAL CARE 11 (September-October 1973): 416-29.

A management control system used in the business world was adapted for use in a neighborhood health center. Management control data were collected and used for a period of one year. The system was accepted by the professionals in the health center and was associated with motivational changes in the health center staff and in productivity within the center. Management control systems, even though exhibiting some limitations in this application, appear to be adaptable to the health system, and may help reduce or eliminate some of the inefficiencies that exist in the system.

Kemeny, John G. "The City and the Computer Revolution." In GOVERNING URBAN SOCIETY: NEW SCIENTIFIC APPROACHES, edited by Stephen B. Sweeney and James C. Charlesworth, pp. 49-62. Philadelphia: American Academy of Political and Social Science, 1967.

The basic premise of the article is that the computer will help us to deal with many of the complexities of modern society and relieve some of the problems of our cities. The evolution of computers can be viewed in three stages--the dawn of computing, the coming of time-sharing, and a computer in every home. Cities have been slow to use computers and have generally done so only for the most elementary tasks, ignoring, for instance, the value of simulation in traffic, pollution, and planning. Time-sharing has permitted all users to take advantage of high-speed computers. This is being done in medical care quality control, crime records, and traffic control. Eventually computers will become available to every citizen, thus reducing many of the functions cities perform and at the same time resolving many of our urban problems.

Kibbee, Joel M. "The Scope of Large-Scale Computer-Based Systems in Governmental Systems." In GOVERNING URBAN SOCIETY: NEW SCIENTIFIC APPROACHES, edited by Stephen B. Sweeney and James C. Charlesworth, pp. 181-96. Philadelphia: American Academy of Political and Social Science, 1967.

Many people expect the computer to provide dramatic improvements in the quantity and quality of public services provided by governments. Computers offer the possibility of developing more accurate and timely information and assisting in a wide range of clerical and engineering functions. However, it is still too early to accurately evaluate the costs and benefits of computers in urban government. Computers are currently being used in a number of program areas and the author briefly reviews some of their applications in the law enforcement field, corrections, training, and administration on city, state, and regional levels. The author suggests that urban management, to be effective, must cut across jurisdictional and functional lines. To achieve this, management must recognize the value of this untapped information source and build it into the information system design.

Kraemer, Kenneth L. "The Evolution of Information System for Urban Administration." PUBLIC ADMINISTRATION REVIEW 29 (July-August 1969): 389-402.

Urban information systems have begun to receive increased attention by urban administrators seeking new ways to cope with complex issues. Four approaches are discussed: the housekeeping approach, the data-bank approach, the model building approach, and the process control approach. Examples of how each approach is used are presented. The evolutionary steps are examined: the processing, analysis, and control capabilities of computers viewed as technical subsystems, creating urban information systems as part of integrated systems, and integration of technical subsystems and administrative processes. The four approaches are viewed as stages in the development of urban information systems and are discussed in terms of linkages and redefinition of the system. Improvements are needed in integrating information technology and decision processes, realigning organization structure, developing personnel, expanding our knowledge about information systems, and changing the social climate in which they are built.

_____. "USAC: An Evolving Intergovernmental Mechanism For Urban Information Systems Development." PUBLIC ADMINISTRATION REVIEW 31 (September-October 1971): 543-51.

The Urban Information Systems Inter-Agency Committee (USAC) is a mechanism for channeling federal resources to improve local government administration. The committee seeks to increase intergovernmental cooperation in urban information systems research and development. The article discusses the conditions and needs for developing USAC: the goals, direction, strategy, and administrative organization. HUD, which administers the program, awarded contracts for integrated municipal information systems to Wichita Falls, Texas, and Charlotte, North Carolina. Other cities receiving contracts for related programs were: Reading, Pennsylvania,

Long Beach, California, Dayton, Ohio, and St. Paul, Minnesota.
The author concludes that the intergovernmental cooperation and
flexible administrative arrangements developed in this program may
prove more important than the substance of the specific city projects.

Larson, Richard C. URBAN POLICE PATROL ANALYSIS. Cambridge, Mass.:
M.I.T. Press, 1972. 289 p.

This study develops a model for the allocation of urban police
patrol forces. The ability of police forces to increase the use of
technology in the use of resources is considered by many to be a
major step forward in improving police-community relations. Citing
fragmentation as a major problem in criminal justice agencies, the
author suggests a closer working relationship between agency administrators and quantitatively trained experts. The police response
system and the difficulties of processing calls for service are discussed and some of the technical suggestions for overcoming police
allocation problems are presented by using a hypothetical city of
200,000.

Lewin, David, et al. THE URBAN LABOR MARKET: INSTITUTIONS, INFOR-
MATION, LINKAGES. New York: Praeger, 1974. 176 p.

This is a study which assesses the role, uses, and functions of labor
market information in the urban environment. The authors develop
and apply conceptual schemes to correctional institutions, vocational
schools, and city government to test the impact of labor market
information on these institutions. They conclude that an improved
labor information system will have a minimal impact in the face of
administrative constraints. Some of the constraints identified are:
informal recruitment channels, low market penetration by the employment service, lack of long-range planning, and the existence
of tight labor markets which impedes job placement for the disadvantaged. Few manpower programs account for these institutional
constraints in their development.

Lukens, Matthias E. "Emerging Executive and Organizational Responses to
Scientific and Technological Developments." In GOVERNING URBAN SOCIETY:
NEW SCIENTIFIC APPROACHES, edited by Stephen B. Sweeney and James C.
Charlesworth, pp. 113-27. Philadelphia: American Academy of Political and
Social Science, 1967.

To understand how urban executives and organizations are responding to scientific and technological developments it is necessary to
determine the extent to which modern management techniques such
as systems analysis, electronic data processing, and operations research have been adopted by these executives and organizations.
Examples are given of jurisdictions now using some of these techniques. Major management concepts are reviewed with the author
concluding that the impact of management on executives has been

overestimated because of executive morals and courage and the fact that many urban decisions are based upon political considerations. The tremendous rate of change will have a professional effect on public-sector executives. Several areas of this impact are outlined as are changes expected for organizations and the field of management theory.

Lundberg, Fred J. "Development of Large Urban Information Systems." MUNICIPAL FINANCE 40 (November 1967): 73-79.

The author cites three reasons why urban governments have not developed and used large-scale information systems--lack of resources, lack of skilled manpower, and data banks being used only for special projects. Eight characteristics are listed as being basic to the design and implementation of a large-scale system. The urban data center in Cincinnati is located at the university to free it from any local governmental restrictions. Different models being used are described, and techniques of combining different systems already in use around the country are presented. Urban data banks are difficult and time-consuming projects but they can be successfully implemented.

Maier, Henry W. "An Overview of Urban Observatories." In GOVERNING URBAN SOCIETY: NEW SCIENTIFIC APPROACHES, edited by Stephen B. Sweeney and James C. Charlesworth, pp. 211-20. Philadelphia: American Academy of Political and Social Science, 1967.

In many cases our cities are governed by tradition and an inability to know and understand all of the available options. We have not applied enough of our understanding of science to the solution of urban problems. We have not developed the necessary arrangements to coordinate and analyze urban data which could begin to build an empirical science of cities. One technique for overcoming our past deficiencies is the creation of field centers and data gathering stations called "urban observatories." These observatories combine the talents of local government and urban universities to: collect basic information on urban development, prepare policy-oriented research on select issues, provide studies to local decision makers, and utilize competent staff from urban study centers and universities.

Mindlin, Albert. "Confidentiality and Local Information Systems." PUBLIC ADMINISTRATION REVIEW 28 (November-December 1968): 509-18.

The use of the computer as a management and technological tool poses many problems for the privacy of citizens and the confidentiality of information. This article focuses on the centralization and multiagency use of confidential governmental information obtained by a single agency for a specific purpose. The four major data systems used by city and county governments are: real property data systems, geographic systems, person systems, and family systems.

Each system is defined and discussed. The author also discusses the sharing of confidential information and the maintenance of record confidentiality in local data systems and governmental records in nongovernmental data systems. Recommendations are offered for creating centralized statistical data systems divorced from operating responsibility and insulated from the pressures for individual record feedback.

_____. "Improvements in Federal Statistical Programs for Small Areas." PUBLIC ADMINISTRATION REVIEW 33 (March-April 1973): 136-45.

Many local governments today, in order to research, plan, administer and evaluate programs in their jurisdictions, use statistical information generated by the federal government. In order to assist subnational units of government, the federal statistical system must become more attuned to the needs of the governments. The author surveys numerous organizations around the country to generate recommendations for changes in the federal government's statistical process. The major changes recommended are: the need for a quinquennial census, improved timeliness and coverage, on-going housing data, improved crime and criminal justice system data, improved data on income and labor force, improved geographic identification, and better communication and organization of federal small-area statistics programs. Each of the recommendations is discussed by the author.

Murphy, Thomas P. "Management Information Systems." In DEVELOPING THE MUNICIPAL ORGANIZATION, edited by Stanley Powers, F. Gerald Brown, and David S. Arnold, pp. 211-26. Washington, D.C.: International City Management Association, 1974.

Management information systems are a vital part of local governmental organizations. They provide the necessary information for managers to coordinate the daily operations of local government and they assist in policy analysis and long-range planning. Management information systems are not used solely by chief administrators. They are of value to councilmen, department heads, and citizens. MIS make major contributions in records storage and retrieval, budget information and control, decision making, data processing, program information, internal communications, and interdepartmental coordination. The author discusses the types of data needed for the systems and the problems of centralization versus decentralization. Human problems encountered in implementing new systems are examined as is the impact of MIS on the organization. The author concludes with a discussion of urban information systems.

Parker, John K. "Information Requirements for Urban Research Programs." In GOVERNING URBAN SOCIETY: NEW SCIENTIFIC APPROACHES, edited by Stephen B. Sweeney and James C. Charlesworth, pp. 241-50. Philadelphia:

American Academy of Political and Social Science, 1967.

> Urban research is conducted by a variety of academics including political scientists, economists, sociologists, psychologists, and anthropologists. Three types of information are needed to conduct urban research: published information, printed but unpublished information, and basic data. However, there are no integrated urban research libraries and the existence of potentially useful documents are known to very few. Examples of these types of materials are presented. Urban research is also hampered by a lack of data on our metropolitan regions. Much of the data that becomes available is often outdated before it can be fruitfully used. Metropolitan data banks could be useful components for urban researchers and practitioners. The major problem confronting the urban observatories will be to achieve effective access to available data.

———. "Tools of Modern Management." In MANAGING THE MODERN CITY, edited by James M. Banovetz, pp. 208-37. Washington, D.C.: International City Management Association, 1971.

> Electronic or automatic data processing systems have become part of the management system of many American cities today. Computers automate vast amounts of paperwork, in a short period of time at reduced costs. They also analyze enormous quantities of information; perform complex mathematical calculations; and improve the ability of urban managers to make decisions, implement programs, forecast results, and evaluate program performance. Several digital computer concepts are discussed as are programming systems. Computers are used in many operating functions such as: process control, support of operations, equipment requirements as well as in records automation, planning, and management information systems. Guidelines and alternatives are offered for introducing computers into local government operations.

Quinn, Robert E. "The Impacts of a Computerized Information System on the Integration and Coordination of Human Services." PUBLIC ADMINISTRATION REVIEW 36 (March-April 1976): 166-74.

> Increasing the delivery and efficiency of human services is a governmental problem often thought to stem from unresponsive bureaucracy, fragmented departmental structure, overlapping in goals duplication of services, and poor planning and evaluation techniques. This article focuses on the integration of services which impacts on funding, planning, reporting systems, measurement criteria, methods of evaluation, and multiservice centers. Focusing on Cincinnati, Ohio, the study reviews the development of an urban information system which involved standardization, autonomy and control, clarification of goals, decision criteria, and organizational linkages. Recommendations are offered for further research, and comments about the power of information and inadequacy of current management techniques are presented.

Saltman, Roy G. "Educating Public Administrators for Managing Science and Technology." PUBLIC ADMINISTRATION REVIEW 34 (July–August 1974): 394–99.

In recent years, several reports have commented on the inability of public administrators to effectively use science and technology in their jobs. Public officials receive a great deal of scientific and technological information which must be incorporated into the decision-making process which affects the quality of government in his/her jurisdiction. Scientific and technological information can be either pervasive, which affects the operation of government as a whole, or it can be more specialized and concern only one public service function. Public administrators need to be trained in new analytical tools, systems approaches, computer utilization, and information science.

Savas, E.S. "Cybernetics in City Hall." SCIENCE 168 (29 May 1970): 1066–71.

The author discusses five basic factors in a cybernetic loop which he attempts to use in analyzing recent developments in New York City. The five are: dynamic characteristics of the process, the information system, administration, goal setting, and disturbances. Several findings are reported. First, the development and implementation of urban systems are not related to the elected terms of office, often causing discontinuity. Second, information often comes to the mayor through a selective or filtered process. If he is to get untainted information, he has to develop an outreach program to the community. Third, local governmental administrators are underpaid and, over the past few decades, this has caused a deterioration in quality. Fourth, goal setting is hampered by the source, quantity, and quality of information available. Fifth, political, economic, and social disturbances do not lend themselves to adjustments that can reasonably be made in urban systems.

Stallings, C. Wayne. "Local Information Policy: Confidentiality and Public Access." PUBLIC ADMINISTRATION REVIEW 34 (May–June 1974): 197–204.

This article discusses a model policy developed in Charlotte, North Carolina, which regulates the collection, storage, use, and dissemination of information. The policy, which can be adopted by any local government, protects privacy while promoting reasonable public access to public documents. The author discusses the administrative structure for decision making and the procedures and techniques for implementing the plan as well as a classification system for information and the varying degrees of access permitted for each classification. The plan can work only if all public officials are committed to privacy and access and are willing to exert pressure on all parties concerned to achieve the twin goals.

Stover, Carl F. "The Roles of Public Officials and Educators in Realizing the Potentials of New Scientific Aids for Urban Society." In GOVERNING URBAN SOCIETY: NEW SCIENTIFIC APPROACHES, edited by Stephen B. Sweeney and James C. Charlesworth, pp. 129-42. Philadelphia: American Academy of Political and Social Science, 1967.

> Focuses on our ability to use new scientific and technological capacities while avoiding new problems these techniques may bring. Much of this depends upon public officials and educators who help to train public officials as well as scientists, engineers, researchers, and the general public. We must develop new perspectives for thinking about the changes that technology brings to our society. Technological change also imposes the burden of choice on decision makers who must be guided by standards if they are to avoid new problems. The use of technology is a political subject and unless it is controlled can lead to an administrative state governed by an elite corps of scientists and managers. We must develop better goals, learn to analyze technology, and be willing to adapt our institutions to the changing demands of technology.

THE STRUGGLE TO BRING TECHNOLOGY TO THE CITIES. Washington, D.C.: Urban Institute, 1971. 80 p.

> This report discusses problems cities encounter when they try to use new technology to provide municipal services. Suggestions for making better use of technological advances include developing an urban applied research center to develop prototypes, aggregate the urban market so industries will find it more profitable to invest risk capital, and undertake development tasks and generate a climate of innovation to make city officials more aware of the benefits of technological innovation.

Taylor, H. Ralph. "Defining and Implementing the Urban Observatories Concept." In GOVERNING URBAN SOCIETY: NEW SCIENTIFIC APPROACHES, edited by Stephen B. Sweeney and James C. Charlesworth, pp. 221-28. Philadelphia: American Academy of Political and Social Science, 1967.

> The author suggests that, in order to build foundations for the large urban areas of the future, we must avoid some of our past mistakes and create a new technology. To date, our efforts in this area have fallen far short of the need. Problems we have experienced have been: inadequate money for urban research, and the allocation of funds to collect fragmented data. We have developed some useful demonstration projects in planning and comprehensive land-use inventories. A new program, called "urban observatories," ties universities and local governments together in an effort to use research, training, and competent personnel to solve urban problems. This partnership is a vital step forward in providing some of the necessary skills to approach urban problems in a systematic manner.

Wilensky, Harold L. ORGANIZATIONAL INTELLIGENCE: KNOWLEDGE AND POLICY IN GOVERNMENT AND INDUSTRY. New York: Basic Books, 1968. 240 p.

> This book analyzes the use, misuse, and nonuse of technological and ideological intelligence in business and government. Intelligence needed to make decisions comprises information, questions, hypotheses, evidence, and insight, which are relevant to a specific policy. Many of the examples used in the book are not drawn from urban areas but the concepts discussed can guide urban managers in the use of intelligence for decision making. The author examines the determinants of uses of various types of experts, structural and doctrinal roots of intelligence failures, and administrative arrangements that facilitate the flow of intelligence. He shows how hierarchy, specialization, centralization, and the nature of the decision all affect the quality of information used in policy making.

C. MANAGEMENT TOOLS

Arnold, David S. "Public Relations." In MANAGING THE MODERN CITY, edited by James M. Banovetz, pp. 377-401. Washington, D.C.: International City Management Association, 1971.

> Public relations is viewed as both a concept and a process. As a concept it means informing, influencing, and measuring. As a process it consists of communicating ideas. The author discusses the difference in public relations activities and ideas between the public and the private sector. Also examined are the differences between public relations and publicity, public opinion, and communication. Public relations is a management responsibility which involves determining attitudes, influencing attitudes, and facilitating communications. The roles of the city council, the chief administrative officer, and the city employees are examined. The news media's role in reporting on governmental activities is discussed as a vital link between city hall and the citizenry. The organization of a public relations department is outlined.

Carvalho, Gerald F. "Installing Management by Objectives: A New Perspective on Organization Change." HUMAN RESOURCE MANAGEMENT 11 (Spring 1972): 23-30.

> The successful installation of management-by-objectives programs requires the development of results-oriented, responsibility-sharing, non-zero-sum game attitudes on the part of all managers. The author focuses on the time lag between initiation of a management-by-objectives program and the achievement of change. Also discussed are the problems which impede rapid and successful implementation of MBO. MBO is viewed as a system of management performance appraisal and steps are outlined to assist managers in installing the program.

Chetkow, B. Harold. "The Planning of Social-Service Changes." PUBLIC ADMINISTRATION REVIEW 28 (May-June 1968): 256-63.

This study examines the intentions of planners and the channels of communication they employ in using priority recommendations to bring about changes in social services. The author focuses on a long-range plan developed by the Community Service Council of Metropolitan Indianapolis. The article discusses and defines concepts and examines how recommendations are communicated to others both inside and outside the council. The goal of implementing social service changes was achieved by using both participant and nonparticipant intervention. The use of priority recommendations was valuable to the staff for information purposes as well as uniting them on specific issues.

Drucker, Peter F. "What Results Should You Expect? A Users' Guide to MBO." PUBLIC ADMINISTRATION REVIEW 36 (January-February 1976): 12-19.

Management-by-objectives requires administrators to establish two sets of objectives. One measures results in terms of management and the other measures results in terms of objectives. Using examples from the private sector, the author discusses the problems involved in establishing objectives and in establishing priorities and applies these to the public sector. MBO must obtain results and these results are defined as understanding the difficulty and complexity of decisions; producing responsibility and commitment within the organization; allocation of resources and personnel effort; and decisions concerning goals, standards, structure, and behavior of the organization.

Hennessy, James J. "The Management of Crime--PPBS and Police Management." THE POLICE CHIEF 39 (July 1972): 62-67.

PPBS and management-by-objectives are discussed as possible methods for restructuring police departments. Historically, police departments have organized by function, beginning with the operating units and using them as hierarchical and dynamic means to achieve a goal. PPBS systems begin with a statement of goals and work downward through a series of subgoals, selecting the best alternative methods to attain these goals. Examples of subgoals are presented and structural tables are included and discussed.

Hoos, Ida R. "Systems Techniques for Managing Society: A Critique." PUBLIC ADMINISTRATION REVIEW 33 (March-April 1973): 157-64.

Systems analysis has been used by governmental agencies for over a decade. During that time few changes have been made in either systems analysis or public agencies. The managerial levels of government have employed the systems approach with little evidence that the scientific management of society is closer to reality. Several problems have been encountered. Social service agencies are so large and complex that they must be broken down into components to be studied or managed. Systems models often cannot replicate real world situations. Objectives in the public sector social service agency may be ambiguous and often are the result of political or value judgments. Data gathering is expensive and time consuming and sometimes does not lend itself to analysis which will produce clear managerial alternatives.

Hoover, Larry T. "Planning-Programming-Budgeting Systems: Problems of Implementation for Police Management." JOURNAL OF POLICE SCIENCE AND ADMINISTRATION 2 (March 1974): 82-93.

The impact of PPBS on the federal bureaucracy is being felt at the state and local levels. Police departments in urban areas are among those departments being affected by PPBS. Some of the questions surrounding the implementation of PPBS concern: the necessity of clearly defined organizational objectives, the relating of programs to objectives, indices establishing output measurement and analysis of the effectiveness of alternative police programs. The author feels that it is presently not possible for PPBS to be implemented in local law enforcement agencies because much data are missing which are needed to analyze the cost effectiveness of program alternatives.

Jackson, John H., and Mathis, Robert L. "Management by Objectives: Promises, Pitfalls and Possibilities." PERSONNEL ADMINISTRATION AND PUBLIC PERSONNEL REVIEW 1 (September-October 1972): 72-75.

The concept of management-by-objectives (MBO) is discussed and two problem areas, control and salary, are examined as potential problem areas for managers to understand. A case study of how to avoid misunderstandings in implementing an MBO program is presented. For the program to be successful, top managers must be willing to implement and maintain a system directed at improving overall performance as well as improving budgetary functions.

Jun, Jong S. "Management by Objectives in the Public Sector: Introduction." PUBLIC ADMINISTRATION REVIEW 36 (January-February 1976): 1-5.

Stating that management-by-objectives (MBO) is one technique for achieving organizational goals by enhancing employee commitment and participation, the author discusses some of the management fads that have been tried in government. Starting in 1970, MBO has emerged as a new management system requiring agencies to formulate goals, initiate action plans for implementation, and assess in quantitative terms the degree to which goals have been achieved. The author discusses some of the underlying theories and examines the organizational elements for an effective MBO program. These include: self-management, communication and feedback process, organizational development and change, policy research, and leadership support.

Katz, Robert L. "Skills of an Effective Administrator." HARVARD BUSINESS REVIEW 52 (September-October 1974): 90-102.

    The purpose of this article is to show that effective administration depends on three basic personal skills which have been labeled technical, human, and conceptual. The effective administrator needs: sufficient technical skills to accomplish the mechanics of the particular job for which he is responsible, sufficient human skills in working with others to be an effective group member and to be able to build cooperative effort within the team he leads, sufficient conceptual skills to recognize the interrelationships of the various factors involved in a given situation, which will lead the administrator to take that action which is likely to achieve the maximum good for the total organization. All three of these skills can be developed.

Kleber, Thomas P. "Forty Common Goal-Setting Errors." HUMAN RESOURCES MANAGEMENT 11 (Fall 1972): 10-13.

    A list of the forty most common mistakes made by organizations in goal setting for a management-by-objectives program is presented. Some of the major errors include: setting goals too high or too low, setting common goals before individual goals are identified, not communicating common goals to lower-level managers, all accepting goals without criticism, and often inflexible goals. The presentation is a guide to managers as to what steps should be taken in setting formal goals.

Lonergan, Wallace G. "Groups and Meetings." In DEVELOPING THE MUNICIPAL ORGANIZATION, edited by Stanley Powers, F. Gerald Brown, and David S. Arnold, pp. 111-24. Washington, D.C.: International City Management Association, 1974.

    Conferences and meetings are a major communications vehicle for managers. The success of meetings often is the result of the knowledge, skills, and attitudes of the managers who lead them. Meetings involve purpose, membership, and leadership. Several types of meetings that are discussed include informational, advisory, and problem-solving meetings. Six specific roles in a meeting are defined as well as who performs these roles. Planning and conducting the meeting involves many factors and often determines the success or failure of the meeting. Included are objectives, invitees, advance information, physical setting and materials, preparation of subject matter, and starting, running, and closing the meeting. A discussion is also presented on how groups work and reach decisions, and the leader's role in these groups.

Mushkin, Selma J. "PPB in Cities." PUBLIC ADMINISTRATION REVIEW 29 (March-April 1969): 167-78.

    Focuses on the techniques of implementing planning-programming-

budgeting systems (PPBS) in cities and counties and the challenges
generated by this practice to both research and education. City
activity in PPB can be traced to New York and Philadelphia and
ten local governments--five cities and five counties--that joined
together in cooperative intergovernmental program application of
the system. The author discusses the evolution of the concept from
the Department of Defense to interested government agencies which
began to think of the benefits of the system for city and county
governments. The application of the system in New York, Philadelphia, and ten local governments is examined. An agenda of
actions that could be undertaken by universities is presented, including: idea generation, research on technology and methodology,
experimentation, and data collection.

Pearson, Fred. "Managing By Objective." In DEVELOPING THE MUNICIPAL
ORGANIZATION, edited by Stanley Powers, F. Gerald Brown, and David S.
Arnold, pp. 174-88. Washington, D.C.: International City Management Asso-
ciation, 1974.

Management-by-objectives is a management tool that looks to the
future by recognizing existing problems and the areas for possible
improvement. The objective-setting process is fundamental to a
program of management-by-objectives. It includes: establishing
priorities, realizing capabilities, and gaining commitment. Effective objective setting includes participation by the employees which,
in turn, creates a feeling of community. Managers learn to discard
some traditional roles such as final arbiter, lone decision maker and
director, and must learn to become better coordinators of resources.
A discussion of workable criteria for stated objectives is presented.
These include: significance, attainability, measurability, and
understandability. The author also outlines a plan for introducing
a management-by-objectives program which discusses facilities, resources, leadership, training agreements, and decisions.

Powers, Stanley P. "Administrative Communication." In DEVELOPING THE
MUNICIPAL ORGANIZATION, edited by Stanley Powers, F. Gerald Brown,
and David S. Arnold, pp. 125-42. Washington, D.C.: International City
Management Association, 1974.

Communication describes the flow of information throughout the
organization and the processes involved. Approaches to the study
of communication center on quantitative theory, content theory,
or a combination of the two. Basic communication and expanded
communications models are presented. Behavioral factors affect the
communications process in many ways. Some of the factors discussed are: experience, attitudes, beliefs, opinions, motivations,
semantic differences, interpretations, situation, person, and self.
One of the most difficult barriers affecting a communications system
is ego protection. All organizations have informal channels of communications, many of which are of great value. Several communication skills are discussed: the art of listening, questioning tech-

niques, and leadership styles and communication.

Rosenbloom, Richard S., and Russell, John R. NEW TOOLS FOR URBAN MANAGEMENT: STUDIES IN SYSTEMS AND ORGANIZATIONAL ANALYSIS. Boston: Harvard Business School, 1971. 298 p.

Using five case studies of how local governments have employed systems analysis and operations research, the authors present a discussion of the applications in a nontechnical manner. The five case studies vary tremendously in the degree to which they were successful. The functional areas discussed include: firehouse location, housing applications, implementation of PPBS, underemployment, and systems management in planning and development. Many of the problems encountered by consultants and public officials have arisen in other cities. Insufficient data, time schedules versus thoroughness of research, bureaucratic infighting, local politics, and fragmented authority affected the applications to some extent. Many of the innovations have great applicability in nonsocial service areas. The last two chapters outline the conditions under which these approaches are most likely to help solve urban problems.

Russell, John R. CASES IN URBAN MANAGEMENT. Cambridge, Mass.: M.I.T. Press, 1974. 556 p.

This casebook in urban management is divided into functional sections with several cases presented in each area. The major issues covered are: housing, narcotics control, public assistance, environmental protection, and decentralization. The first section is a collection of introductory cases designed to allow students to analyze techniques used in specific issue areas. These techniques include cost-benefit analysis and cost-effectiveness analysis. Readers are placed in the position of urban analysts or urban managers, and can increase their familiarity with the process of developing urban programs, implementing change, and managing the day-to-day problems in different urban services.

Sherwood, Frank P., and Page, William J., Jr. "MBO and Public Management." PUBLIC ADMINISTRATION REVIEW 36 (January-February 1976): 5-12.

This article defines MBO as a tactical and instrumental method of coping with specific managerial needs. The concept implies specificity in stating objectives, establishment of feasibility, relatively short time period, measurement of results, definitive resource allocations, and reassessment and restatement of objectives. The authors discuss the background of MBO by tracing it through several agencies and discussing some of the published studies. MBO in the Nixon administration is reviewed as are the questions of data and objectivity, closed systems, and leadership. The authors conclude

that MBO in one form or another is a good management practice
and will be continued. They offer another approach which retains
the concept of MBO but utilizes a different management strategy.

Stuart, Darwin G. "Urban Improvement Programming Models." In DECISION-
MAKING IN URBAN PLANNING, edited by Ira M. Robinson, pp. 343-76.
Beverly Hills, Calif.: Sage Publications, 1973.

A programs-objectives matrix is one of the most commonly used
methods for evaluating alternative urban plans. This matrix balances alternative public investment programs against specific goals
and objectives. Problems arise when different units of measurement
are used for different objectives and programs. Urban improvement
and public investment programming models are not the optimal solution to urban decision making. They do provide one approach,
from among many options, that can be used to determine the allocation of resources.

Szanton, Peter L. "Systems Problems in the City." OPERATIONS RESEARCH
20 (May-June 1972): 465-73.

If urban problems are to be meaningfully resolved, the approach
of operations researchers must be changed. More interdisciplinary
skills must be mobilized. Systems engineers and operations researchers must join with statisticians, economists, sociologists,
lawyers, politicians, and active community leaders to solve these
problems. Linkages must be developed with management consultants,
university urban institutes, consulting engineers, and research firms
in order to develop new theories--not just more studies. The goal
of these new approaches is a growth in practical and analytical
studies that can be acted upon by legislative bodies and implemented by administrators.

"Team Management in Local Government." MANAGEMENT INFORMATION
SERVICE REPORT. Washington, D.C.: International City Management Association, July 1973. 12 p.

Team management is gaining popular acceptance in a number of
local governments today. This innovative management concept
involves individuals in a process of group decision making and
working together. The basic management tools used to implement
this concept are: information systems, planning-programming-
budgeting, and management-by-objectives. The experience of
several cities suggests a wide variety of approaches to team management, ranging from periodic team-building sessions to formally
structured management teams.

Webb, Kenneth, and Hatry, Harry P. OBTAINING CITIZEN FEEDBACK: THE
APPLICATION OF CITIZEN SURVEYS TO LOCAL GOVERNMENTS. Washington,
D.C.: Urban Institute, 1973. 105 p.

More and more local officials are beginning to use citizen surveys to assess the quality of municipal services. This management tool can provide valuable information on services by age, ethnic group, and income level. The citizen survey can also help explain why citizens are not using certain services, which services are deficient, which are satisfactory, and what types of services are needed. The authors discuss some inherent problems in survey research and cost estimates and illustrate both good and poor techniques in implementing citizen surveys.

Chapter 4

PERSONNEL MANAGEMENT

A. GENERAL PERSONNEL ISSUES

Bassett, Glenn A. "Exemployee Turnover Measurement and Human Resources Accounting." HUMAN RESOURCES MANAGEMENT 11 (Fall 1972): 21-30.

Human resources accounting and turnover are discussed by integrating two systems into one. Payroll turnover is distinguished from position turnover and the impact of position on payroll is assessed. The actuals costs of turnover are difficult to determine but accounting for human resources acquisition and development expenses can be instituted. This is the beginning point for a human resources accounting system. Turnover measurement and human resources accounting complement each other and should be combined into one system.

Beaumont, Enid F. "A Pivotal Point for the Merit Concept." PUBLIC ADMINISTRATION REVIEW 34 (September-October 1974): 426-30.

Two major criticisms of the civil service system have been voiced recently. One claims that civil service has moved too far in protecting employees and the second asserts that traditional methods no longer permit a reasonable response to changing manpower requirements. The article examines the two criticisms by reviewing the findings of social science research in the humanistic side of organizations and concludes that current research, reform proposals, and existing practices are in conflict. Topics discussed include: better management, tenure, productivity, layoffs, written examinations, incentives, and innovation. The author suggests the merit system is at a critical point and only major reform, not minor reorganization, will help it survive.

Brown, F. Gerald, and Saunders, Robert J. "Training." In DEVELOPING THE MUNICIPAL ORGANIZATION, edited by Stanley Powers, F. Gerald Brown, and David S. Arnold, pp. 160-73. Washington, D.C.: International City Management Association, 1974.

Even though municipal budgets allocate 60 to 80 percent of their funds for personnel, there is not a very strong commitment to training the employees. This task is left to society at large or to the individual. Three types of training are discussed: big-picture training, functional training, and applied behavioral science training. Big-picture training involves the general education development of employees. Functional training can be broken down into three sections: orientation training, technical training for functional specialties, and management and supervisory training. Behavioral science training includes: agenda building, data collection, feedback, and problem-solving techniques. Planning a training program involves an initial commitment to the concept. Training needs must be assessed, and the authors discuss several options available and some of the shortcomings of each. Once the training program has been selected, it must be geared to employees as adults, not children, and as workers, not students.

Coleman, Charles J. "Personnel: The Changing Function." PUBLIC PERSONNEL MANAGEMENT 2 (May-June 1973): 186-93.

Thirty-two personnel administrators in a large metropolitan area were queried. The data were used to analyze the change in the personnel function. The results indicate a change in the personnel occupation is evidenced by a shift in focus toward the salaried employee, who has developed greater influence within the organization. Greater influence is manifested principally by greater employee involvement in the organizational decision-making process. The results of this study suggest the components of a model that may explain the repeated findings of increasing staff power in organizations.

Dinunzio, Michael, and Hall, Nancy. "Manning Tomorrow's Cities. A Special Report." NATION'S CITIES 11 (June 1973): 25-40.

This report summarizes a conference attended by local government experts to assess the problems cities are having in meeting their professional staff needs. The conference discussion centered on three major areas: the role of local government for the next ten to fifteen years, including changes forced by federal and state action; methods necessary to cope with changes and to move local government out of its passive reactor status toward innovation and leadership; and how to best project professional staff needs and insure the hiring of professionals who can build the capacity of both the chief executive and the governmental institution itself.

Finch, Wilbur. "Paraprofessionals in Public Welfare, A Utilization Study." PUBLIC WELFARE 34 (Winter 1976): 52-57.

The shortage of trained manpower which affected the implementation of welfare programs was overcome by a better utilization of resources, particularly paraprofessional manpower. This study reports on research conducted in a California welfare department where many weaknesses in the use of paraprofessionals were uncovered. The roles of the paraprofessionals were poorly defined at the administrative level, requiring the individual social workers to develop work assignments. Many workers were assigned tasks which did not make full use of their skills and abilities. Transfers were numerous and frequently reduced the skill utilization of the workers. More careful planning is required if paraprofessionals are to play a useful role in these agencies.

Floyd, Picot B. "Some Aspects of Staffing for the Urban Crisis." PUBLIC ADMINISTRATION REVIEW 31 (January-February 1971): 36-42.

City managers must begin to change their patterns of recruitment and staffing if they are to be able to cope with current urban problems. The author suggests that improvements are needed if municipal employment is to be upgraded, and new staffing patterns in the manager's office are presented. The article discusses new ways of managing, professionalization, training opportunities, employee organizations, employment of minorities, and joint appointments with higher-education institutions. Some conclusions reached are: higher salaries to attract more competitive people, more innovative recruitment and training methods, more attention to training resources within their own communities, greater professionalization among decision makers, more flexible interactions with employee organizations, and greater attention to minority employment.

Harrison, Bennett. PUBLIC EMPLOYMENT AND URBAN POVERTY. Washington, D.C.: Urban Institute, 1971. 63 p.

The author examines the relationship between public employment and the disadvantaged, and concludes that the economic status of the poor would be improved if there were an increase in public service jobs. Several factors are used to support this argument. Public service jobs require relatively little skill and the entry-level pay is higher than poor people are apt to receive in other jobs. The central city location of most public service jobs makes them readily accessible for the urban poor.

Haskell, Mark A. THE NEW CAREERS CONCEPT: POTENTIAL FOR PUBLIC EMPLOYMENT OF THE POOR. New York: Praeger, 1969. 110 p.

This book focuses on the concept of restructuring jobs as a way of reducing poverty. Using health services as an example, the author examines supply and demand factors and then applies the "new careers" concept to nine different cases, ranging from veterans' hospitals to teaching hospitals, to train nurses to perform tasks formerly done only by doctors. Many hospitals have already begun developing new careers ladders and have started restructuring their occupational classifications. New educational programs are needed to support both the reclassification project and the new careers program. This education must come from unions, professional associations, government agencies, and universities. The new careers concept is applicable in other agencies such as police, housing, and sanitation.

Heisel, W. Donald. "Personnel Administration." In MANAGING THE MODERN CITY, edited by James M. Banovetz, pp. 318-46. Washington, D.C.: International City Management Association, 1971.

Many of the services a city performs are the direct result of the quality of the system through which personnel were hired. All administrators involved in human resources activities are engaged in personnel administration. Personnel administration usually involves a personnel department and in many cities an independent civil service commission. The role of the supervisor in personnel administration is discussed in terms of motivation, performance assessment, and the handling of grievances. Other subjects examined include: recruitment, selection, appointment, position classification, and pay administration. Relations with unionized employees are viewed from the reasons for unionism, areas of union activity, negotiations, communications, and grievance procedures.

Kirkpatrick, Samuel A.; Morgan, David A.; and Lyons, William. "Municipal Training Needs and Personnel Practices: Implications for Program Planning and Policy Making." MIDWEST REVIEW OF PUBLIC ADMINISTRATION 8 (January 1974): 3-16.

This article tries to clarify the relationships between a municipality's interest in employee training and its personnel practices and, at the same time, to determine the extent to which these are related to specific city characteristics. The findings are based on a survey of seventy-two Oklahoma cities with populations in excess of 2,500. A basic assumption of the study is that improved local public services may be related to advancements in training and personnel systems among localities, and that public policy makers need a better grasp of the relationships between these important aspects of city government. Cities can be differentiated with respect to overall interest in training, and definite preferences among cities for particular training activities can be identified.

Lewin, David. "Aspects of Wage Determination in Local Government Employment." PUBLIC ADMINISTRATION REVIEW 34 (March-April 1974): 149-55.

A major criterion in the determination of local governmental salaries is the prevailing wage principle. Recently economic and political considerations have prompted local governments to pay the same wages, for comparable jobs, as private industry pays. Citing data from about ten large cities, the author shows that public employee wage rates are more egalitarian than private employee wages.

Local governments pay higher salaries to unskilled, semiskilled, and skilled craft workers but generally pay less for professional, managerial, and executive employees than the private sector. A case study of local governments in the Los Angeles metropolitan area indicates the fragmented nature of the decision-making process, and the final decision for wage rates, residing in political boards and commissions, contributes to the wage-rate differentials observed in the study.

Lutz, Carl F. "Efficient Maintenance of the Classification Plan." PUBLIC PERSONNEL MANAGEMENT 2 (July-August 1973): 232-41.

The author suggests that the classification process can become more efficient if a continuous-review procedure is instituted, paper work is limited, and field audit time is minimized. He describes how classification plan administration can be implemented to meet the above criteria. And he focuses on the merits of a continuous-review program, organizing for classification administration, the basic processes, techniques and forms involved, the elimination of frills from class specifications, and the training strategies for the classification staff.

Miller, Glenn W. "Manpower in the Public Sector." PUBLIC PERSONNEL REVIEW 30 (January 1972): 50-55.

The number of civilians working for all levels of government increased dramatically in the 1960s. Employment in state and local government appears to be a major growth industry for the 1970s. However, state and local government personnel policies have proved deficient in the areas of wages, salaries, and employee unrest. The article focuses on state and local government employees, except those in the field of education. The author discusses problem areas such as: wages and salaries, turnover, retention, public image of government jobs, attracting high-level personnel, moonlighting, minority group employment, and the financing of state and local services. The projected increase in state and local employment levels makes it imperative that public sector officials engage in more manpower planning programs.

Mulcahy, Charles C. "Municipal Personnel Problems and Solutions." MARQUETTE LAW REVIEW 56 (Spring 1973): 529-49.

New state legislation which allows municipal employees to organize and bargain with their municipal employers, requires local governments to re-examine their traditional personnel programs. Local governmental departments rarely work together on personnel issues. This leads to fragmented provision of public services. This article offers guidelines for the initiation of effective municipal personnel programs. Recommendations include: centralizing personnel responsibility, from a policy and administrative perspective,

in a personnel committee; and guidelines for the committee to prepare bargaining and post-bargaining practices, training sessions,
and reprimand procedures.

Rosenblum, David H. "Public Personnel Administration and Politics: Toward a
New Public Personnel Administration." MIDWEST REVIEW OF PUBLIC ADMINIS-
TRATION 7 (April 1973): 98-110.

The current status of public personnel administration is reviewed
and new directions are suggested to help make it more useful to
the public sector as a whole. Public personnel administration is
related to scholarly developments in the fields of political science
and public administration. Also discussed are the narrow scope of
the public personnel field and its commitment to the merit system.
Public personnel administration has the potential to make significant
contributions to political science and public administration if it becomes more self-conscious and methodologically sophisticated as
well as adopting a more political focus.

Rutledge, Philip J. "Can Local Government Afford Not to Pay the Price."
PUBLIC MANAGEMENT 57 (November 1975): 4-8.

Equal opportunity has become the law of the land in employment.
Many public agencies, more through inadvertence than through
conscious intent, are in affect violating this policy. Many federal,
state, and local agencies are charged with enforcement of anti-
discriminatory laws and many local governments are finding out why
they must take affirmative action in this area. Being found guilty
of discriminatory practices could lead to suspension of general
revenue-sharing funds and other grant monies needed by cities.

Savas, E.S., and Ginsburg, Sigmund G. "The Civil Service: A Meritless
System?" PUBLIC INTEREST 32 (Summer 1973): 70-85.

After ninety years of civil service law, the authors feel the time
has come to make major changes in the civil service system. The
vast changes which have occurred in the public sector during this
period require a new look at the merit system. The major components and shortcomings of the present civil service system in New
York City are examined. The areas discussed are: jobs, recruitment practices, examinations, selection procedures, promotions, and
motivational rewards. The growing support for collective bargaining is a prime reason for reforming the public personnel systems.
Prospects for achieving reform are discussed.

Stone, Clarence N., and Feldbaum, Eleanor G. "Blame, Complacency and
Pessimism: Attitudes and Problems Among Selected Street Level Administrators
in Two Suburban Counties." ADMINISTRATION AND SOCIETY 8 (May 1976):
79-106.

Social service employees work in potentially frustrating conditions.

Their reactions to job stress may differ. Results of survey data suggest that personal characteristics are an important intervening variable between job stress and employee reaction. Agencies, however, are not equally receptive to all reactions. Social agencies seem to reward complacency. The authors conclude that employees who define their work objectives as attaining extrinsic rewards will be satisfied and remain with their agencies. Employees seeking intrinsic rewards will be frustrated and will leave their agencies.

Thompson, Frank J. "Bureaucratic Responsiveness in the Cities: The Problem of Minority Hiring." URBAN AFFAIRS QUARTERLY 10 (September 1974): 40-68.

Surveys the nature of urban bureaucratic responsiveness to the needs of the poor, particularly the minority poor. Discussed are reasons for lack of response, factors that encourage responsiveness, and strategies to encourage bureaucratic responsiveness. The discussion is tied together by a case study of Oakland, California which focuses on the response of the city fire department to demands for more jobs for minorities. Reasons for lack of responsiveness are found to be: lack of incentives to change practices, no-risk attitude of bureaucrats, middle-class bias of the bureaucracy, and a lack of minority groups' resources and skills. Several suggestions are offered for overcoming the static nature of urban bureaucracy.

B. UNIONS AND LABOR-MANAGEMENT RELATIONS

Anderson, Arvid. "The Structure of Public Sector Bargaining." In PUBLIC WORKERS AND PUBLIC UNIONS, edited by Sam Zagoria, pp. 37-52. Englewood Cliffs, N.J.: Prentice-Hall, 1972.

Questions concerning the composition of the bargaining unit, the scope of bargaining, the authority to bargain for the employer, and the legal rules for bargaining often predetermine the results of bargaining. The author discusses the types of bargaining used and the criteria applied in their selection. He feels these units vary considerably but are generally based upon private sector standards. The question of who bargains for the employer is examined by presenting a variety of examples. Discussed are the role of a labor relations office and the position of the jurisdiction's legal officer. When the structure and the personnel are in place, the political jurisdiction must concern itself with the scope, timetable, and criteria for bargaining. All of these components are necessary for the public sector to keep pace with the rapidly expanding public union movement.

Crabtree, James S. "Development, Status and Procedures for Labor Relations." In DEVELOPING THE MUNICIPAL ORGANIZATION, edited by Stanley Powers,

F. Gerald Brown, and David S. Arnold, pp. 249–66. Washington, D.C.:
International City Management Association, 1974.

> Over the past twenty years, increasing numbers of public sector
> employees have been joining unions or associations. The author
> reviews several scholarly studies which try to explain the movement
> toward employee organization. Included are discussions of the
> evolution of two major approaches adopted by state and local gov-
> ernments. These are the meet-and-confer approach and collective
> bargaining. Disputes over interests and rights often lead to an
> impasse and occasionally to strikes. In order to avoid work stop-
> pages, alternative mechanisms have been developed. These include:
> compulsory arbitration, voluntary arbitration, mediation, and fact
> finding. The need to hear and resolve grievances is also examined,
> outlining five different formats that can be employed. Where
> grievances cannot be amicably settled, there is a need for an ap-
> peals process.

Feuille, Peter, and Long, Gary. "The Public Administrator and Final Offer
Arbitration." PUBLIC ADMINISTRATION REVIEW 34 (November–December
1974): 575–83.

> The growth of unionization and collective bargaining in the public
> sector has made labor relations one of the most important parts of
> the local administrator's job. The article examines the concept of
> final-offer arbitration as it has been used in Eugene, Oregon to
> negotiate labor contracts. Several variations are possible in final-
> offer arbitration and each approach has a different impact upon
> incentives to bargain and to arbitrate. The author discusses the
> final-offer system, the unique feature of dual offers, entire package
> selection, selection criteria, the tripartite panel, and the time-
> table provisions. The Eugene system is constructed so as to en-
> courage bargaining at each step in the process and, since different
> procedures produce different outcomes, comparison between cities
> is often impossible.

Flynn, Ralph J. PUBLIC WORK, PUBLIC WORKERS. Washington, D.C.: New
Republic, 1975. 112 p.

> The author believes there should be a national labor relations act
> for public employees similar to the Wagner Act which guided the
> development of labor-management relations in the private sector.
> The growing number of strikes in the public sector and several
> cases of injustice are cited as reasons for this new approach.
> Public sector workers want to be able to influence and participate
> in management decisions in order to improve their conditions and
> the services to their clients. Productivity measures are being writ-
> ten into many union contracts. Sound labor-manager relationships
> can continue to produce innovations.

Gould, William B. "Labor Relations and Race Relations." In PUBLIC WORKERS AND PUBLIC UNIONS, edited by Sam Zagoria, pp. 147-59. Englewood Cliffs, N.J.: Prentice-Hall, 1972.

> The author suggests that since public unions are a relatively new phenomenon they may be able to avoid many of the discriminatory practices historically evident in the private sector unions. A brief discussion of some legal cases attacking discrimination is presented along with 1971 data showing the disparity between the black population in ten large cities and the black members of each city's police force. The author also examines the community's interest in union practices and the growing number of black caucuses within municipal unions. A brief discussion of several major unions with high black membership is presented. These include transit workers, police, fire fighters, and teachers.

Hayes, Frederick O'Reilly. "Collective Bargaining and the Budget Director." In PUBLIC WORKERS AND PUBLIC UNIONS, edited by Sam Zagoria, pp. 89-100. Englewood Cliffs, N.J.: Prentice-Hall, 1972.

> There is a natural conflict of interest between the municipal union and the director of the budget. The unions represent an external force that exerts great pressure on the ability of managers to control the budget. The author discusses the bargaining process by examining some of the differences in the process between small and large cities. Charts and diagrams are presented to illustrate the analysis of direct costs. Collective bargaining adds a great deal of uncertainty to the budget process and makes it difficult for management to change work rules or initiate productivity measures. Many of these problems are compounded by the fact that union members occasionally reject the contracts their leaders have worked out. Municipal unionism has made it much more difficult for managers to make rational decisions and it has added an element of inflexibility to local government. However, collective bargaining stands as a moderate compromise between managerial autocracy and worker militancy.

Horton, Raymond D.; Lewin, David; and Kuhn, James W. "Some Impacts of Collective Bargaining on Local Government: A Diversity Thesis." ADMINISTRATION AND SOCIETY 7 (February 1976): 497-516.

> The growth of public employee unionism in recent years has focused the attention of both scholars and practitioners on labor relations, collective bargaining, and the process involved in bargaining decisions. Little attention has been paid to the impact of collective bargaining on local government management. The authors use a diversity-of-impacts theory that suggests several patterns of bargaining outcomes. Five components of public management are analyzed: compensation, personnel administration, service provision and delivery, government structure, and politics. The thesis is tested in bargaining outcomes in New York, Chicago, and Los Angeles. The

authors conclude that the diversity in state and local government labor relations processes suggest the federal government should shy away from enacting laws to regulate state and local labor relations. Another approach should be found to deal with public employee strikes rather than simply prohibiting them.

Jones, Ralph. CITY EMPLOYEE UNIONS: LABOR AND POLITICS IN NEW YORK AND CHICAGO. Cambridge, Mass.: Ballinger, 1976. 272 p.

Stating that political environment may be an important variable in determining the existence and maintenance strategies of large public sector unions, the author analyzes the relationship between the political environment of the city and the organizational behavior of city employee labor unions. The study traces the evolution of city employee unions in New York and Chicago. Using interviews and direct observation, the author examines the strategies of the unions to maintain their membership, organizational rivalries, the use of professional organizers, and value of collective bargaining.

_____. PUBLIC SECTOR LABOR RELATIONS: AN EVALUATION OF POLICY-RELATED RESEARCH. Cambridge, Mass.: Ballinger, 1976. 320 p.

This study is a summary and an evaluation of current research pertaining to public sector labor relations. The major issues discussed are employer organizations, unit determination, scope of bargaining, union security, the merit system, conflict resolution, and the impact of collective bargaining on wages, hours, and working conditions. The author outlines areas where more research is needed and suggests ways for conducting the research. An annotated bibliography of over 300 documents is included at the end of the study.

Juris, Harvey A., and Feuille, Peter. POLICE UNIONISM: POWER AND IMPACT IN PUBLIC SECTOR BARGAINING. Lexington, Mass.: Lexington Books, 1973. 228 p.

Data on the growth of police unionism was collected from twenty-two urban areas around the country. The study focuses on six major areas: the nature of police employee organizations, the nature of the collective bargaining process in the police services, the impact of police unions on policy formulation, unions and professionalization, the impact of unions on the ability of the chief of police to manage and control the department, and the relationship between police unions and black officers' organizations. The authors conclude that unionism will continue to grow and that conflict will continue over wages, hours, working conditions, and the relationship of the police to the minority community. These struggles will be resolved through the bargaining process as well as in the legislative and administrative arenas.

Kochan, Thomas A.; Huber, George P.; and Cummings, L.L. "Determinants of Intraorganizational Conflict in Collective Bargaining in the Public Sector." ADMINISTRATIVE SCIENCE QUARTERLY 20 (March 1975): 10-23.

Several models of organizations and theories of behavior within organizations assume common goals among members. Other models and theories assume that incompatible goals exist within organizations. This study summarizes field work conducted in 228 city government organizations that engaged in collective bargaining with locals of the International Association of Fire Fighters. Results of the study suggest several approaches for resolving conflict in the municipal collective bargaining process. Conflict must not only be resolved between the union and the city but among the diverse interests within both. Failure to resolve these conflicts within the management decision-making process means they will surface in the negotiations process.

Livingston, Frederick R. "Collective Bargaining and the School Board." In PUBLIC WORKERS AND PUBLIC UNIONS, edited by Sam Zagoria, pp. 63-76. Englewood Cliffs, N.J.: Prentice-Hall, 1972.

Collective bargaining has grown more rapidly in public education than in any other area of governmental activity. Almost every state in the country recognizes the right of the school boards to negotiate with teachers. School boards are unique in that they perform both executive and legislative functions. This presents many difficulties when it comes to collective bargaining, because of the traditionally closed nature of this process. The scope of what is negotiable is much broader in school districts than in other units of government primarily because teachers are professionals and have an interest in and expertise about many policy decisions which nonprofessional employees don't place on the bargaining table. Collective bargaining is also complicated because of the close relationship between teachers and parents. The author discusses the problems concerning teacher strikes, composition of the school board, and the role of the superintendent.

Macy, John W., Jr. "The Role of Bargaining in the Public Service." In PUBLIC WORKERS AND PUBLIC UNIONS, edited by Sam Zagoria, pp. 5-19. Englewood Cliffs, N.J.: Prentice-Hall, 1972.

Even though public service employment has been growing at a rapid rate and public service strikes have become impediments to the orderly administration of government, citizens and public officials appear to have paid very little attention to the role of unions in the public service. The complexity and magnitude of the subject have obscured a clear understanding of labor-management relations. Several aspects of the setting in which public unions operate are discussed: the balance of benefits and obligations, the roles of civil service and the legislative body, differences between public and private sector, blurred lines between manage-

ment and unions, and neglected working conditions. The author
outlines a series of policies, standards, and procedures to guide
the actors involved in seeking effective solutions to management-
labor problems.

Maier, Henry W. "Collective Bargaining and the Municipal Employer." In
PUBLIC WORKERS AND PUBLIC UNIONS, edited by Sam Zagoria, pp. 53–62.
Englewood Cliffs, N.J.: Prentice-Hall, 1972.

Several factors put pressure on the mayor of a large city for the
allocation of funds. Among these are: the prevailing public
sentiment; the physical, economic, and social components of the
city; and the costs of municipal manpower to provide the services
needed. In the area of manager-employee relations, the mayor
often has much less power than is realized. This is mostly due to
the system of checks and balances which divides powers among a
variety of actors. States often impose limitations that restrict the
ability of local governments to raise revenues or bargain on certain
issues. In all of these cases, the public sector is at a disadvantage
when compared to the private sector. The author offers several
suggestions based upon his own experiences as mayor of a large city.

Nesvig, Gordon T. "The New Dimensions of the Strike Question." PUBLIC
ADMINISTRATION REVIEW 28 (March–April 1968): 126–32.

The number of work days lost due to strikes in the public sector
escalated dramatically in the 1960s. Not all of this increase can
be explained by the growth in numbers. With a leveling off of
jobs in the private-sector, blue-collar work force, the labor movement turned its attention to the public sector. The labor movement came into conflict with long established professional associations of teachers, firemen, and policemen and began to compete
for dues and loyalties. This competition heightened tension and
has had much to do with public sector employee unrest. The author also discusses work stoppages and antistrike laws and concludes
that public sector managers and employee groups should learn that
a strike is an admission of failure on both sides.

Posey, Rollin B. "The New Militancy of Public Employees." PUBLIC ADMIN-
ISTRATION REVIEW 28 (March–April 1968): 111–17.

In the post-World War II era the growth of unionization of public
employees has increased at a rapid rate. The growth has been
particularly evident in larger cities. With the growth in public
employee unionization has come a more militant attitude in govern-
ment-employee negotiations. A number of cases where public employees have struck are cited. Particular attention is paid to the
unionization and resulting strikes in the public education field.
The author discusses some of the reasons for increased militancy
and the special problems that exist in the public sector which are

not common to other areas of employer-employee relations.

Raskin, A.H. "Politics Up-Ends the Bargaining Table." In PUBLIC WORKERS AND PUBLIC UNIONS, edited by Sam Zagoria, pp. 122-46. Englewood Cliffs, N.J.: Prentice-Hall, 1972.

> This article begins with an historical look at the relations between mayors and city unions in New York City up to the Lindsay administration. The nature of labor-management relations changed dramatically in 1966 when Lindsay became mayor and attempted to reform the highly politicized bargaining structure that existed in the city. The author discusses the background, politics, and conflict resolution of the three major strikes in New York City in the 1960s: the transit strike, the sanitation strike, and the teachers' strike. The author feels that the labor-management history of the 1960s in New York has serious implications for diminished management rights, racial and ethnic pressures, employee exodus from the city, and the threat of selective strikes.

Silbiger, Sara. "The Missing Public-Collective Bargaining in Public Employment." PUBLIC PERSONNEL MANAGEMENT 4 (September-October 1975): 290-99.

> Municipal employee unionism has advanced steadily over the years, though the question of union power in the structure of city governance has seldom become a political issue. In New York City, collective bargaining among public employees has achieved an unusually high level of development. What is still missing is the connecting link between the structure of municipal labor relations and the public interest. A mayor is the only person who can raise the public's understanding of how collective bargaining affects all the citizens. This in turn will make it easier for future elected officials to resist unwarranted demands.

Stenberg, Carl W. "Labor Management Relations in State and Local Government: Progress and Prospects." PUBLIC ADMINISTRATION REVIEW 32 (March-April 1972): 102-7.

> Labor-management relations in state and local governments have become a major issue of conflict in the intergovernmental system. The author reviews the growth, size, and strength of public employee unions on both the local and state levels over the past decade and a half. He reviews several proposals put forth by the Advisory Commission on Intergovernmental Relations and other legislation sponsored by organizations trying to cope with the problem. Several specific recommendations are offered concerning the role of professionals, antistrike legislation, multijurisdictional collective negotiating and worker productivity. Each of these issues will have to be resolved if a workable balance is to be achieved between the rights of the employees and the responsibilities of the public employers to the citizens.

Weitzman, Joan. THE SCOPE OF BARGAINING IN PUBLIC EMPLOYMENT.
New York: Praeger, 1975. 384 p.

> The focus of this book is on the collective bargaining process and
> the impact it will have on legislative and executive decision mak-
> ing with respect to the allocation of resources and power. Several
> risks involved in the bargaining process are discussed for elected
> and appointed officials and the public. The scope of bargaining
> as developed in state law is analyzed for eleven states. Also
> reviewed are major court cases and relevant literature on the sub-
> ject. A case study is presented on the bargaining process over
> class size in the New York State educational system. Citizen in-
> volvement in the negotiating process is still a serious issue and the
> author suggests several ways citizens can be included.

Wellington, Harry H., and Winter, Ralph K., Jr. THE UNIONS AND THE
CITIES. Washington, D.C.: Brookings Institution, 1971. 217 p.

> The authors believe the public sector is not just like another indus-
> try. Public employee unions often wield too much political power
> which may negatively affect the city. Many other groups in the
> city have demands they want acted upon just as the unions do.
> The book focuses on the theory, practice, organization, and pro-
> cess of collective bargaining. The major difference between the
> public and private sector unions is the degree of political power
> each is subjected to by unions. Since public sector unions often
> provide services under a legalized monopoly arrangement, there is
> little fear that strikers will lose their jobs or that the cost of set-
> tling the strike will make the service too expensive to purchase.

Zack, Arnold M. "Impasses, Strikes, and Resolutions." In PUBLIC WORKERS
AND PUBLIC UNIONS, edited by Sam Zagoria, pp. 101-21. Englewood Cliffs,
N.J.: Prentice-Hall, 1972.

> The 1960s marked the beginning of a rapid spread of public sector
> unionism. The author cites several reasons for this growth includ-
> ing: low wage rates, more militant workers, rising civil disobedi-
> ence in the country, and the general success of several illegal
> strikes which pointed up the fact that the power to strike was more
> important than the right to strike. Presented is a brief discussion
> of the legislative reaction to illegal strikes and the evolution of
> collective bargaining machinery. There is an examination of direct
> negotiations and the types of appeal machinery available with a
> discussion of the mediation approach. Also discussed are the ad-
> vantages and disadvantages of fact-finding and compulsory arbitra-
> tion.

Zagoria, Sam. "Labor Relations Management." In DEVELOPING THE MUNICI-
PAL ORGANIZATION, edited by Stanley Powers, F. Gerald Brown, and David
S. Arnold, pp. 267-78. Washington, D.C.: International City Management
Association, 1974.

The author provides general guidelines for labor relations management for the chief administrator, department heads, personnel office
and other management officials. Discussed are the stages of unionization from the period before the union is established up to and
through the orientation of supervisory personnel to the terms and
conditions of the contract accepted by both management and labor.
Special attention is paid to attitudes towards unionization—for,
against, and neutral. The author examines how to prepare for
negotiations and how the negotiations should be conducted. He
concludes with a discussion of impasse procedures to be used when
negotiations become stalemated.

C. PRODUCTIVITY

Bushey, Harold T. "Work Analysis and Work Environment." In DEVELOPING
THE MUNICIPAL ORGANIZATION, edited by Stanley Powers, F. Gerald Brown,
and David S. Arnold, pp. 227-44. Washington, D.C.: International City
Management Association, 1974.

Work analysis is a management process which helps to clarify needs
and objectives and to increase performance, efficiency, and effectiveness. It provides managers with the needed flexibility to ad-
just the work unit and the flow of work to changing needs and
goals. Several charts and diagrams are presented illustrating the
different topics discussed. These are: work distribution; work flow;
operations analysis; work layout; forms design and space planning,
furniture, and equipment. Most of the tools illustrated and described are designed to give managers a systematic way of looking
at work in their organizations. Managers must still be able to
identify problems, gather information, and make decisions based
upon the available alternatives.

Chitwood, Stephen R. "Social Equity and Social Service Productivity." PUBLIC
ADMINISTRATION REVIEW 34 (January-February 1974): 29-35.

This article focuses on current attention being paid to increasing
productivity in the public sector and the evolution of this trend
as it relates to earlier public management movements. Productivity
measures historically have neglected to question social equity as it
pertains to the distribution of services. This article identifies some
of the relationships between these two concepts by examining the
dimensions of social equity, its relationship to public decision making, and the standards for measuring social equity. The author concludes that as governmental institutions continue to deliver more
public services it will become increasingly important for public
officials to define and articulate their views on social equity in
the distribution of public services.

DeLadurantey, Joseph C., and Knowles, Lyle. "The New Management Team: Performance Evaluation on Trial." POLICE CHIEF 60 (October 1973): 18-23.

In the past decade the role, duties, and responsibilities of the law enforcement officer have changed greatly. However, the methods and procedures of evaluating the performance of the individual officer have remained basically unchanged. The role of the supervisor, the subordinate, and the manager are discussed in terms of performance measurement systems. Recommendations are offered for instituting an employee evaluation system.

Greiner, John M. TYING CITY PAY TO PERFORMANCE: EARLY REPORTS ON THE EXPERIENCES OF ORANGE, CALIFORNIA AND FLINT, MICHIGAN. Washington, D.C.: Labor-Management Relations Service, 1974. 26 p.

In trying to cope with demands for more and better services, pay increases, and more rewarding jobs in a time of increasing taxpayer resistance, a number of local governments are trying to improve productivity through performance-oriented employee incentives. This study examines the efforts of two cities which have generated much public interest in their performance-oriented programs. The Flint, Michigan program rewards waste collectors for reduced overtime and increased productivity, while the Orange, California program rewards policemen through wage increases by reducing the crime rate in four categories. The report discusses the origin of these programs, how they operate, and the impact and effectiveness of these plans.

Greiner, John M.; Bell, Lynn; and Hatry, Harry P. EMPLOYMENT INCENTIVES TO IMPROVE STATE AND LOCAL GOVERNMENT PRODUCTIVITY. Washington, D.C.: National Commission on Productivity and Work Quality, 1975. 157 p.

This study discusses the use of employee incentives, in state and local government, to improve productivity and employee morale. Several incentive systems are examined including attendance, career development, competition and contests, education benefits, job enrichment, merit increases, performance bonuses, piecework, safety awards, suggestion awards, task systems, and varying work standards and hours. The results were obtained from a survey of state and local governments and a follow-up on some programs. In some cases, evaluations of the programs are included. The report presents some findings and suggestions for planning, implementing, and evaluating state and local government employee incentive programs.

Hamilton, Edward K. "Productivity: The New York City Approach." PUBLIC ADMINISTRATION REVIEW 32 (November-December 1972): 784-95.

The New York City productivity program was designed to maintain and improve the quality of service to citizens at a time when the work force was being reduced. Public reports are issued quarterly to inform public officials and citizens of what types and quality of service are being provided. Several obstacles to implementing a productivity program are discussed and the evolution of New York's program from 1965-72 is recounted. New York set four major goals in their productivity program--reducing unit costs, improving the deployment of resources, improving government organization processing and procedures, and technological innovations. Within each major goal area, programs are outlined such as rat control, park cleaning, sanitation vehicle maintenance, fire response, police dispatch, sanitation deployment, capital construction, and computer use. While problems still need to be resolved, the public has come to expect a periodic, detailed statement of the output and input factors in service delivery.

Hatry, Harry P. "Issues in Productivity Measurement for Local Government." PUBLIC ADMINISTRATION REVIEW 32 (November-December 1972): 776-84.

Productivity measurements are important resources in determining how effective action taken by local governments has been. Unfortunately, productivity measurement programs in local government have not been implemented in large numbers. This article highlights the need for productivity measurement in cities and discusses the difficulties involved in trying to define and measure outputs in social service functions. The measurement of input is discussed by suggesting three alternatives: man-hours or man-years of effort, cost in constant dollars and cost in current dollars without deflating for price-level changes. The author presents an illustration of ten service functions and suggested workload measures, citizen impact measures, and pertinent local conditions that should be considered in measuring productivity. Two examples--solid waste collection and police crime control--are presented.

Hatry, Harry P., and Fisk, Donald M. IMPROVING PRODUCTIVITY AND PRODUCTIVITY MEASUREMENTS IN LOCAL GOVERNMENT. Washington, D.C.: National Commission on Productivity and Work Quality, 1971. 73 p.

This study summarizes the major issues in productivity and productivity measures in local government with special emphasis on the comparisons between political jurisdictions. Reviewing current programs and practices, the authors do not find adequate comparative data or national data for any local governmental functions. They recommend approaches for developing such data, to increase efficiency and effectiveness in local government, and suggest problem areas to be considered when comparing productivity data in different local governments.

Hirsch, Gary B., and Riccio, Lucius J. "Measuring and Improving the Productivity of Police Patrol." JOURNAL OF POLICE SCIENCE AND ADMINISTRATION 2 (June 1974): 169-84.

Past studies of police productivity have focused on broad measures, such as crime rate per capita or the number of police officers per capita. This study develops a framework of goals, objectives, and activities within which the performance of a police department's patrol function can be assessed. A process is presented for measuring the productivity of patrol activities, diagnosing the causes of poor productivity, and taking the most effective action to improve patrol productivity. Suggestions based on programs being used by several agencies are offered for productivity improvement in each area in which poor performance is discovered.

Holzer, Marc. "Police Productivity: A Conceptual Framework for Measurement and Improvement." JOURNAL OF POLICE SCIENCE AND ADMINISTRATION 1 (December 1973): 459-67.

A framework for the comprehension and analysis of police productivity is presented. Police productivity indexes are defined as: internal output, external output, and effectiveness of output. Five catalysts found in police literature on productivity are discussed. They are: productivity bargaining, capital investment, awareness of innovation, management audits, and the principles of management. Factors which might impede productivity measurement are discussed. The author concludes that the utility of police productivity measurement is largely a function of acceptance by patrolmen.

Horton, Raymond D. "Productivity and Productivity Bargaining in Government: A Critical Analysis." PUBLIC ADMINISTRATION REVIEW 36 (July-August 1976): 407-14.

Productivity bargaining has been proposed as a means of increasing productivity in government, particularly at the state and local level. However, both the research and the experience with productivity bargaining point up a number of conceptual and implementation problems. Productivity increases measured in output must be measured against per unit of input. Increasing productivity in a poorly delivered public service may be counterproductive. Using New York City's experience with productivity bargaining, the author discusses the experiences with police, fire, and sanitation workers. The results were marginal. Managers have to realize the difference between production and productivity and understand that productivity bargaining has definite limitations as a management tool.

Katzell, Raymond, et al. "Improving Productivity and Job Satisfaction." ORGANIZATIONAL DYNAMICS 4 (Summer 1975): 69-80.

Many techniques are available for improving the attitudes and performance of workers in their jobs, but most of these approaches focus on a partial aspect of the workers' relationship to their jobs—financial incentives, control over work, and social relationships. Usually no one of these techniques will significantly affect both productivity and job satisfaction. To achieve large-scale and enduring improvements, managers have to develop a combination of methods. There does not appear to be one program that can improve both productivity and job satisfaction in all situations. To achieve this goal, numerous and far-reaching changes must be made before the desired effects become visible. However, managers are often constrained by political factors and tend to proceed slowly.

Kessler, Clemm C. "Influencing Employee Behavior." In DEVELOPING THE MUNICIPAL ORGANIZATION, edited by Stanley Powers, F. Gerald Brown, and David S. Arnold, pp. 84-101. Washington, D.C.: International City Management Association, 1974.

Motivation is a difficult topic to deal with partly because there is a lack of agreement on the term and partly because it involves both biological and psychological factors. The author reviews some of the empirical and theoretical research in the area of motivation. Also included are theories and applications of several different approaches such as: social interaction approaches, material incentive plans, supervisory and leadership behavior, job modification, and participatory management and accountability. The concept, nature, and control of rewards are discussed as motivating factors as is the element of punishment. The author concludes that good managers do not use any one system but draw from all approaches to maximize resources to the fullest extent.

Parker, John K. "Administrative Analysis." In MANAGING THE MODERN CITY, edited by James M. Banovetz, pp. 255-94. Washington, D.C.: International City Management Association, 1971.

This chapter focuses on the nature, purpose, and techniques of administrative analysis by examining work measurement, administrative statistics, records management, and organization for administrative planning and analysis. Over a dozen methodological steps are outlined and several approaches to administrative analysis are discussed. Samples of work simplification and work distribution charts are presented. Work progress charts and office layouts are illustrated as techniques for improving efficiency. The uses and applications of work measurement are discussed as ongoing programs designed to aid the budget process, administrative control, and the public information function.

Ross, Joel E., and Murdick, Robert G. "People, Productivity and Organizational Structure." PERSONNEL 50 (September-October 1973): 8-18.

Productivity has become an important issue to managers today. It can be increased most effectively by stepping up organizational and management restructuring, particularly in terms of the effects on human resources. The authors discuss traditional, new, and emerging forms of organizational structure and recommend an adaptive climate in which the applicable components of each structure can be incorporated where necessary.

Ross, John, and Burkhead, Jesse. PRODUCTIVITY IN THE LOCAL GOVERN-MENT SECTOR. Lexington, Mass.: Lexington Books, 1974. 192 p.

Taxpayers are becoming increasingly concerned about local tax rates. When tax rates rise, citizens want to know whether the quantity and quality of services have improved and if local government is operating more efficiently and more effectively. Using data on government expenditures over time, the author analyzes changes in local government, productivity, and output. The changes analyzed include costs, workload, productivity, and effectiveness. Local officials can use this study as a guide for determining the extent of changes in local government employee productivity.

Staudohar, Paul D. "An Experiment in Increasing Productivity of Police Service Employees." PUBLIC ADMINISTRATION REVIEW 35 (September-October 1975): 518-22.

Approaches to improving productivity in police forces have included changes in technology, changes in organization, and increasing employee motivation. This report examines a program to increase employee motivation that was developed by the city of Orange in California and the local police association. The incentive plan provided salary increases if there were reductions in rape, robbery, burglary, or auto theft over prescribed time periods. Experience with the plan indicates that performance incentives can help in reducing the reported number of specific crimes. However, while total crime rates went down, two categories of targeted crime did increase. Better crime reporting systems and external auditing would insure the accuracy of the results. Greater attention is also needed in areas of crime prevention and community relations.

Chapter 5

URBAN DECENTRALIZATION

A. THEORETICAL APPROACHES

Aronowitz, Stanley. "The Dialectics of Community Control." SOCIAL POLICY
1 (May-June 1970): 47-51.

Blacks have begun to redefine their objectives and develop a new
concept of political alliances. Decentralization has begun to
question hierarchical arrangements as well as the representative
nature of the bureaucracy and has led to demands for community
control. Proponents see services being administered by indigenous
community leadership; resource allocations from federal, state, and
local governments; and the development of political and social
leadership as the major benefits of community control. Problems
in community control center on definitions and limits of community
and power and the intangible results of a volatile national economy.
Community control also prevents citywide alliances and sets oppressed
groups fighting among themselves.

Bresnick, David. "Decentralizing the City: Who Gets Control?" NATIONAL
CIVIC REVIEW 62 (October 1973): 486-90.

Changing demographic patterns have tended to concentrate large
numbers of people in metropolitan areas. This has complicated
the service delivery systems of these areas. The author shows that
the concept of two-tiered government is becoming more and more
popular as metropolitan areas seek new ways to deliver services.
This trend towards decentralization cannot continue if cities are
considered creatures of the state.

_____. "The Other Side of Decentralization: New York City." NATIONAL
CIVIC REVIEW 64 (February 1975): 70-78.

Current efforts aimed at governmental reorganization in New York
City concentrate on decentralization. As public issues become
more complex, local governments require a more informed input
from citizens. The scope of issues confronting the city can become

more manageable if people who know the issues best can articulate
their needs to local government. Cities in turn can present their
case to state governments better, which could lead to a more coordinated effort to solve problems in large metropolitan areas.

Fesler, James W. "Approaches to the Understanding of Decentralization."
JOURNAL OF POLITICS 27 (August 1965): 536-66.

Part of the problem in trying to understand the concept of decentralization derives from the assumed dichotomy between centralization and decentralization. This type of thinking often impedes
critical analysis, particularly in situations where decentralization
might actually tighten control. Decentralization is often thought
to be more democratic, but the author suggests this clouds the real
issues of area and function and whether conversion from security
maintenance and revenue extraction functions to economic and
social development functions is possible. The inherent conflicts
in these issues necessitate much more research on the problems of
decentralization.

Haider, Donald. "The Political Economy of Decentralization." AMERICAN
BEHAVIORAL SCIENTIST 15 (September-October 1971): 108-29.

Discusses some historical aspects of the conflict over centralization
and decentralization, citing this as a virtual war between the old
and new reformers. Noting that the costs of decentralization are
extreme, politically and economically, the author predicts an end
to this movement. Decentralization is progressing in some cities,
not solely in terms of power and authority, but more in the area
of administrative flexibility and access to information.

Hallman, Howard. ADMINISTRATIVE DECENTRALIZATION AND CITIZEN
CONTROL. Center for Governmental Studies, Pamphlet no. 7. Washington,
D.C.: March 1971. 27 p. Paperbound.

The major issues in this study are the concepts of administrative
decentralization and citizen control and the complex issues which
are associated with each. The author discusses the concept of decentralization as it relates to administrative discretion in areas such
as personnel, budgeting, purchasing, and operating policy. Also
discussed are the problems inherent in the centralization-decentralization dichotomy which particularly affects employees, delegation
procedures, coordination, evaluation, and planning. Citizen politics is reviewed in elections, advisory committees, and neighborhood boards. The author concludes that there is no easy solution
to the distribution of political and administrative power in our
system, unless we simultaneously respond to the issues of legitimacy,
factions, accountability, bargaining, and a more precise definition
of what constitutes a community.

_____. COMMUNITY CORPORATIONS AND NEIGHBORHOOD CONTROL.
Center for Governmental Studies, Pamphlet no. 1. Washington, D.C.: January
1970. 12 p. Paperbound.

> The concept of decentralization is viewed differently by various
> actors in the intergovernmental system. While most practitioners
> agree on the theory, federal officials, governors, mayors, and
> citizen activists all disagree on how much administrative and polit-
> ical power should be decentralized and which components in the
> system should be the recipients of this power. The author reviews
> community action programs in Washington, D.C. and New York
> City, and model cities programs in Oakland and Dayton and then
> compares the two approaches. He suggests that leadership, unity,
> and technical knowledge are key ingredients in achieving success.
> There should be experiments and more flexibility to see what types
> of community organizations function best. Most important, how-
> ever, is the time needed for these new organizations to gain ex-
> perience and to learn to use their new grants of power.

Hart, David K. "Theories of Government Related to Decentralization and
Citizen Participation." PUBLIC ADMINISTRATION REVIEW 32 (October
1972): 603-21.

> Differing views concerning the theoretical basis of decentralization
> exist in the fields of political science, public administration, and
> administrative theory. There is little agreement on definitions,
> implementation, or implications. The value of citizen participa-
> tion is discussed as well as its disadvantages. It is often difficult
> to determine what motivates people to participate in the political
> process. More research must be conducted on the complex prob-
> lems of decentralization and citizen participation and what is the
> appropriate mix if we are to have a participatory democracy.

Herbert, Adam W. "Management Under Conditions of Decentralization and
Citizen Participation." PUBLIC ADMINISTRATION REVIEW 32 (October 1972):
622-37.

> Examines for public management, the theoretical framework of
> citizen participation and decentralization and the implications of
> both. Citing several studies in the field, the author describes
> three processes in a managerial approach to decentralization. The
> socioemotional process, the integrative process, and boundary-
> exchange process highlight the need for several managerial skills
> required by public administrators. It becomes the obligation of
> schools of public administration to begin training pre-service and
> in-service managers in the development of these essential skills.

Johnson, Bert W. "Governance of the Municipality: Fracture and Divorce."
PUBLIC ADMINISTRATION REVIEW 31 (March-April 1971): 187-91.

> The author states that local government is fractured among 81,000

units that are competing for citizen support and financing sources. Within these units there is a divorce between school and nonschool functions. Almost all proposals for eliminating fracture and divorce are met with stiff resistance by some interest groups seeking to preserve the status quo. The author suggests creating neighborhoods within political units based upon junior high school area boundaries. This approach would open up communication channels between citizens and government and would assist local governments to make administrative changes to improve the delivery of urban services. The neighborhood concept can also help establish a framework for organized citizen involvement and help to educate citizens about their government.

Kaufman, Herbert. "Administrative Decentralization and Political Power." PUBLIC ADMINISTRATION REVIEW 29 (January-February 1969): 3-15.

Three major values are discussed as components of the administrative system: executive leadership, representation, and neutrally competent bureaucrats. These values fluctuate in their importance to different groups at different times. Minority groups have attacked the system because it appears to reward only the powerful groups and impedes changes needed by other groups. The result of this growing minority dissatisfaction has been a demand for administrative decentralization. The author suggests that the three major values follow a cycle, decentralization being a manifestation of inept bureaucratic implementation. This is turn will lead to stronger executives with centralized power. At some point there will be a cry for greater representation within the elected body and councils will be strengthened. In attempting to remove politics from administration there will be more responsibility invested in the bureaucracy.

Kristol, Irving. "Decentralization and Bureaucracy in Local Government." In THINKING ABOUT CITIES: NEW PERSPECTIVES ON URBAN PROBLEMS, edited by Anthony H. Pascal, pp. 69-80. Belmont, Calif.: Dickenson, 1970.

The article begins with a discussion of the mandate for popular participation in the Model Cities Program and its impact upon decentralized administration at the local level. Decentralization, according to the author, has become a current solution to urban problems. The author feels that liberals have picked the right problem, but the wrong time. Decentralization became a mechanism for moving populism from consultation to active participation. Using the New York City school system as an example, the author argues that decentralization failed and resulted in a reduction in funding for many of the social service programs involved. While decentralization has failed to reform our large bureaucratic organizations and the school systems in particular, it has also lost sight of the fact that the civil service system has played a major role in integrating many middle-class minority members into American society.

Decentralization is an important and valid objective but it will have greater significance in the long run.

Levy, Frank, and Truman, Edwin M. "Toward a Rational Theory of Decentralization: Another View." AMERICAN POLITICAL SCIENCE REVIEW 65 (March 1971): 172-79.

The nature of the organization being examined often affects the analysis of the process of decentralization. Comparing decentralization features of organizations that produce economic and government or public goods can be misleading. The major differences in the two types of organizations are examined. In economic organizations producers and consumers agree on the goods to be produced while in government organizations there is often substantial disagreement. Economic organizations usually establish information flows in compact numerical form which is not the case in government organizations. Prices are used to measure private organization performance while government organizations deal with less precise statistics.

Liebman, Lance. "Metropolitanism and Decentralization." In REFORM OF METROPOLITAN GOVERNMENTS, edited by Lowdon Wingo, Jr., pp. 43-56. Baltimore: Johns Hopkins University Press, 1972.

The theme of this article is that metropolitanism and decentralization can be implemented simultaneously. Using a two-tier governmental system, the lower level would be the neighborhood unit with responsibility for decisions on specific services. Minorities in a metropolitan area usually feel their power is being diluted when they are consolidated with the white suburbs in a new governmental unit. The author asserts that with power delegated to neighborhood units, minorities would not necessarily be giving up their newly acquired power. The author suggests that decentralizing the decision-making process will increase understanding between public officials and clients, increase governmental efficiency, and make political leaders more responsible. This in turn would bring in new managers to implement the changes which are necessary.

McAllister, Donald M. "Equity and Efficiency in Public Facility Location." GEOGRAPHICAL ANALYSIS 8 (January 1976): 47-63.

Urban planners should consider both equity and efficiency effects in determining the size of urban public service centers and the distance between the centers. There are no objective means for determining the relative importance of equity and efficiency. However, theoretical empirical and simulation evidence indicates that equity is more sensitive than efficiency to the selection of size and spacing within a wide range of alternatives. Planners and administrators should recognize that the equity criterion is important in the design of public service systems and requires more attention than it has received in the past.

Margolis, Julius. "Decentralization and Urban Programs." In THINKING
ABOUT CITIES: NEW PERSPECTIVES ON URBAN PROBLEMS, edited by Anthony
H. Pascal, pp. 49–68. Belmont, Calif.: Dickenson, 1970.

Focus is on the increasing trend of cities to seek help from the
state and federal levels and whether this trend implies increased
centralization of authority and administration in lieu of local decision making. The debate over centralization versus decentralization concerns fiscal transfers from federal agencies to local governments. While there is no optimal decentralization model, the author analyzes the arguments for this approach, citing societal pref-
erence and greater administrative efficiency. He also discusses the
difficulties involved in trying to objectively assign functions to a
specific level of government. The issues of externalities, incentives, and information are examined in light of their impact upon
centralized and decentralized systems.

Rein, Martin. "Decentralization and Citizen Participation in Social Services."
PUBLIC ADMINISTRATION REVIEW 32 (October 1972): 687–700.

The article begins with a theoretical framework of service delivery
and the debate surrounding the various service delivery systems.
Two conflicting philosophies, labeled the universalist-formalist
position and the selectivist-discretionary approach, are analyzed
as delivery systems. Citing that decentralization and service delivery are linked, the author suggests that they should reinforce
each other to ascertain citizen needs and develop programs to
service those needs. The problems surrounding service delivery
might be resolved by using a special coordinator, integration without coordination, integration with coordination, or comprehensive
care organized around a single function.

Schmandt, Henry J. "Municipal Decentralization: An Overview." PUBLIC
ADMINISTRATION REVIEW 32 (October 1972): 571–88.

The author contends that dividing the city into small subsections
will not solve our urban problems. Neighborhood governance is
reviewed in the context of its theoretical framework as well as
organization, size, boundaries, powers, functions, and finance.
Doubts are raised about the efficacy of neighborhood government
to solve major social problems by controlling service delivery or
through political organization. Urban areas are thought to be too
large and too complex for this to be feasible.

Shalala, Donna E., and Merget, Astrid E. "The Decentralization Option."
In ORGANIZING PUBLIC SERVICES IN METROPOLITAN AMERICA, edited by
Thomas P. Murphy and Charles R. Warren, pp. 141–51. Lexington, Mass.:
Lexington Books, 1974.

Governmental institutions that were shaped by the reform movement
have in the past ten years come under increasing attack. Some

critics have argued for the metropolitanization of local government while others have supported a movement for decentralization. This chapter describes and compares some of the approaches to local governmental decentralization. Four different views of decentralization are presented: the ideologues, the analysts, the model builders, and the reformers. Several justifications for decentralization are discussed including: political, psychological, administrative, and economic. The authors conclude their discussion by comparing and contrasting the arguments of centralization and decentralization.

Shepard, W. Bruce. "Metropolitan Political Decentralization: A Test of the Life-Style Values Model." URBAN AFFAIRS QUARTERLY 10 (March 1975): 297-313.

This is a test of a model developed by Oliver Williams which suggests that life-style values are causal agents. Families value certain life-styles and the regulation of these values is dependent upon residential location. Another proposition offered is that the extent of decentralization is associated with the degree of heterogeneity in the community because heterogeneity is a possible threat to life-style value maintenance. The propositions are tested with the dependent variable conceptualized as educational decentralization. The findings are inconclusive which is attributable partially to the life-style measures employed. Further research is recommended to explain political decentralization.

Smith, Bruce L.R. "Introduction to Decentralization." AMERICAN BEHAVIORAL SCIENTIST 15 (September-October 1971): 3-14.

The author defines three types of decentralization. These include: administrative decentralization, in which the delegation of authority is from higher to lower levels within an organization or unit of government. Community control, in which authority is delegated to both lower levels within the organization and also to groups outside the government. And citizen involvement, which encompasses a variety of techniques that allow individuals access to the institutions of government. The movement for greater participation is in four areas: policy making, the citizen as a consumer, paraprofessionals involved in the administration of services, and mobilizing new constituencies to bring pressure on politicians to change the administrative system. The future trend is towards more openness, representativeness, and change in the American political system.

Thomas, William C., Jr., and Hillebroe, Herman E. "Administrative Centralization Versus Decentralization and the Role of Generalists and Specialists." AMERICAN JOURNAL OF PUBLIC HEALTH 58 (September 1968): 1620-32.

Many local health departments have decentralized, however, even those with a long history of experimentation are beginning to doubt the efficacy of this concept. The authors discuss the administrative

mechanisms involved in decentralization and the role of generalists
and specialists in this program. It is difficult to define precise
principles because the issues are so complex. The functions of
central offices and field offices become blurred when examined
against the roles of specialists and generalists in these offices.
Generalist decision makers seem to have many advantages over
specialists in several levels of the administrative structure. The
major difference is the range of programs or specialties with which
a person is familiar and how diversified and varied his experience
is.

Wolfinger, Raymond E. "Why Political Machines Have Not Withered Away and
Other Revisionist Thoughts." JOURNAL OF POLITICS 34 (May 1972): 365-
98.

This article suggests that machine politics still exists in America
and presents a definition of machine politics linked to incentives
for political participation. Explanations for the existence of machines and for their demise are analyzed. The author discusses
the political machines in New Haven, Connecticut and defines
machine politics. Research discussing the difficulty of assessing
patronage is presented. A typology of two-dimensional incentives
is developed based upon tangible-intangible and routine-substantive
characteristics. Many of the functions performed by political machines in the past for the poor and the needy are still required.
In addition, the machine performs services for many business and
professional groups who seek to advance their causes.

Yin, Robert K., and Lucas, William A. "Decentralization and Alienation."
POLICY SCIENCES 4 (September 1973): 327-36.

Proponents of decentralization assert that this new approach to the
delivery of public services will reduce alienation. A number of
cities have implemented decentralization programs but the research
on these efforts has been fragmented. The authors analyzed 1970
national survey data from the University of Michigan's Survey Research Center to test if efficacy-powerlessness is related to participation rather than trust-distrust. The evidence seems to rule out
the possibility that decentralization will increase trust in government. Neither participation nor awareness of local decision making
is related to trust. No evidence is available to indicate that decentralization improves service outputs.

Zimmerman, Joseph F. "Community Building in Large Cities." ADMINISTRA-
TION 20 (Summer 1972): 71-87.

Three major steps that can promote a sense of community in low-
income neighborhoods are presented. Establishment of mechanisms
to improve neighborhood-city hall communications, administrative
decentralization, and devolution of certain political powers to newly

organized neighborhood governments are the three techniques.
Little city halls are the mechanism to improve communications
between citizens and their local government. Administrative decentralization requires dividing the city into uni or multi-functional
administrative districts which permits decisions to be made on less
than a citywide basis. Political, economic, and administrative
criteria for guiding these decisions are also presented.

B. STRUCTURAL ALTERNATIVES

Barton, Allen, et al. DECENTRALIZING CITY GOVERNMENT: AN EVALUA-
TION OF THE NEW YORK CITY DISTRICT MANAGER EXPERIMENT. Lexington,
Mass.: Lexington Books, 1977. 279 p.

This evaluation of New York's program of decentralization examines
problem areas such as environmental quality, unemployment, crime,
poverty, racial conflict, and the demand for community control.
The authors describe the goals of urban decentralization and the
programs planned by the city Office of Neighborhood Government.
Eight stages in the District Manager Program are identified and
evaluated as are several projects initiated by the Office of Neighborhood Government. An analysis is made of program costs and
resource allocation. Findings are presented on the relationship between community leaders and the neighborhood office personnel
from city government. The attitudes of local governmental officials
participating in the program are discussed. The authors conclude
with an analysis of what has been learned from the New York City
experiment with decentralization.

Bloch, Peter B., and Specht, David. NEIGHBORHOOD TEAM POLICING.
Washington, D.C.: Government Printing Office, 1973. 154 p.

This is a study of neighborhood team policing in eight cities--
Holyoke, Massachusetts; Albany, New York; New York City; St.
Petersburg, Florida; Los Angeles; Oxnard, California; Cincinnati;
and Detroit. Neighborhood team policing is a concept which de-
centralizes police operations by giving increased authority to neighborhood chiefs who are usually lieutenants with full responsibility
for their areas. The goals of the program are to improve police-
community relations, increase police effectiveness in preventing
and controlling crime, and increase job satisfaction to police officers. Advantages and disadvantages of this concept are discussed
and guidelines for planning and implementing this program are presented.

Costikyan, Edward N., and Lehman, Maxwell. RESTRUCTURING THE GOV-
ERNMENT OF NEW YORK CITY: REPORT OF THE SCOTT COMMISSION
TASK FORCE ON JURISDICTION AND STRUCTURE. New York: Praeger,
1972. 128 p.

The task force recommends 30±35 independent communities with locally elected councils, responsibility for service delivery, and budgetary power. The citywide government would be responsible for those functions requiring sizable resources and a coordinated approach. Service delivery personnel would be more visible and hopefully more effective. A new policy-making unit would be created consisting of a city council composed of local representatives and a policy board headed by the mayor. This board would also mediate interdistrict and district-city conflicts. Duplication of services will be minimized and the units closest to the citizens, in most cases, will be given the authority to deliver the services.

Fantini, Mario, and Gittell, Marilyn. DECENTRALIZATION: ACHIEVING REFORM. New York: Praeger, 1973. 170 p.

The authors begin with a brief history of the concept of decentralization. They view decentralization as a reaction to centralization, that took place in the early 1900s, which tried to eliminate corruption. As centralization increased, the decision-making process became more inaccessible, irresponsible, and unresponsive to community needs. Decentralization is attempting to redirect the decision-making process by limiting the role of the professionals and giving more power to the community.

The authors analyze experimental educational programs in New York, Detroit, Chicago, and Washington, D.C. to evaluate the degree of success decentralization programs have achieved. The case studies are followed by plans and strategies for reform. Three alternatives are offered and the authors suggest a plan in which reform goes from top to bottom and from bottom to top. In this way all parties involved are brought together in the planning, development, and implementation of the reform program.

The book concludes with a discussion of the future of decentralization. Since the concept of decentralization is a political means of seeking change and since public education is the main vehicle of political socialization in America, any reform will ultimately test the system as we know it now.

Fantini, Mario; Gittell, Marilyn; and Magat, Richard. COMMUNITY CONTROL AND THE URBAN SCHOOL. New York: Praeger, 1970. 268 p.

During the 1960s many inner-city residents turned their anger and frustration toward the urban school system. Viewing the school system as a ladder to social and economic success, they began to see that the schools had failed in integration and compensatory programs and had become a detriment to their children. Those communities turned to decentralization and community control as a means of moving the system toward quality education. The authors trace this movement and analyze the development of the community control concept. Several alternatives to school reform are

discussed as are the governance and policy-making procedures of
the school system. The political and administrative conflicts inherent in implementing a community control experiment are presented by reviewing three demonstration districts in the system.
The results of experiments were inconclusive but the authors feel
the community control concept will grow steadily.

Farr, Walter G.; Liebman, Lance; and Wood, Jeffrey S. DECENTRALIZING
CITY GOVERNMENT: A PRACTICAL STUDY OF A RADICAL PROPOSAL FOR
NEW YORK CITY. New York: Praeger, 1972. 242 p.

A study of a decentralization proposal for New York City. Examines whether institutional change can help improve the quality of
urban life, whatever the level of available funds. Two-tiered and
metropolitan governmental structures are discussed as possible techniques for solving areawide problems while permitting the satisfaction of local needs. Problems encountered include: failure of
most citizens to cooperate with government in improving their own
environment; everyone feels their neighborhood pays a fair share in
taxes but receives less than a fair share in services; lack of understanding and identification with government; and minority group
feelings that bureaucrats are insensitive to their needs. Restructuring government requires balancing political and social values.
Decentralizing government involves the transfer of responsibility
and some budget authority. Adjusting the personnel system to the
decentralized structure might create problems with the unions.

Foley, Fred J., Jr. "The Failure of Reform: Community Control and the
Philadelphia Public Schools." URBAN EDUCATION 10 (January 1976): 389-
414.

School reform in the late 1960s and the early 1970s tried to make
schools more responsive to their clients by shifting basic decision-
making responsibility to locally elected community boards. Some
success had been achieved in New York City and Detroit. A program of decentralization was attempted in Philadelphia in 1969.
The superintendent lacked control over personnel and financial resources and was opposed by teachers, parents, and civil rights
groups. Several demonstration projects were initiated to help mobilize community support. A Commission on Decentralization was
created but it also failed to mobilize the necessary support. The
program of decentralization failed because nonwhite and lower-
income communities did not support it.

Gittell, Marilyn. "Decentralization and Citizen Participation in Education."
PUBLIC ADMINISTRATION REVIEW 32 (October 1972): 670-86.

The article begins with a historical review of citizen participation
in local school systems focusing on the role of boards of education,
parent groups, and civic groups involved in the local school process.

Several community control plans implemented in the 1960s are discussed. Most of the efforts in the urban school reform movement
have attempted to increase citizen participation while trying to
decentralize the large school bureaucracies. The author concludes
that decentralization can only be achieved if it follows an incremental pattern of increasing participation and opening the process
of decision making in the school system.

Gittell, Marilyn, et al. LOCAL CONTROL IN EDUCATION: THREE DEMON-
STRATIONS IN SCHOOL DISTRICTS IN NEW YORK CITY. New York: Praeger,
1972. 152 p.

This is an evaluation of three school districts in New York City,
one black, one Puerto Rican, and one integrated poor neighborhood.
The evaluation focuses on two areas. First, the new community
school boards, the membership, and their affect on parents and
students. Second, the impact on policy as a result of this community participation. The composition of the school boards produced a more change-oriented policy-making body. Time was
spent on policy and educational problems and the boards became
very active on these issues. Parents gained enough knowledge to
be confident in their participation on policy issues. Many personnel changes were made by the boards but the record of new appointments was not very successful. Innovative programs were
started and student attitudes in these three districts showed marked
improvement over comparable districts. Academic achievement also
showed a marked increase.

_____. SCHOOL BOARDS AND SCHOOL POLICY. New York: Praeger,
1973. 169 p.

An examination of school decentralization, school boards, and
school policy in New York City. The major areas discussed are
school policy which includes budget, personnel and curriculum,
and community participation; and the community school boards.
The authors believe the major problems emanating from the decentralization program are the ambiguity of the legislation, the
retention of political power by the United Federation of Teachers,
and the unequal ethnic composition of the community school boards.
Decentralization was intended to redistribute political power and
make the school system more effective. The authors find little
evidence to support either assumption. The community school
boards have limited powers but rarely exercise even these powers.
The teachers union has been able to exert a great deal of influence
over the local school boards and thus has maintained or expanded
its power base.

Glasgow, Douglas. "Patterns in Welfare: Bureaucracy to Neighborhood Services."
JOURNAL OF BLACK STUDIES 2 (December 1971): 171-87.

This article criticizes the public welfare system because of its in-adequate, inappropriate, and mislocated services which systemati-cally destroy the ability of black clients to become self-reliant and reduces the ability of people to work for change. The author recommends decentralizing welfare services from central bureaucra-cies to neighborhood locations. An example is given using a pilot project in Los Angeles County which has instituted neighborhood family day care centers.

Johnston, Ray E., and Moore, Charles H. "School Decentralization, Community Control and the Politics of Public Education." URBAN AFFAIRS QUARTERLY 6 (June 1971): 421-46.

Proposals for school decentralization and local control have two major goals. First, increased levels of participation in school decisions by citizens of local neighborhoods and, second, changing the nature of the educational product. Using the Detroit school system as a case study, the authors see achieving these vital goals only through structural reform and political activity.

LaNoue, George, and Smith, Bruce [L.R.]. "The Political Evaluation of School Decentralization." AMERICAN BEHAVIORAL SCIENTIST 15 (September-October 1971): 73-93.

The vast number of school systems in the United States makes our educational system one of the most decentralized in the world. Citing examples in New York City, Detroit, Los Angeles, and Washington, D.C., the authors highlight the major differences of the politics of school decentralization. However, there are also many similarities in curriculum, integration, professionalism, and community control of policy which might lead to more experimen-tation in the future.

_____. THE POLITICS OF SCHOOL DECENTRALIZATION. Lexington, Mass.: D.C. Health, 1973. 284 p.

Utilizing a case study approach, the authors focus on the policy problems of school decentralization efforts in St. Louis, Detroit, Washington, D.C., New York City, and Los Angeles. The com-mon political themes in these cities are the initiation of the de-centralization movement in the quest for community control and the need for the state legislature eventually to resolve many of the conflicts. The decentralization movement is thought to be diminish-ing as interest in community control wanes. In their analysis, the authors discuss the responsiveness of governmental institutions, the sensitivity of bureaucracies to minority demands and what types of policy decisions lead to what types of policy outcomes. The de-velopment of the school decentralization movement is also traced.

Lawson, Simpson. "The Pitiful History of the Pilot Neighborhood Center Program." CITY 6 (March-April 1972): 53-57.

This article is part of a series which examines some of the federal urban programs initiated as part of the Great Society program of the Johnson administration. It focuses on the conceptual development, the federal planning, and the implementation of the neighborhood center program. The program was launched as a demonstration project in fourteen cities to subsidize neighborhood centers offering integrated services to multiproblem families. Conflicting priorities on the federal level and disputes on the neighborhood level concerning the role of the centers in the community hampered implementation. Several evaluations of the program by private and public officials are summarized.

Newsome, Moses. "Neighborhood Service Centers in the Black Community." SOCIAL WORK 18 (March 1973): 50-54.

The operations of neighborhood service centers in the black community are discussed and analyzed. The author reviews the centers' goals, funding sources, organizational structure, and strategies and highlights how these factors relate to each other and to the black community. Priorities of neighborhood service centers have to be reordered if the centers are to become meaningful components of the community. This is a necessity because blacks feel their fundamental problems are systemic and structural and these problems are generated by oppressive features of the political, economic, and social institutions.

Nordlinger, Eric A. DECENTRALIZING THE CITY: A STUDY OF BOSTON'S LITTLE CITY HALLS. Cambridge, Mass.: M.I.T. Press, 1972. 310 p.

It is assumed that the quality of public life will be improved only when power is redistributed downward through governmental structures. Most decentralization efforts have three goals: increased governmental responsiveness, reduction of citizen alienation, and the improvement of city services. Four major decentralization models are available to local governments: bureaucratic, representation, governmental, and little city halls. Assessment of the four models and the three goals finds the bureaucratic model least effective, the representative model next, and the little city halls and governmental models rated best. This study analyzes the little city hall model as implemented in Boston.

Nordlinger, Eric A., and Hardy, Jim. "Urban Decentralization: An Evaluation of Four Models." PUBLIC POLICY 20 (Summer 1972): 359-96.

Decentralization of local government is discussed as a current and viable approach to solving some of the urban problems plaguing cities today. Four models are described: bureaucratic, advisory, governmental, and the little city hall models. Their strengths and

weaknesses are assessed according to the stated objectives of increased governmental responsiveness, decreased citizen alienation,
and improved city services. The authors conclude the little city
hall model is most effective in meeting the objectives.

O'Donnell, Edward J. "The Neighborhood Service Center." WELFARE IN RE-
VIEW 6 (January-February 1968): 11-21.

Neighborhood service centers which are also meeting places, rally-
ing points, and springboards for new ideas, are seen as integral
components in the decentralization process. While citizens begin
to have more of a voice in how their neighborhoods are governed,
there is still the problem of integrating and coordinating the services to be delivered by professionals. The author feels that clients
must become a part of the process of service delivery or else the
system will not work. Some early experiments in neighborhood
service centers are discussed as is the role of private efforts. The
key to making the system work is to insure that providers and consumers work together in the planning and implementation stage of
service delivery.

Rebell, Michael A. "New York's School Decentralization Law." JOURNAL
OF LAW AND EDUCATION 2 (January 1973): 1-39.

The major legal and administrative developments of the first thirty
months of the implementation of New York's school decentralization law are analyzed in four key areas: curriculum, budget, personnel, and collective bargaining. In each of these areas, a similar pattern emerges. Negotiation, confrontation, and litigation
are used by community board activists and community organizations
working together to obtain specific powers from the central board
of education. The city board of education, despite its public commitment to decentralization, emerged as the major obstacle to
achieving decentralization.

Schiff, Martin. "Community Control of Inner-City Schools and Educational
Achievement." URBAN EDUCATION 10 (January 1976): 415-28.

Community control was an experiment tried in several school districts after the failure of integration efforts. Following the Ocean
Hill-Brownsville teachers strike, New York City passed a school
decentralization program in 1969. Thirty-two school districts were
given responsibility for elementary and junior high school education.
Some of these autonomous districts were taken over by militant factions and in some cases corruption and incompetence were obvious.
The author feels decentralization was a temporary political solution,
taken instead of addressing the real social problems of the ghettos.

Schmandt, Henry J. "Decentralization: A Structural Imperative." In NEIGH-
BORHOOD CONTROL IN THE 1970S: POLITICS, ADMINISTRATION AND

CITIZEN PARTICIPATION, edited by George Frederickson, pp. 17-35. New York: Chandler, 1973.

Decentralization is examined as a problem of organization and administration with special reference to the service delivery system. The author focuses on the various models of decentralization, the impact of each on the behavior of bureaucrats and constituents, and the relationship of each model to the stated goals of neighborhood control. The different models analyzed are: exchange model, bureaucratic model, modified bureaucratic model, developmental model, and the governmental model. The results of decentralization can be categorized as therapy, service, or political. The first relates to the psychological effects of neighborhood control on individuals; the second concerns the responsiveness of the service delivery system; and the third involves the mobilization of political power.

Shalala, Donna E., and Merget, Astrid E. "Decentralization Plans." In ORGANIZING PUBLIC SERVICES IN METROPOLITAN AMERICA, edited by Thomas P. Murphy and Charles R. Warren, pp. 153-77. Lexington, Mass.: Lexington Books, 1974.

Several plans describing varying degrees of decentralization are reviewed. Two major criteria are used as analytical measures for the extent of decentralization. These are: scale or size of the decentralized units, and authority-functional, policy-making and fiscal authority delegated to each unit. The decentralization plans discussed include: New York City's decentralization through coordination, Dayton's decentralization through planned variation, the New York City school system's single function decentralization, two-tier models suggested by the Advisory Commission on Intergovernmental Relations and the Committee for Economic Development, the minigovernments of Indianapolis, and the total reorganization plan of London.

Warren, Roland; Rose, Stephen M.; and Bergunder, Ann F. THE STRUCTURE OF URBAN REFORM: COMMUNITY DECISION ORGANIZATIONS IN STABILITY AND CHANGE. Lexington, Mass.: Lexington Books, 1974. 235 p.

This is a study of the structure of urban reform and the implications for strategies of social change. It discusses the structures and processes with which urban reform movements must cope if they are to succeed. The study focuses on the role played by community decision organizations in Oakland, Denver, San Antonio, Detroit, Columbus, Atlanta, Newark, and Boston. The authors examine the social problems of the city and the patterns of organizational response. They develop a basis for assessing the Model Cities program and its underlying theory of collaborative liberal reform.

Washnis, George J. LITTLE CITY HALLS. Center for Governmental Studies, Pamphlet no. 6. Washington, D.C.: January 1971. 33 p. Paperbound.

This report is the result of a survey conducted by the Center for
Governmental Studies and the International City Management Association to determine the extent of decentralization in American
cities. Following the survey, field surveys were made in twelve
cities selected as a representative sample by size, region, form of
government, and types of decentralization. The twelve cities
selected were: Atlanta; Baltimore; Boston; Chicago; Columbus,
Ohio; Houston; Kansas City, Missouri; Los Angeles; New York;
Norfolk; San Antonio; and San Francisco. The field study was
directed at three principal aspects of decentralization: a description of the program in each city, politics and citizen participation,
and agency performance and coordination. The author's conclusions
and recommendations suggest that urban problems and attempted
solutions can be seen in many cities of different size and location.
Ten generalizations about decentralization activities are offered.

Yates, Douglas. NEIGHBORHOOD DEMOCRACY: THE POLITICS AND IM-
PACTS OF DECENTRALIZATION. Lexington, Mass.: Lexington Books, 1973.
202 p.

Examines the politics and the impact of decentralization programs
in urban government. Evaluates these experiments and discusses
why certain efforts fail and others succeed. Four major questions
are analyzed. Does decentralization make government more responsive and have an impact on neighborhood problems? Does it
strengthen representation and internal democracy? Does it produce
strong political leadership in the neighborhood? And does it reduce feelings of powerlessness and alienation from government?
Decentralization is traced historically and the current demands are
analyzed. The concept of decentralization is examined and several
different forms are identified. Seven decentralization experiments
in New Haven and New York City are analyzed. The case studies
are used for a comparative analysis of initiatives, impacts, representation, and internal democracy. Four different styles of neighborhood leadership are identified with an examination of these
styles and the impact of political structure on the leadership styles.
Citizen and government support for decentralization programs is
examined.

_____. "Political Innovation and Institution Building: The Experience of De-
centralization Experiments." In THEORETICAL PERSPECTIVES ON URBAN POLI-
TICS, edited by Willis D. Hawley et al., pp. 146-75. Englewood Cliffs, N.J.:
Prentice-Hall, 1975.

Decentralization of local government has been hailed as a promising
method of urban reform. Still there is little agreement in the literature or in public discussion of what decentralization involves, what
impact it will have, and what techniques are most likely to bring
it about. The focus of this article is on what determines the success or failure of innovations in participatory government and how

ideas of decentralization and participation are implemented and endure as neighborhood institutions. Different degrees of decentralization are found in all political systems, ranging from intelligence operations to political resource allocation. Nine different types of decentralization existing in American cities are discussed. The author examines the power relations in neighborhood experiments and analyzes decentralization innovations from 'the viewpoints of social conditions, structural determinants, task orientation, and costs. Political skills and resources are also reviewed.

Yin, Robert K.; Hearn, Robert W.; and Shapiro, Paula M. "Administrative Decentralization of Municipal Services: Assessing the New York City Experience." POLICY SCIENCES 5 (March 1974): 57-70.

New York City's Office of Neighborhood Government was created in 1971 to coordinate efforts to decentralize municipal operations. The decentralization was primarily administrative in nature with emphasis on expanding neighborhood management. The study examines decision making at the district level. The focus was on the nature of decision-making responsibilities in five municipal agencies and the degree to which district officers acted as autonomous managers before and after administrative decentralization was implemented. The results indicate that major shifts in responsibilities occurred in only one management function--interagency communication.

Yin, Robert K., and Yates, Douglas. STREET-LEVEL GOVERNMENTS: ASSESSING DECENTRALIZATION AND URBAN SERVICES. Lexington, Mass.: Lexington Books, 1975. 276 p.

Five decentralized projects are discussed. The five service areas are: public safety, health, multiservice programs, education, and economic development. Each of the areas is constituted differently, with its own agency-client relationships and its own ground rules and strategies. Decentralization implies more services being distributed at the street level and, during the 1960s, it caused much conflict in urban administration. The goals were to improve services or to increase control in the service area. Opponents saw it as a force that would undercut local governmental authority. This study reports on 250 decentralization programs over the last ten years.

C. CITIZEN PARTICIPATION

Aleshire, Robert A. "Power to the People: An Assessment of the Community Action and Model Cities Experience." PUBLIC ADMINISTRATION REVIEW 32 (September 1972): 428-43.

The participatory rights of citizens in a democracy are examined in the historical context of the 1960s, the War on Poverty legislation, and the resulting programs such as Community Action Programs and Model Cities. Each of these programs was supposed to increase citizen expectation while delivering very little of what was promised. Frustration evolved from the promise-delivery gap and citizens became extremely negative about self-help programs. Institutions which fail to involve citizens in the planning and policy-making process in the future are not likely to survive.

Archer, Dane, and Marx, Gary T. "Citizen Involvement in the Law Enforcement Process." AMERICAN BEHAVIORAL SCIENTIST 15 (September-October 1971): 52-72.

The rising demand for increased citizen participation in the law enforcement process is viewed as a desire for more involvement in planning, control, and delivery of services which affect the lives of citizens. Data on organizational arrangements and different citizen group activities is presented with a recommendation that citizen groups be encouraged to participate and to assist the police in their community law enforcement process.

Arnstein, Sherry R. "A Ladder of Citizen Participation." JOURNAL OF THE AMERICAN INSTITUTE OF PLANNERS 35 (July 1969): 216-24.

The author begins by discussing what citizen participation is--namely the redistribution of power to people excluded from the political and economic processes. She presents a typology of participation, arranged in the format of eight steps on a ladder. The eight steps are: manipulation, therapy, informing, consultation, placation, partnership, delegated power, and citizen control. Steps 1-2 are labeled nonparticipation. Steps 3-5 are called tokenism. Steps 6-8 constitute degrees of citizen power. Each step is described and examples are provided. Many of the arguments against community control are cited, but the author concludes that all other efforts of this type apparently have failed.

Babcock, Richard F., and Bosselman, Fred B. "Citizen Participation: A Suburban Suggestion for the Central City." LAW AND CONTEMPORARY PROBLEMS 32 (Spring 1967): 220-31.

The authors suggest that central cities might profit from utilizing a suburban idea in the solution of some urban problems. The concept discussed is decentralization and it involves creating neighborhood boards of compliance and appeal, made up of neighborhood residents with the power to set standards, enforce them, and grant variances where necessary. Each board would have its own staff of engineers, planners, and attorneys who would provide information and assistance. The neighborhood board should be a better judge of disputes involving landlords, property owners, and tenants. Decentralized boards of this type should help improve housing conditions, zoning, and land use in neighborhoods.

Benz, Loretta N. "Citizen Participation Reconsidered." SOCIAL WORK 20 (March 1975): 115-19.

> This article examines the concept of citizen participation as a strategy in community organization. The author asserts that feelings of alienation are very common in the community which, in turn, leads to fragmentation and impedes both planning and organizing activities. Using Des Moines, Iowa as a case study, she highlights one of the basic flaws of the citizen participation movement: community programs must be operated under the bureaucratic guidelines of the agency administering the program. In most cases, these governmental agencies stifle rather than assist citizen participation activities.

Boone, Richard W. "Reflections on Citizen Participation and the Economic Opportunity Act." PUBLIC ADMINISTRATION REVIEW 32 (September 1972): 441-56.

> Begins with a brief history of the Economic Opportunity Act of 1964. The impact and the controversy surrounding the mandate for citizen participation extend far beyond the programs associated with the act. Government did not wholeheartedly support the War on Poverty and, therefore, the poor never were given a meaningful opportunity to make decisions. The token efforts made actually co-opted the leaders of the poor and did nothing to meld power and participation which is essential if the poor are to be involved in decision making.

Brody, Stanley J. "Maximum Participation of the Poor: Another Holy Grail?" SOCIAL WORK 15 (January 1970): 68-75.

> Americans have become involved in a number of efforts to improve the delivery of services. These include: public housing programs, citizen mobilization activities, and manpower and training programs. The latest thrust seems to be increasing the participation of area residents in programs affecting their communities. The major problem concerns transforming the administrative structure of service delivery to increase the support and involvement of clients without decreasing the skills administrators bring to their jobs. The author classifies the poor into upper-class poor, middle-class poor and poor poor and discusses the problems in each category. The real problem of participation is with the poor poor and how to involve them in programs.

Brooks, Wendy Goepel. "Health Care and Poor People." In CITIZEN PARTICIPATION: EFFECTING COMMUNITY CHANGE, edited by Edgar S. Cahn and Barry A. Passett, pp. 110-28. New York: Praeger, 1971.

> Not only poor people, but most American citizens have been excluded from participating in and influencing the field of health care. The poor tend to suffer more and get sick more because

they are poor. The source of the problem is defined as the role of medical education, where health policy is set, what the poor see in medical care, and why people don't organize themselves on the issue of health care. Poor people participate in health care issues in two areas. First, where they are employed by health care agencies and, second, where they are asked as consumers to help design and direct federally funded community health centers. The author discusses the role of the poor in each situation. As employees they are working as technician aides and community health aides. The Office of Economic Opportunity has begun including the poor in location decisions, training programs, scope of health services offered, community-staff relations, and commitment to see the program work.

Burke, Edmund M. "Citizen Participation Strategies." JOURNAL OF THE AMERICAN INSTITUTE OF PLANNERS 34 (September 1968): 287-94.

The major conflict in citizen participation is between the concept of democracy and the need for expertise. The choice of strategies for citizen involvement is also a difficult problem. There is no one strategy of citizen participation but rather several strategies defined in terms of objectives. The specific strategy is dependent upon the capability of the organization and the environment in which it functions. Several strategies discussed are: education-therapy, behavioral-change, staff-supplement, and community-power strategy. The author concludes that conflict strategies are not very effective in dealing with government agencies that stress coordination and cooperation. This is particularly true in planning agencies.

Cahn, Edgar S., and Cahn, Jean Camper. "Citizen Participation." In CITIZEN PARTICIPATION IN URBAN DEVELOPMENT: CONCEPTS AND ISSUES, edited by Hans B.C. Spiegel, pp. 211-24. Washington, D.C.: NTL Institute for Applied Behavioral Science, 1968.

The concept of citizen participation raises questions of skepticism and distrust because it is always possible to find important decision-making steps occurring before citizens were involved. What needs to be addressed is whether choices were foreclosed and what were the consequences of the choices made. Another critical issue involving citizens and organizations is the amount of resources to be devoted to the democratic process. The authors discuss some of the myths surrounding the relationship between professional bureaucrats and clients who are consumers of services. The values of citizen participation are presented--promotion of dignity, utilization of untapped manpower, and the increase in knowledge. Citizen participation is deeply involved with rights and values which are characteristic of the democratic process.

_____. "Maximum Feasible Participation: A General Overview." In CITIZEN PARTICIPATION: EFFECTING COMMUNITY CHANGE, edited by Edgar S. Cahn and Barry A. Passett, pp. 9-62. New York: Praeger, 1971.

Citizen participation involves many dangers and many risks, but it has demonstrated that it can make major contributions to the quality of life. The authors assert that the values of citizen participation outweigh the liabilities, risks, and dangers. The risks of citizen participation are discussed with examples from different cities around the country. The values of citizen participation are viewed as mobilization of resources, a source of knowledge, and as an end itself. The values are illustrated with examples from around the country also. Several dimensions of the concept of citizen participation are: the right of effective speech, the right to be wrong, the right to be different, the right to influence decision making, the right to contribute, the right to consume with dignity, and the right to a continuing share in society's burdens and benefits. Each of these is discussed with explanatory examples.

Cary, Lee J. "Resident Participation." COMMUNITY DEVELOPMENT JOURNAL 5 (April 1970): 73-78.

The major premise is that direct participation of people in planning, developing, and implementing goals is a basic element in community development. Many of the programs of the War on Poverty established broad national goals which made resources available to numerous communities. These programs and resources increased citizen participation and decision making at the local level.

Cole, Richard L. CITIZEN PARTICIPATION AND THE URBAN POLICY PROCESS. Lexington, Mass.: Lexington Books, 1974. 178 p.

This book reports the findings from two surveys. The first part of the book is based upon a 1970 survey conducted by the Advisory Commission on Intergovernmental Relations in cities over 50,000 population. The author examines eight factors and tests them in nine hypotheses to determine which factors are associated with citizen participation. He finds three factors--city size, level of suburbanization, and percentage of black population--strongly associated with citizen participation. The author also surveyed about 400 citizen activists in 26 cities from the original study to determine participants' motives and levels of trust or satisfaction in government performance. Concern with their neighborhood was the prime motivating factor. Political trust in government rises with participation and then drops off. The author concludes that we should not attempt any more large-scale decentralization efforts.

Cunningham, James V. "Citizen Participation in Public Affairs." PUBLIC ADMINISTRATION REVIEW 32 (October 1972): 589-602.

The author discusses the history of citizen involvement in public affairs both in the United States and abroad. The American experience covers the period from the Jackson era to the 1964 War on Poverty Act. Citizen participation is defined and examined in light of an increased information flow which enables citizens to respond to both internal and external influences. The author concludes that citizen participation will increase in urban areas and become a powerful force in society.

Godbey, Geoffrey. "Recreation Advisory Councils and the Poor." PARKS AND RECREATION 7 (November 1972): 28-34.

This study examines citizen participation in recreation advisory councils in Philadelphia and the effects of the socioeconomic status of geographic areas within the city on that participation. The findings are related to three variables: representativeness, effectiveness, and participation. The findings indicate that citizens participate on recreation advisory councils both within and outside of poverty areas. There are definite differences in the types of participation and the author concludes that poverty area councils are unlikely to function successfully with middle-class councils.

Greenstone, J. David, and Peterson, Paul E. RACE AND AUTHORITY IN URBAN POLITICS: COMMUNITY PARTICIPATION AND THE WAR ON POVERTY. New York: Basic Books, 1973. 326 p.

Using a single public policy issue--citizen participation in the Community Action Program of the War on Poverty--the authors examine the workings of authority and race structures in urban life. They focus on the politics of the project in five major American cities and discuss the factors which affected the development of each city's action program. The book focuses on the effect of machine and reform structures on minority group organizations and the failure of these groups to appreciate the significance of racial cleavage in urban politics. The impact of bureaucratic influence on community participation and an analysis of politics, race, and community is presented. The five cities studied are: New York, Chicago, Los Angeles, Detroit, and Philadelphia.

Hallman, Howard W. "Federally Financed Citizen Participation." PUBLIC ADMINISTRATION REVIEW 32 (September 1972): 421-27.

In the past twenty years the federal government has begun requiring citizen participation in many federally funded programs. Citing programs such as urban renewal, juvenile delinquency, community action programs, and model cities, the author reviews the citizen participation process in each program. Funding in the area of citizen participation is increasing rapidly in many different programs. This renewed emphasis on citizen participation could help institutionalize an orderly process for greater citizen involvement.

Herman, M. Justin. "Citizen Partnership with Renewal Bureaucrats is the Order of the Day." JOURNAL OF HOUSING 25 (January 1968): 25-28.

Examines citizen participation in light of what works and what doesn't work. The factors which contribute to successful citizen participation are: the need for recognized leadership, involvement in the beginning of planning, consistency in goals, acceptance by the city for equal and honest participation in planning and executing the development program, and administrative support while the services are being delivered to the neighborhood. Citizen participation usually doesn't work when the following factors exist: community apathy and indifference, high turnover in community leadership, and demands for recognition by minor groups in the implementation phase. A case study of a successful project is presented.

Howard, Lawrence C. "Decentralization and Citizen Participation in Health Services." PUBLIC ADMINISTRATION REVIEW 32 (October 1972): 701-17.

Citizen involvement in health services is increasing because consumers want to be included in determining health policy, participating in management, and articulating their views on the changing nature of health in general. The author discusses the differences between health care and medicine and suggests that politics is the strategy to be used in changing the health care system. Political issues examined are: regionalization, decentralization, participation, consumerism, neighborhood health centers, evaluation, and public policy. The author concludes that knowing what we want to achieve is only half the problem. Development of the managers and new management tools is the other half. Training pre-service and in-service health managers is the role of the Schools of Public Affairs.

Johnson, Carl F. A STUDY OF CITY-WIDE CITIZEN PARTICIPATION IN TEN CITIES. Washington, D.C.: National Citizen Participation Council, 1975. 182 p. Paperbound.

This study is in two parts. Part one is a review and assessment of the literature on citizen participation, which covers the historical development of the concept, the community action programs of the 1960s, the urban renewal and Model Cities programs, and the most recent activities in cities. Part two presents the results of a ten-city study of citizen participation efforts in Albuquerque; Dayton; Des Moines; Helena; Norfolk; Portland, Oregon; Tucson; Plainfield, New Jersey; Worcester, Massachusetts; and Metropolitan Dade County, Florida. Comparative data is presented on citizen education, budgets and funding, staffing, selection of board members, and technical assistance.

Kloman, Erasmus [H.]. "Citizen Participation in the Philadelphia Model Cities Program: Retrospect and Prospect." PUBLIC ADMINISTRATION REVIEW 32 (September 1972): 402-8.

This essay is a case study of the Philadelphia Model Cities Program which presents a retrospective evaluation of the issues and an appraisal of the future prospects for citizen participation in the program. It discusses the misunderstanding and ambiguity surrounding the concept of citizen participation and how this generated many problems for the program. Only if some of the mistakes of the past can be converted into positive action in the future will citizen-oriented programs have a chance to reach their stated objectives.

_____. "Public Participation in Technology Assessment." PUBLIC ADMINIS-TRATION REVIEW 34 (January–February 1974): 52–61.

Public administrators face conflicting pressures in implementing the programs passed by legislative bodies. On the one hand, technological advances have created complex interactions between physical and social factors in society. On the other hand, there is an increasing demand to make the decision-making process more democratic by including greater citizen involvement. The problem facing public managers is how to optimize the impact of technology and the potential of public involvement. Citizens have become active through litigation, organized groups, and assessing the impact of technological development. Case studies of their activities are presented in the Regional Plan Association of New York, the Metropolitan Fund in Detroit, the New York State Department of Transportation, and the Boston Transportation Planning Review Program.

Lazar, Irving. "Which Citizens To Participate in What?" In CITIZEN PAR-TICIPATION: EFFECTING COMMUNITY CHANGE, edited by Edgar S. Cahn and Barry A. Passett, pp. 92–109. New York: Praeger, 1971.

Begins with an examination of the ways in which citizens participate and how individual citizens learn the array of organizational skills that are essential to a community organization. The concept of a community organization is analyzed in terms of what is a group, the purposes of groups, and the membership of groups. Groups do not originate in a vacuum, they are formed because of the community setting or their environment. Membership in groups is discussed by examining the types of people who join according to concentrations of active members. Various types of participation are listed and several strategies of participation are discussed. The author briefly reviews the Office of Economic Opportunity's strategies for participation and concludes that, while the experiment was generally unsuccessful, both the experience of organizing community groups and the changing moral in the ghetto were positive results.

Lowenstein, Edward R. "Citizen Participation and the Administrative Agency in Urban Development." SOCIAL SERVICE REVIEW 45 (September 1971): 289–301.

Planners and administrators should be more interested in involvement of neighborhood people in the planning and implementation of urban development programs. The advantages and disadvantages of citizen participation are presented. A major problem is how to reconcile efficient program implementation with the diverse demands of citizen groups. One response has been for agencies to manipulate the behavior of local citizen groups to minimize their inputs in the decision-making process. Several proposals for minimizing conflict between agencies and citizen groups are offered and the author concludes that failure to involve citizens will deprive many agencies of a valuable resource and possibly impede program development and implementation.

Marshall, Dale Rogers. "Public Participation and the Politics of Poverty." In RACE, CHANGE AND URBAN SOCIETY, edited by Peter Orleans and William Russell Ellis, Jr., pp. 451-82. Beverly Hills, Calif.: Sage Publications, 1971.

Places the ideology of public participation in historical perspective and discusses the origins of participation in the War on Poverty. Analyzing participation in poverty programs is achieved by reviewing several studies which examine variables such as political factors, city size, minority population, form of government, political parties, and the mobilization capability of minority groups. Participation takes the following forms: employment in poverty programs, membership and advisory committees or area councils, shared power arrangements, and social action. Three types of conflict have resulted from participation efforts. They are: advisory, coalitional, and adversary. Assessing the impact of increased participation on programs, agencies, and participants is difficult. Problems of poverty have not been lessened and the impact upon the programs has been minimal. Little impact has been made on local government agencies but there have been positive results for the participants, psychologically, educationally, and politically.

_____. "Who Participates in What? A Bibliographical Essay on Individual Participation in Urban Areas." URBAN AFFAIRS QUARTERLY 4 (December 1968): 201-16.

This is a bibliographical essay on individual participation in urban areas divided into three sections: mass society, social participation patterns, and political participation patterns. The trends in these three areas are assessed and the author poses possible implications of increasing urbanization for the patterns of individual participation in urban America and the political system in general. Many citizens participate to a high degree in a variety of ways. Instead of looking at who participates, researchers should focus on how people participate, and the differences between small and large groups.

Miller, S.M., and Rein, Martin. "Participation, Poverty and Administration." PUBLIC ADMINISTRATION REVIEW 29 (January-February 1969): 15-25.

The authors discuss the evolution of the term "maximum feasible participation" and outline the arguments of the major groups which supported the concept. The problems raised for administrators from the concept are particularly evident in personnel practices, professional discretions, policy development, and new mechanisms of accountability. Each of these problems has caused local administrators to make adjustments in the operation of their departments and to alter their thinking about bureaucrat-client relations. Demands for increased participation will continue to stir up unrest and highlight the need for change. Large organizations will have their traditional practices challenged as the conflict between greater participation and efficiency intensifies.

Mogulof, Melvin B. CITIZEN PARTICIPATION: THE LOCAL PERSPECTIVE. Washington, D.C.: Urban Institute, 1970. 182 p.

Examines citizen participation from the local level by observing six city or county agencies in the far West. These were: a neighborhood health services center; a Model City agency; an OEO-supported legal services center; a public housing tenants' council; an urban renewal project area committee; and a community mental health center. The report begins with a discussion of local structures for participation and influencing decision making. Included also is a discussion of representation and different aspects of participation. An analysis is presented of the impact of these agencies on the minority community, how these agencies interact with other agencies, and the federal-local relationships that exist. The author concludes that citizen participation is operational, it can be observed, and it appears to be working and to be having a favorable impact upon community tension and conflict.

Montgomery, John D., and Esman, Milton J. "Popular Participation in Development Administration." JOURNAL OF COMPARATIVE ADMINISTRATION 3 (November 1971): 358-83.

This article focuses on popular participation of the poor in governmentally sponsored development and social action programs. Participation is defined as exerting influence on administrative behavior and on outputs of official action. Types of participation and the evaluation of participation programs are analyzed. Professional public administrators are urged to increase their own effectiveness by making greater use of citizens and the resources they bring to the decision-making process. Six dimensions of participation are identified: scope, size, frequency, salience, directness, and initiative. Several myths concerning participation are outlined and administrators are urged to review both program variables and environmental factors when considering the possibilities for public participation.

Myren, Richard. "Decentralization and Citizen Participation in Criminal Justice."

PUBLIC ADMINISTRATION REVIEW 32 (October 1972): 718-38.

The article is divided into three subsections: decentralization and
citizen participation in police agencies, in prosecution and adjudi-
cation, and in corrections. Programs in each subsection are examined to assess the involvement of citizens. The lack of pre-
service education is cited as a major drawback to effective policing
and citizen participation in the criminal justice system. The author
concludes his article by suggesting five areas that must be developed
by colleges and universities if they are to train students for careers
in the criminal justice system. These areas are: the nature of
crime and its relationship to other kinds of deviance as well as to
conformity; the nature of society's reaction to crime, both historically and in the present, which requires exploration of all formal
and informal and legal and governmental theories of crime; in-depth
consideration of criminal justice systems as one social control mechanism; the nature of personal, organizational, and institutional change
as well as the mechanisms for achieving such change; and the design of research necessary to expand our current knowledge of criminal justice systems.

Onibokun, Adepoju G., and Curry, Martha. "An Ideology of Citizen Participation: The Metropolitan Seattle Transit Case Study." PUBLIC ADMINISTRA-
TION REVIEW 36 (May-June 1976): 269-77.

This is a case study of planning and participation involving the
Metropolitan Seattle Transit System. The article examines some
of the underlying assumptions of citizen participation to determine
the extent to which citizens and planners share similar opinions on
the observed and expected role of citizens in the planning process.
Once the transit study had been approved, a questionnaire was administered to 52 citizens from among the 1,300 who attended the
citizen participation discussion meeting. A similar questionnaire
was administered to 10 of the 12 professionals involved in the
study. Expectations of the two groups differed but both felt their
expectations had been met. Citizens were aware of the sections
of the plan where their influence was felt. Citizen satisfaction is
greatly influenced by knowledge of the issue, previous involvement
in community affairs, and willingness of professionals to accept
citizen ideas and suggestions.

Piven, Frances F. "Participation of Residents in Neighborhood Community Action Programs." SOCIAL WORK 11 (January 1966): 73-80.

Agencies seeking to involve citizens in the policy-making process
must be aware that community organizations often lack resources,
skills, and knowledge about developing organizations and training
and maintaining leadership. Many of the citizens are apathetic,
doubtful of their ability to affect their lives or simply overwhelmed
by daily crises which threaten their ability to survive. Several
steps are needed to insure an ongoing qualitative input by citizens.

These include: providing specific services; providing staff and facilities to community organizations; and seeking out existing ethnic, religious, or occupational groups as a base for organizing and encouraging the initiation of social protest action when warranted. Several suggestions are offered for ways to have citizens participate but all of these must be weighed against the essential questions of who should participate and how can this participation be developed and maintained.

Riedel, James A. "Citizen Participation: Myths and Realities." PUBLIC ADMINISTRATION REVIEW 32 (May-June 1972): 211-20.

The rising demand for citizen participation has developed from a real or imaginary belief of citizens that government has failed to respond adequately to their needs and demands. The author discusses some of the realities of citizen participation and concludes that most people participate in the government process in one way or another though many people participate in a passive manner. Several postulates about citizen participation are examined, dealing with interest, alienation, responsiveness, and resistance. Many government agencies have sought citizen involvement by creating advisory committees. These committees are almost always controlled by the agencies and can be classified as advisory, supportive, put-off, or put-on. The author concludes that the problem is a political one, not a structural one, and the reallocation of power will create many conflict situations between citizens and agencies. A public education program informing citizens of the opportunities and channels for involvement, as well as avenues for redress of grievances might be more productive.

Rosenbaum, Nelson M. CITIZEN INVOLVEMENT IN LAND USE GOVERNANCE: ISSUES AND METHODS. Washington, D.C.: Urban Institute, 1975. 100 p.

Asserting that citizen involvement is increasing in the movement for greater government control in land use decisions, the author provides a framework for evaluating citizen participation programs. The report examines the difficulties and opportunities available to public officials engaged in such programs. These are: public preparation, citizen participation, and government accountability. Several examples of techniques from here and abroad are presented as well as recommendations on how and when specific techniques can be used most effectively.

Seaver, Robert C. "The Dilemma of Citizen Participation." In CITIZEN PARTICIPATION IN URBAN DEVELOPMENT: CONCEPTS AND ISSUES, edited by Hans B.C. Spiegel, pp. 61-71. Washington, D.C.: NTL Institute for Applied Behavioral Science, 1968.

Citizen participation in local governmental public affairs has become a fact of political life. The issue confronting local officials is not whether to have citizen participation but whether to incorporate it as a formal stage in the policy-making process. Planning and urban renewal have used citizen participation but there never has been any real agreement on who should participate, how, and with what degree of influence. Many difficulties confront officials trying to implement citizen participation plans. These include: goal definition, adequate community representation, staff assistance, and meeting the expectations of the community. One way the author sees of overcoming these problems is for the planning and renewal agencies to work closer with community groups. This would reduce ambiguous goals and high expectations and provide the necessary staff and resources.

Steggert, Frank X. COMMUNITY ACTION GROUPS AND CITY GOVERN-MENTS. Cambridge, Mass.: Ballinger, 1975. 128 p.

Local governments have recently become aware of the growing impact of citizen groups on the policy-making process. This report of the Urban Observatory Program examines organized citizen participation in urban areas and discusses which kinds of citizen groups influence the decisions in city governments. Areas studied are: types of groups engaged in activities with local government, issues that ignited initial involvement, and estimates of group effectiveness. The author studies characteristics which influence the degree of citizen participation in the ten-city study and concluded that social class, race, age, and length of residence have a significant relationship to membership in community action groups.

Stenberg, Carl W. "Citizens and the Administrative State: From Participation to Power." PUBLIC ADMINISTRATION REVIEW 32 (May-June 1972): 190-98.

Reviews the emergence and development of the concept of citizen participation from post-World War II to the present. Analyzes several federal programs, including Community Action and Model Cities programs, which helped to increase citizen participation. Citizens are examined as adviser-persuaders, partner-adversaries and finally as advocates of increased decentralization. The discipline of public administration is challenged to help increase awareness within the bureaucracy to meet the changing and expanding role of citizens in local government.

Strange, John H. "Citizen Participation in Community Action and Model Cities Programs." PUBLIC ADMINISTRATION REVIEW 32 (October 1972): 655-69.

Using as a starting point the intense political conflicts of the 1960s, the author reviews the mandate for maximum feasible participation by examining the community action programs and agencies and the Model Cities program with respect to their attempts to increase citizen involvement in community affairs. The weaknesses inherent in the poverty and Model Cities programs are detailed. The article concludes with an analysis of citizen participation in terms of its objectives, necessary conditions, techniques, and future prospects.

_____. "Community Action in North Carolina: Maximum Feasible Misunderstanding, Mistake or Magic Formula?" PUBLIUS 2 (Fall 1972): 51-73.

This is a study of eleven community action agencies in North Carolina. All of the agencies are private, nonprofit organizations receiving funds from the Ford Foundation. Most of the agencies operated programs that provided services to the community. Most of their activities were in programs such as Headstart, Neighborhood Centers, and Neighborhood Youth Corps. All of the agencies studied have provided new services for the poor and have helped to allocate resources to fight poverty. Each agency has opened up new opportunities for the poor and disadvantaged to participate in community decision making affecting the delivery of services.

_____. "The Impact of Citizen Participation on Public Administration." PUBLIC ADMINISTRATION REVIEW 32 (September 1972): 457-70.

The article begins with a history of citizen participation up to the War on Poverty Act in 1964, which mandated maximum feasible participation of the poor in community action programs. Three major problems have arisen concerning participation in poverty programs. Who is to participate? How much will they participate? What constitutes participation? Citizen participation is analyzed in terms of the techniques used to increase participation, and the impact upon participants, the programs, and the community.

Straub, Daniel H. "Institutionalizing Citizen Participation." In DEVELOPING THE MUNICIPAL ORGANIZATION, edited by Stanley Powers, F. Gerald Brown, and David S. Arnold, pp. 288-97. Washington, D.C.: International City Management Association, 1974.

Citizen participation has become a familiar term if not a reality to most city administrators. It becomes increasingly necessary for administrators to face the issue of participation by citizens in decision making. The author advances some guidelines for managers for the equitable inclusion of citizens in the decision-making process. Four philosophical approaches to citizen participation are defined: cooptation theory, consultation theory, educational-social therapy theory, and the community power theory. The recent history of participation is examined as well as who participates. The author presents a decision diagram intended to help local government administrators. Specific suggestions and several organizational and administrative mechanisms are discussed.

Thursz, Daniel. "Community Participation: Should the Past Be Prologue?" AMERICAN BEHAVIORAL SCIENTIST 15 (May-June 1972): 733-48.

Several sources of support for the concept of community participation are discussed including mental health stress upon community participation as a means of reducing alienation and powerlessness. Other issues discussed are the poverty program view of community participation as a means of enfranchising the poor, and social service agency use of client organizations as a mechanism for increasing service effectiveness. Community organization is viewed in terms of the effect of increased numbers of community groups upon social policy. Also discussed is the evolution of the nature and role of community groups in community life.

Van Meter, Elena C. "Citizen Participation in the Policy Management Process." PUBLIC ADMINISTRATION REVIEW 35 (December 1975): 804-12.

Two major needs of management are information to develop policies and information to determine if policies are being implemented effectively. An organized citizen-management system can provide much of the information required by management. Citizens should make inputs which help managers make policy and should monitor policies and report on their effectiveness at the client level. There is a discussion of citizen participation as implemented in Cincinnati with the support of the city manager and an examination of citizen participation based upon the National Revenue-Sharing Monitoring Project in sixty local and six state governments. Citing evidence from both projects, the author reviews ad hoc and permanent citizen participation mechanisms, the institutional constraints on citizen participation, technical assistance needs, and the balance between small group needs and the public interest.

Van Til, Jon, and Van Til, Sally Bould. "Citizen Participation in Social Policy: The End of the Cycle?" SOCIAL PROBLEMS 17 (Winter 1970): 313-23.

This paper examines the concept of citizen participation in urban renewal, the War on Poverty, and the Model Cities program. Six different interpretations emerge from their study: elite coalition, politics of reform, citizen advice, pluralist participation, client participation, and grass roots participation. An examination of the three program areas leads the authors to conclude that current citizen participation efforts are reaching a stalemate with the elites. Successful participation efforts emerge in specific situations. Only recently have the poor been able to make a meaningful input into how resources are to be allocated in the community. Citizen participation has to take on new institutional forms that will adequately represent the poor and involve them in the political and social structure.

Washnis, George J. "Community Involvement . . . Why?" PUBLIC MANAGEMENT 57 (December 1975): 2-6.

The strengthening of the democratic system is the strongest argument for increasing citizen participation. Disadvantages are outweighed by opportunities for citizens to participate in decision making, convey ideas to governmental officials, and debate public issues periodically. Citizen involvement can help local officials gain consensus on issues and also helps to reduce differences of opinion between contending factions. This involvement process means fewer decisions will be challenged later in the process. True participation means at least three levels of involvement: citywide or area-wide committees, special project boards, and block organizations. This approach means participation can be a meaningful component for improving city services and increasing effective communications.

D. COMMUNITY ORGANIZATION

Alexander, Ernest R. "Goal Setting and Growth in an Uncertain World: A Case Study of a Local Community Organization." PUBLIC ADMINISTRATION REVIEW 36 (March-April 1976): 182-91.

This is a case study of a community organization in Racine, Wisconsin which engaged in a participative planning process to establish goals and a strategy for achieving them. The focus of the study is on the relationship between the goal-setting process and goal displacement during the implementation phase. The organization failed to assess the future availability of resources and, as the organization grew and developed, priorities were set based upon available resources rather than the originally agreed upon objectives. Goal setting is a complex process which requires a realistic approach to what is feasible, a community education program, and a long-term commitment to development of an interactive process with local public officials.

Alinsky, Saul D. RULES FOR RADICALS: A PRAGMATIC PRIMER FOR REALISTIC RADICALS. New York: Random House, 1971. 196 p.

This is a handbook for people seeking to become full-time community organizers in poor neighborhoods. The major theme of the book is the promotion of conflict as a means to building powerful community organization which can reallocate resources. Problems discussed include leadership, communication, programs, and tactics. The development of multiple-issue, community-based organizations is seen as a long-term, continuous project which can be terminated by expectations of either easy or quick victories. The development of community organizations is related to concepts of social change and the relationship of ends and means.

Austin, David M. "Resident Participation: Political Mobilization or Organizational Co-optation?" PUBLIC ADMINISTRATION REVIEW 32 (September 1972): 409-20.

This is an analysis of community representation in community action agencies in twenty cities with populations between 50,000 and 800,000. The focus of the study is on the target-area members on the policy board and the activities of the target-area associations and advisory groups recruited and sponsored by the community action agency. The findings are broken down into the similarities and differences among the agencies. Topics researched include participation levels, characteristics of board members, and constituency representation. The conclusions are presented in three separate areas: the relation of federal policy on resident participation found in the agencies, the impact of resident participation within the local community, and the relation of resident participation to the general issue of citizen participation in a democracy.

Bailey, Robert, Jr. RADICALS IN URBAN POLITICS: THE ALINSKY APPROACH. Chicago: University of Chicago Press, 1974. 208 p.

This book analyzes the methods and philosophy of the late Saul Alinsky. Focusing on a West Side Chicago community group, the author examines the founding structure, and the activities of the organization by comparing these with alternative forms of community-based groups. Much of the research is based upon personal experiences of the author in the community as well as hundreds of interviews with residents and organization activists. The author reviews several models of protest including rent strikes and protest marches. Readers receive penetrating insights into some of the major actors in protest politics such as organizers, slum lords, politicians, and bureaucrats.

Bell, Daniel, and Held, Virginia. "The Community Revolution." PUBLIC INTEREST 16 (Summer 1969): 142-77.

The Kennedy-Johnson administrations fostered a revolution in the political structure of urban life through passage of the War on Poverty Act in 1964. The neighborhood organization became a major bargaining unit in urban political life. The three major communal systems in urban life have now become the reform-minded civic groups, the service-oriented fraternal organizations, and the neighborhood organizations. Urban minorities have made gains in the past thirty years but they have not gained real entry into the urban political structure. Power and resources will only come to communities over time. They must develop mechanisms for political bargaining much as the trade unions did. This includes the traditional striving to gain relative advantages. But this political bargaining will have to be confined to the boundaries of acceptable societal action so chaos does not ensue.

Brager, George, and Specht, Harry. "About the Process of Community Work." In COMMUNITY ORGANIZING, pp. 67-87. New York: Columbia University Press, 1973.

No theory of community organization has as yet been developed to help in the task of ordering the elements that go into community work. Questions and hypotheses about the social process must be formulated with an eye towards understanding the behavior of the worker and how he/she may affect the process in a particular way. Stages in the process include socialization groups which teach values, expectations and behaviors; peer groups which develop a sense of belonging; and organizational-development groups which have social, political, and action goals. Primary goals should be to change organizations in the interests of the constituents of the community. Community workers must understand their own roles and be able to assess the needs of groups in different stages of the process.

Bridgeland, William M., and Sofranko, Andrew J. "Community Structure and Issue-Specific Influences: Community Mobilization Over Environmental Quality." URBAN AFFAIRS QUARTERLY 11 (December 1975): 186-214.

To study citizen mobilization in 124 Illinois communities, sets of community structure variables and issue-specific variables were measured. Little support is found for either in explaining community mobilization. The study raises questions of whether incidents produce mobilization or whether a mobilized citizenry generates incidents. In some communities, clearly identifiable projects mobilize the citizens. In others, routine activities trigger incidents.

Brieland, Donald. "Community Advisory Boards and Maximum Feasible Participation." AMERICAN JOURNAL OF PUBLIC HEALTH 61 (February 1971): 292-96.

Maximum-feasible-participation may interfere with more significant involvement of the poor by diverting the attention of the poor to funding for neighborhood programs instead of seeking major social reforms. Many community reform movements are blunted and divided because leadership is given official status on community advisory boards. Representation on the boards is achieved without community participation and often board members will begin to lose touch with the community. Boards give advice but have little or no control over the finances or administration of programs. Conclusions are boards must be structured and empowered to bring complaints and recommendations to top management. Rotation of board leadership is essential to continued development of community leadership and boards should have clear policy-making power on those issues which affect their local constituents.

Eisinger, Peter K. "The Urban Crisis as a Failure of Community: Some Data." URBAN AFFAIRS QUARTERLY 9 (June 1974): 437-61.

Examines the urban crisis as perceived by those closest to the problems, the residents of urban areas. An attitudinal survey is used to test the hypothesis that the major symptom of the urban crisis is the failure of community-sustaining norms and institutions, rather than problems of poor service delivery, congestion, and fiscal decay. Failure of community was defined as "improper behavior in public places" resulting in crime, racial tension, and delinquency. Residents of Milwaukee were asked about important problems facing the city, but contrary to a similar study conducted in Boston, respondents cited the conventional problems of housing, taxes, and unemployment as being of paramount concern. The concept of community did not emerge as strong as it had in Boston.

English, Gary. "The Trouble with Community Action." PUBLIC ADMINISTRATION REVIEW 32 (May-June 1972): 224-31.

The community-action program was launched as a major new approach to social innovation and community change. Problems have arisen among such factors as the community political environment, the legislative vehicles provided to implement programs, and the established goals. The author discusses some of the problems that have arisen with governing boards, staffing, conflict with governmental agencies, and administrative regulations. The conclusions drawn from this essay are: adequate funds are a necessity if these agencies are to survive, state agencies must become supportive of local community-action efforts, training programs are needed to insure a supply of qualified community leaders, and periodic meetings of community-action personnel must be arranged so they can exchange ideas and experiences.

Greenberg, Stanley B. POLITICS AND POVERTY: MODERNIZATION RESPONSE IN FIVE POOR NEIGHBORHOODS. New York: Wiley, 1974. 275 p.

This is a series of case studies of five poor urban neighborhoods in Detroit, Philadelphia, Atlanta, Belmont, Ohio, and San Jose, California. Included are two northern black communities, one southern black community, one white community, and one Mexican-American community. The author discusses the evolution of each community, focusing on the immigration, job seeking, urban development, and frustration. Each community reacts differently to similar conditions. The responses range from violence to disaffection with the political system. The author feels the key to understanding poverty is learning the traditional life patterns, political and ideological beliefs, and levels of awareness of the different groups in urban areas. This will indicate the forms of political expression most likely to occur.

Grosser, Charles F. "Community Organization and the Grass Roots." SOCIAL WORK 12 (October 1967): 61-67.

The United States is a welfare state which allocates services and resources to all segments of the population except the poor. Voluntary agencies, often funded in part by the city, also provide services to the poor. These agencies are often run by professionals and businessmen who are out of touch with the needs and the problems of the people they serve. With federal programs mandating participation of the poor there has been a much greater effort to involve the clients in planning and delivery strategy. Increasing the involvement of the powerless in the planning and organization of programs may extend the benefits of the welfare system and increase the dimensions of pluralism in our society.

_____. NEW DIRECTIONS IN COMMUNITY ORGANIZATION: FROM ENABLING TO ADVOCACY. New York: Praeger, 1973. 239 p.

Social welfare policy and administration has taken on a different character in the wake of the civil rights movement and the new militancy of the social work clients. Social work institutions have to begin defining clients as active consumers, otherwise the schism between clients and practitioners will grow. Individual rehabilitation must be coupled with strategies to improve the individual's relationship with the social work institutions interacting with him. Several organizational change elements of the 1950s, '60s and '70s are analyzed with respect to the degree of change and the response of communities and institutions to each.

Grove, Walter, and Costner, Herbert L. "Organizing the Poor: An Evaluation of a Strategy." SOCIAL SCIENCE QUARTERLY 50 (December 1969): 643-56.

The life-styles and perspectives of the poor are attributable to financial status and the poverty culture. Many intervention programs are based on the belief that self-help organizations are an essential ingredient to breaking the poverty culture. Participation, it is felt, helps to alleviate feelings of powerlessness and leads to other changes in perspective and behavior. The authors evaluated a poverty program in Seattle and concluded: (1) indigenous organizers without guidance become frustrated, (2) hard-core residents are not the ones usually recruited, (3) dissatisfied residents usually lack the knowledge necessary to deal with the causes of their dissatisfaction, (4) incremental process of community change often heightens frustration and alienation and (5) local neighborhood units are ineffective mechanisms for dealing with the problems of the poor. More attention should be paid to institutional contributions toward goal achievement and less to the socioemotional factors leading to psychological change.

Hunt, Martin H. "Parents-Teachers Alliance: An Alternative to Community Control." INTEGRATED EDUCATION 14 (March-April 1976): 35-37.

The continuing struggle over centralization and decentralization of the schools is not just a question of political control, it involves

integration and educational reform also. Deep frustrations in black
communities have fostered many of the proposals for community control. Teachers also find themselves powerless to effect change.
An alliance of parents, teachers, and students would allow for more
options whether decisions are made by the community, teachers, or
administrators. The community control movement failed to realize
that in antagonizing teachers it lost a powerful ally and created
another obstacle to reaching its goals.

Krickus, Richard J. "Organizing Neighborhoods: Gary and Newark." DISSENT
19 (Winter 1972): 107-17.

Two case studies are presented in which white working-class neighborhoods were organized to combat established power bases which
had been negligent in responding to community needs. These new
organizations were needed to replace intermediate organizations
which had always helped these communities. However, the political machine, the partronage system, and the local churches now
have fewer resources or they have been severely limited in their
effectiveness. The democratic left has discounted or ignored the
ethnic communities and, therefore, these organizing efforts have
been undertaken. It is still not too late for liberal government
leaders to recognize the needs and the importance of these communities and to begin to work with them in their organizing movement.

Levens, Helene. "Organizational Affiliation and Powerlessness: A Case Study
of the Welfare Poor." SOCIAL PROBLEMS 16 (Summer 1968): 18-32.

Many of the poor feel powerless, believing there is really nothing
they can do to relieve the circumstances of the extreme poverty
in which they live. This view presents an attitudinal barrier for
mobilizing the poor to opportunities to assist them in advancing
higher on the socioeconomic ladder. Many believe that by involving the poor in meaningful self-help community activities this attitudinal barrier can be lowered. This study focuses on one chapter
of the Welfare Recipients League--women receiving AFDC. A
sample of league members was identified as was a control sample
of nonmembers. Interviews were conducted with both groups and
the results support the hypothesis that poor people active in community organizations feel more efficacious than nonmembers. Community organization members also felt they had greater control over
their lives than nonmembers.

Marx, Gary T., and Archer, Dane. "Community Self-Defense." SOCIETY
13 (March-April 1976): 38-43.

As local police forces become less able to deal adequately with
the crime problem, private citizen patrols have begun to assume
some of the responsibility. The effectiveness of these community

self-defense groups has not been analyzed but there appears to be strong support for them in many low-income areas. The primary function of the patrols is deterrence. Little is known about why citizens want to join these groups but the police have failed to keep order and provide security and the patrols have emerged. Police forces have responded either with encouragement or opposition. Many of the self-defense groups fail to survive because of a lack of formal organization, no clear direction, and a lack of continuing support.

Newberg, Herbert B. "Building Local Citizen Alliances to Reduce Crime and Create a Fairer and More Effective Criminal Justice System." JOURNAL OF URBAN LAW 49 (February 1972): 443-83.

A National Alliance on Shaping Safer Cities was created to find new ways to process and reduce crime and to insure a fairer and more effective criminal justice system. The goal of the alliance was to create local citizen groups allied with the national organization but autonomous in their communities. The focus of the article is on the importance of the local alliances and the problems inherent in organizing effectively to induce change in the cirminal justice system. The author discusses the interdependent institutions which comprise the criminal justice system including: police, judges, courts, prisons, and corrections officials. The role of the police in the community is discussed with respect to how they view themselves and how they are viewed by the poor, the young, the blacks, and the middle-class residents. Many recommendations are offered for citizen action in bringing about change in the criminal justice system as well as suggestions for improving police-community relations.

O'Brien, David J. NEIGHBORHOOD ORGANIZATION AND INTEREST GROUP PROCESSES. Princeton, N.J.: Princeton University Press, 1975. 368 p.

Neighborhood organizations of the poor have not failed because of inherent social, psychological, or cultural characteristics. They failed because the organizers did not understand interest-group formation. Poor people in communities have interests in common, but they are also self-interested persons trying to cope with their problems. Many current political issues are local in nature and involve conflict between agencies and clients or among groups. Several federal programs mandate local involvement and control. Urban renewal is an example cited. This program benefits politicians, businessmen, and the poor with the former having much more power than the poor.

_____. "The Public Good Dilemma and the 'Apathy' of the Poor Toward Neighborhood Organization." SOCIAL SERVICE REVIEW 41 (June 1974): 229-44.

The lack of enthusiasm by poor people toward neighborhood organizations was one of the great paradoxes of the 1960s. The author feels the apathy of the poor has been misinterpreted because of a lack of understanding of interest-group formation. The obvious needs of the poor, contrasted with their apathy toward social service programs, has created what the author calls the public good dilemma. The author suggests giving poor people the necessary resources with which to purchase the benefits they desire.

Parr, Arnold R. "Organizational Response to Community Crises and Group Emergence." AMERICAN BEHAVIORAL SCIENTIST 13 (January–February 1970): 423-29.

When a disaster strikes a community many emergency organizations respond and begin to cope with the crisis. Fire, police, and hospitals are examples. In some crisis situations, emergent community groups respond and assist the efforts of the emergency organizations. This article examines the nature of organizational response during crisis and the conditions created which encourage the emergence of new groups. Eleven major community crises were selected; six were characterized by group emergence and five had no new groups formed. Data was collected through semistructured, tape-recorded interviews and the two sets of crises were compared. Three characteristics are offered which explain the emergence of new groups: interorganization coordination, organizational authority structure, and organizational demands and response capability.

Washnis, George J. COMMUNITY DEVELOPMENT STRATEGIES: CASE STUDIES OF MAJOR MODEL CITIES. New York: Praeger, 1974. 415 p.

Most of this study examines case studies of the Model Cities program in Boston, Chicago, Dayton, Indianapolis, Newark, New York, Savannah, and Seattle and the impact the program has had on relieving urban problems in each city. Focuses on the objectives, organization, and methods of the program as it affects local government. The author believes only a few gains have been made in achieving the goals of the program. Both citizens and public officials have benefited from the program even though many components of the program were underfunded. The program was flexible and the author feels that a block grant approach would help streamline the funding.

E. NEIGHBORHOOD GOVERNMENT

Altshuler, Alan. COMMUNITY CONTROL: THE BLACK DEMAND FOR PARTICIPATION IN LARGE AMERICAN CITIES. New York: Pegasus, 1970. 238 p.

Focuses on the demands of blacks in urban areas for community control of public services in their communities. The central questions addressed are who demands community control, how does community control relate to the history of urban areas, what is the impact on good government values, what options are available in establishing neighborhood government, and what are the costs and benefits of the proposed options? The author answers each of these questions by citing both the proponents and the critics of community control. Special attention is paid to the practical problems of accountability, finances, personnel, contracting, and the federal role in dealing with community control within cities. The author concludes that community control is a necessary and feasible program for our cities.

Hallman, Howard W. NEIGHBORHOOD CONTROL OF PUBLIC PROGRAMS: CASE STUDIES OF COMMUNITY CORPORATIONS AND NEIGHBORHOOD BOARDS. New York: Praeger, 1970. 226 p.

This is a study of thirty community-controlled organizations that developed as a result of public pressure. Many of the organizations reviewed are community corporations while others are neighborhood boards and community-action groups. All are popularly elected, choose their own staffs, and allocate funds within their neighborhoods. Evaluation of the programs includes both performance and the feelings of those involved. Most of the groups surveyed appeared to be doing as well or better than decentralized operations without resident control. There is a strong willingness on the part of the community members to work together though administrative problems do exist. New strategies and styles are required to deal with different types of centralization.

_____. "Neighborhood Government Can Work." PLANNING 40 (July 1974): 16-19.

Many cities around the country are beginning to organize neighborhood governments within their boundaries. The units are governed by representative bodies elected by the residents and exercise power delegated to them by the city and the state. This arrangement allows responsibility for need assessment and service provision to be assigned as close as possible to the clients to be affected. Small units of government provide basic services while larger units provide specialized activities. The author contends that the quality of life in cities would improve if neighborhood governments were viewed as political institutions and could make inputs along with bureaucracies, politicians, developers, and other specialized interest groups.

_____. NEIGHBORHOOD GOVERNMENT IN A METROPOLITAN SETTING. Beverly Hills, Calif.: Sage Publications, 1974. 302 p.

The first section of the book examines the theory and practicality of neighborhood government by examining case studies around the country. The cases are reviewed with respect to community participation, small-scale administration, shared power, and competitive power. Several intermediate steps are discussed as part of management decentralization. These are: neighborhood city halls and multiservice centers, citizen participation in decentralized administration, neighborhood policy boards, and neighborhood corporations. Each of these is illustrated with cases of practical applications. The author favors a neighborhood government concept and analyzes how to organize neighborhood government, operate it, and finance it. The relationship of local government to the neighborhood is examined and the application of these ideas to several major cities is discussed. The book concludes with a discussion of suburban governments, metropolitan areas, and the role of state and federal government agencies.

Hamilton, Charles V. "Neighborhood Control and Urban Governance." In NEIGHBORHOOD CONTROL IN THE 1970S: POLITICS, ADMINISTRATION AND CITIZEN PARTICIPATION, edited by George Frederickson, pp. 249-58. New York: Chandler, 1973.

The author views neighborhood control as a response to the crisis of legitimacy in local government. Many people no longer believe in the institutions which govern them at the local level. Neighborhood government becomes a goal of people who seek to make public policy more responsive to needs of groups previously excluded from the decision-making process. Problems arise over the definition of "neighborhood" and the determination of which groups in the community represent that community. The goal of a united, monolithic black community is a myth that has never existed and probably never will. The electoral process is not always the best technique for selecting community representatives since many citizens are alienated from this process. Even under a system of neighborhood control, ultimate power will still reside with the national government. Neighborhood control is not a panacea, since it will not solve many of the practical problems confronting urban America.

James, Ronald J. "National Strategies for Neighborhood Control and Citizen Participation." In NEIGHBORHOOD CONTROL IN THE 1970S: POLITICS, ADMINISTRATION AND CITIZEN PARTICIPATION, edited by George Frederickson, pp. 179-94. New York: Chandler, 1973.

Local governments in the United States are neither efficient nor economical. Cities are characterized by little citizen involvement, less local democracy, and meaningless individual self-determination. While neighborhood control may not be the answer to all of our urban problems it probably won't be worse than the existing system and it will force us to think about new approaches to old problems. The author reviews three major programs which sought to strengthen neighborhood control: the Economic Opportunity Act of 1964, the Model Cities Act of 1966, and the Community Self-Determination Act which never passed Congress. Also discussed are questions of radical decentralization, the politics of achieving neighborhood control, and the personal and political costs involved.

Kotler, Milton. "Neighborhood Government." LIBERATION 19 (Spring 1976): 119-25.

New studies in public administration show the inefficiency of large centralized administrations of public goods and services. The larger a local government becomes, the more agreements it enters into, not fewer. Under the circumstances, the neighborhood unit could become the basic unit of urban life and furnish services superior to those now provided by traditional urban governments. Using the Shaw-Cardoza area in Washington, D.C., the author shows this area paid approximately 45 million dollars in taxes in 1969 but received only 35 million dollars in public services and welfare. The neighborhood might have fared better using intercommunity agreements to provide public services. A good model to examine is the autonomous suburban government.

_____. "Rise of Neighborhood Power." FOCUS 4 (December 1975): 4, 5, 8.

The new Community Development Block Grant program has been used in several cities to permit grant funds to be spent in ways which are useful to community groups. In Washington, D.C., voters passed a charter referendum establishing advisory neighborhood councils which will advise the government on public policy in areas such as planning, recreation, and social services. In Simi Valley, California, the council created five neighborhood council districts similar to town meetings. Similar programs have been developed in the Chinese community in New York City and in a black community in Greenville, Mississippi.

_____. "The Road to Neighborhood Government." NEW GENERATION 51 (Summer 1969): 7-12.

The author comments on several approaches which have been advocated for local governments to begin assisting the poorer neighborhoods. Among these are Saul Alinsky's organizing techniques, SDS's revolutionary tactics, black nationalism, which seeks autonomous control over territory, and liberal approaches calling for little city halls based on improved human resources delivery systems. All of these mistake the true goal of the neighborhood, which is liberty, for improved service delivery. The author believes in developing neighborhood corporations which will draft their own constitutions to guide their governance and set their tax rates. This is the only way the imperial stranglehold of the downtown can be broken.

Perry, David C. "The Suburb as a Model for Neighborhood Control." In NEIGHBORHOOD CONTROL IN THE 1970S: POLITICS, ADMINISTRATION

AND CITIZEN PARTICIPATION, edited by George Frederickson, pp. 85-99. New York: Chandler, 1973.

Evaluates the viability of the strategy of neighborhood control to give inner-city residents increased power over their own affairs. The author suggests that this entails transplanting the suburban model of community governance to the inner city. The suburban model includes cultural identity, sufficient economic resources, and governmental mechanisms which respond to citizen needs. Each of these factors is discussed and documented with examples and charts. The deterioration of American cities will not be arrested and reversed in the near future. Modification of local governmental structure is essential. This modification will entail providing inner-city residents with the same control over services that affect their daily lives as suburban residents now enjoy.

Shalala, Donna E. "Neighborhood Government: Has the Time Come?" NATIONAL CIVIC REVIEW 61 (April 1972): 185-89.

Focuses on the growing movement for greater neighborhood control of government and the opposing point of view advocating increased centralization of control through metropolitan or regional governments. An analysis is presented of one major proposal for a two-tiered governmental system—one regional level and another a set of community districts for neighborhood governments. The functional sharing of power presented is illustrated by examples in land use, planning, and the provision of sewage disposal services.

_____. NEIGHBORHOOD GOVERNMENT: ISSUES AND PROPOSALS. New York: American Jewish Committee, 1971. 48 p.

This monograph focuses on several major themes. Can neighborhood government make it possible for citizens on all levels to participate in decision making which affects their lives? Can a neighborhood government system avoid becoming a replica of machine government? Is the neighborhood government movement the best way to achieve quality services and will this movement diminish or increase group conflict? The major questions are discussed in terms of the old and new debate over neighborhood government, the justification for the movement, how power is to be allocated, the size of neighborhood units, the governmental structure, political representation, and staffing. Several plans for variations on neighborhood government are presented.

Strange, John H. "Local Strategies for Attaining Neighborhood Control." In NEIGHBORHOOD CONTROL IN THE 1970S: POLITICS, ADMINISTRATION AND CITIZEN PARTICIPATION, edited by George Frederickson, pp. 167-78. New York: Chandler, 1973.

Assuming the desirability of decentralized decision making and neighborhood or community control, the author focuses on the actions, plans, strategies, and tactics to be used in implementing such a political-administrative arrangement. Protest is seen as one strategy that can work better at the neighborhood level than at any other level of government. Another strategy that can be used successfully in some cases is pragmatic compromise which enables residents to achieve some of their goals. Neighborhoods also have many historical arguments on their side which can be used to achieve some of their goals. Neighborhoods also have many historical arguments on their side which can be used to achieve neighborhood control. The author discusses several benefits to be derived from the implementation of community control and examines the costs of decentralizing versus not decentralizing. Several general strategies for achieving neighborhood control are presented.

Yates, Douglas. "Neighborhood Government." In THE CITY IN THE SEVENTIES, edited by Robert K. Yin, pp. 119-27. Itasca, Ill.: F.E. Peacock, 1972.

Examines the definition of neighborhood government, its origins, benefits, and deficiencies; major obstacles to achievement; and problems related to local democracy and community development. The author outlines several characteristics which must be present if there is to be a real increase in local autonomy and power. The obstacles to neighborhood government are cited as: the increase in time, energy, and personal resources required; the potential conflict with existing neighborhood organizations; and the competition among some local government agencies to deliver services in the neighborhood government is posed and the author concludes that the concept may be a long-range, desirable goal but it is unlikely to be attainable in the near future.

Zimmerman, Joseph F. "Are Neighborhood Governments a Desirable Institutional Change?" ASPO PLANNING 38 (October 1972): 224-31.

Citizen discontent with local government has resulted in greater participation in neighborhood units. Many neighborhood residents feel that a system of neighborhood government opens up the decision-making process to them. These advocates believe a sense of community will be revitalized at the local level. Critics argue that neighborhood government will reinforce parochialism, minimize citywide concerns, and eventually dismember the city. The arguments for neighborhood government espoused by blacks and whites are presented. Also discussed is the legislation for neighborhood government recently passed by Indianapolis.

_____. THE FEDERATED CITY: COMMUNITY CONTROL IN LARGE CITIES. New York: St. Martin's Press, 1972. 114 p.

The movement for neighborhood government was one of the most significant political events of the 1960s. Supporters of the movement want a federated city with substantial grants of power given to neighborhoods to determine their own service needs, while the city government performs a different set of functions. The author proposes a set of criteria for determining neighborhood size or boundaries for service delivery. Included are: administrative and fiscal capacity, who would benefit, population, accountability, and accessibility. Case studies of community control movements in New York City and Detroit are presented and an examination of bureaucratic resistance to the challenge of its authority is analyzed. The author concludes that if changes can be effected in the bureaucracy so that it becomes more sensitive and responsive the movement for neighborhood government will subside.

_____. "Heading Off City Hall--Neighborhood Wars." NATION'S CITIES 8 (November 1970): 18-21.

In the 1960s, there was a call for a new reform movement which would strengthen the neighborhood unit. Claims have been advanced that centralizing power in city hall does not increase economies in scale, provide more equitable tax distribution, improve the planning process, or increase the levels of service. Several proposals advanced for greater metropolitan governmental control contain provisions for neighborhood level units. Administrative response to the reform movement has generated complaint centers, mini-city halls, and new techniques for increasing minority representation in government. All of these responses will help reduce tensions and minimize conflict between city hall and the neighborhoods.

_____. "Neighborhoods and Citizen Involvement." PUBLIC ADMINISTRATION REVIEW 32 (May-June 1972): 201-10.

A new reform movement is emerging in local government which suggests that power has become too centralized and bureaucracies unresponsive. The reformers would like to see power devolved to the neighborhood level. The author offers a counter suggestion, labeled "the federated city," which would insure that groups denied access to the system would become more involved. Structural reform historically has accomplished little. The author recommends more innovation in the development and allocation of financial resources as well as a change in administrative procedures if we are to combat urban problems successfully.

Chapter 6

URBAN BUREAUCRACY

A. SERVICE DELIVERY SYSTEMS

Aberbach, Joel D., and Walker, Jack L. "The Attitudes of Blacks and Whites
Toward City Services: Implications for Public Policy." In FINANCING THE
METROPOLIS: PUBLIC POLICY IN URBAN ECONOMIES, edited by John P.
Crecine, pp. 519-38. Beverly Hills, Calif.: Sage Publications, 1970.

During the 1960s, urban problems were brought to the public's attention through a series of riots in our major cities. Many of these
problems were caused by racial tensions and the growing dissatisfaction of citizens with the quantity and quality of public services
delivered. This report analyzes data collected from white and
black respondents in Detroit in 1967 and '68. The degree of satisfaction with five city services by race is presented, showing greater
black dissatisfaction for all services. When asked about their neighborhood services in relation to other parts of the city, blacks felt
their neighborhoods were worse. Fewer blacks than whites felt that
city officials would respond to complaints. Blacks also had a more
negative view of police behavior and police performance. Vigorous
efforts to end discrimination and more funds to provide more and
better services are necessary to ease the tensions in urban areas.

Anderson, R. Dennis. "Toward the Equalization of Municipal Services: Variations on a Theme by Hawkins." JOURNAL OF URBAN LAW 50 (November
1972): 177-97.

Alternative approaches to correction of the disparity in the provision
of municipal services are presented. Included are both constitutional
and extraconstitutional approaches. Hawkins v. Town of Shaw, a
class action suit against the public officials of Shaw, Mississippi,
citing discrimination on the basis of race and wealth in providing
municipal services, is analyzed. The Shaw case has provided a
model for several other service inequities suits in local governments
around the country. A unique feature of the Shaw case was the
use of statistical evidence, introduced by the plaintiffs, to demonstrate the extent of the service disparities.

Aram, John D., and Stratton, William E. "The Development on Interagency Cooperation." SOCIAL SERVICE REVIEW 48 (September 1974): 412-21.

Interagency cooperation in the health and social services field is a rare occurrence. Documentation of successful cooperation efforts is even more difficult to find. This article examines a successful planning effort, involving twenty local agencies, which coordinated their services to the aged in a local public housing project. Discussed are the significant factors involved in the initiation of the cooperative activity and the factors involved in the planning process that contributed to the program's success. Interviews with participants were analyzed to reach conclusions which highlight the dynamic quality of social processes involved in institutional change.

Benson, Charles S., and Lund, Peter B. NEIGHBORHOOD DISTRIBUTION OF LOCAL PUBLIC SERVICES. Berkeley, Calif.: Institute of Governmental Studies, 1969. 181 p.

This is a study of how neighborhoods make use of publicly financed services. Cities are composed of socially and economically heterogeneous neighborhoods which establish distinct patterns of public service consumption. Taxes paid by residents of any one neighborhood support not only services desired by that neighborhood but also services that are used by other neighborhoods in the city. The authors contend that rates of participation in local public service activities are related to income, education, and occupation. Six service areas are examined to test their hypothesis: police, health, inspection, library, recreation, and school services. The study was conducted in Berkeley, Califomia. The findings indicate that socioeconomic variables account greatly for the degree of involvement of selected households in specific local public services.

Bernard, Sydney E. "Why Service Delivery Programs Fail." SOCIAL WORK 20 (May 1975): 206-11.

The author hypothesizes that service delivery programs usually fail because their goals are too grandiose and the tools for implementation too inadequate. Several factors make it difficult to deliver services effectively and therefore social change is impeded. Many social service institutions start out with expectations and plans that are impossible to achieve thus leaving the local citizens frustrated and apprehensive. Using the Drug Abuse Program of the 1960s and 1970s, the author shows that often programs of this type start off quickly and with great expectations. However, after a short period, they slow down and their goals are redefined. Several suggestions are offered for overcoming the difficulties plaguing our current social service delivery programs.

Boettcher, Richard E. "The Service Delivery System: What Is It?" PUBLIC WELFARE 32 (Winter 1974): 45-50.

This article examines the various meanings of the term "service delivery system" as it is now used in social welfare literature. A
sample of the literature is reviewed to illustrate the various dimensions discussed by those who use the term. Two levels of meaning
for the service delivery system construct are defined and a model
of the organization as a service delivery system is presented. The
implications of this model for social welfare planning and intervention are discussed.

Burby, Raymond J.; Weiss, Shirley F.; and Zehner, Robert B. "A National
Evaluation of Community Services and the Quality of Life in American New
Towns." PUBLIC ADMINISTRATION REVIEW 35 (May-June 1975): 229-39.

This is a study of thirteen privately developed new communities.
Each of the new communities was paired with a nearby suburban
area to compare location, stage of development, age, type, and
price range of housing. Three types of comparisons are made in
evaluating new community service systems: facilities and services,
indicators of performance, and citizen satisfaction with the quality
of services and facilities. The services evaluated are primary education, health care, recreation, shopping, and transportation. The
conclusions indicate that new communities are not the panacea for
the urban service delivery problem. However, there is some evidence to suggest that where public agencies become involved in
the community development process, the public-private partnership
has proved effective.

Fitch, Lyle C. "Increasing the Role of the Private Sector in Providing Public
Services." In IMPROVING URBAN MANAGEMENT, edited by Willis D. Hawley
and David Rogers, pp. 264-306. Beverly Hills, Calif.: Sage Publications, 1974.

Concentrates on increasing the role of the private sector in performing services that otherwise have to be provided by public sector
agencies. Two major areas are discussed. First are public interest
services supplied to constituents and financed by taxes. Second is
the promotion of economic development in the urban ghettos. Three
factors have contributed to the increasing possibility of the private
sector assuming more responsibility for providing services. These
are: the rapidly increasing cost of state and local government,
the inability of local governments to cope with growing demands,
and the belief that public bureaucracies are less efficient than
private firms. The author discusses the political process versus the
market process in allocating resources and the advantages and disadvantages of providing services in the bureaucracy versus contracting with private firms.

Fowler, Floyd J. CITIZEN ATTITUDES TOWARD LOCAL GOVERNMENT SER-
VICES AND TAXES. Cambridge, Mass.: Ballinger, 1974. 276 p.

This report is part of the Urban Observatory Program of the National

League of Cities. It represents a national effort of intercity and university-government cooperation to conduct a large-scale research project. The results are based upon 4,300 interviews with a sample of adults in 10 major American cities. Citizens were asked a series of questions about their views and feelings on city government, city services, and city problems. Highlighting the patterns of agreement and difference in cities, it assists public officials in understanding the satisfaction level in their cities.

Hirsch, Werner Z. "The Supply of Urban Public Services." In ISSUES IN URBAN ECONOMICS, edited by Harvey S. Perloff and Lowdon Wingo, Jr., pp. 477-525. Baltimore: Johns Hopkins Press, 1968.

Focuses on the provision of tangible public services by urban governmental agencies. Services are viewed as resource-using activities which produce pecuniary and nonpecuniary benefits. The quantity and quality of urban public service production are difficult to measure. Output requires defining the basic service unit and estimating the number of units produced in a year. Some service outputs, such as water, are relatively easy to measure while others, such as social services, are difficult to measure. Determining the quality of the service is equally difficult. Urban public service cost and cost functions are discussed as are economies of scale related to governmental consolidations. The author analyzes the nature of urban public service supply functions including who supplies the service and what criteria are used to make this determination. Examples are used to illustrate the major concepts discussed.

Jones, Bryan D., and Kaufman, Clifford. "The Distribution of Urban Public Services: A Preliminary Model." ADMINISTRATION AND SOCIETY 6 (November 1974): 337-60.

This article proposes a distributional model explaining the variance in the level of service delivery. It does not focus on interjurisdictional disparities, such as those between the central city and its suburbs. Rather, it focuses on the distribution of services within a single jurisdiction and seeks to explain intrajurisdictional disparities. The level of service delivery is defined as a product of the socioeconomic composition of the residential neighborhood and the needs and demands the residents generate for services. The model assumes that need affects the level of demand and that socioeconomic status of the population helps to define the level of both needs and demands. Feedback links exist from level of service delivery to needs, demands, and population characteristics. Two types of service delivery systems are suggested by the model.

Kahn, Alfred J. "Public Social Services: The Next Phase--Policy and Delivery Strategies." PUBLIC WELFARE 30 (Winter 1972): 15-24.

Policy and delivery mechanisms for a broad range of social services are discussed in the context of separation of services and payments. Arguments are presented for a universal social service system designed to provide a balance of case services reached through diagnostic channels and public social utilities providing communal services. Senior citizen centers are used as an example and a model service network is presented. The model includes an access system, a generalist social service office, and specialized programs.

_____. "Service Delivery of the Neighborhood Level: Experience, Theory, and Fads." SOCIAL SERVICE REVIEW 50 (March 1976): 23-56.

Social service delivery systems at the local level have recently been characterized by style, hope, and the feeling that the system might be used for many other reasons. In the past twenty-five years, we have attempted to solve the service delivery problem by requiring more expert practitioners, better supervision, integration of social science and behavioral concepts, and multidisciplinary practices. Some of the reforms implemented have had the promise of success but little was known of the actual contribution they might make to better services. Criteria for current and final evaluations of social service programs must be developed by consumers, legislators, professionals, administrators, and researchers.

Levine, Daniel U. "Are the Black Poor Satisfied With Conditions in Their Neighborhood?" JOURNAL OF THE AMERICAN INSTITUTE OF PLANNERS 38 (May 1972): 168-71.

This is a study summarizing data collected in 1970 from high school students attending predominantly black high schools in poverty areas of four large cities and one small southern city. The study focuses on attitudes toward local neighborhood services and conditions. The findings indicate that only a minority of respondents feel positive about local housing, education, law enforcement, or conditions in general. The findings suggest that dissatisfaction with local neighborhood services is fairly widespread among youth and young adults in predominantly black poverty neighborhoods.

Lineberry, Robert L. "Equality, Public Policy and Public Services: The Underclass Hypothesis and the Limits to Equality." POLICY AND POLITICS 4 (December 1975): 67-84.

Many academics and practitioners suspect that the provision of urban services is a function of the racial class or political traits of specific communities and neighborhoods. This article tests the underclass hypothesis in San Antonio, Texas which has a large poor minority population and a highly centralized power structure. The intramunicipal distribution of two services--fire protection and parks-- is examined. The pattern appears to be one of distributed inequality, but the inequalities are not related to underclass variations in neighborhoods. The author poses questions about the underlying concept of equality in the distribution of services.

Margolis, Julius. "The Demand For Urban Public Services." In ISSUES IN
URBAN ECONOMICS, edited by Harvey S. Perloff and Lowdon Wingo, Jr.,
pp. 527-65. Baltimore: Johns Hopkins Press, 1968.

The author starts from the assumption that urban public services are
poorly supplied. He examines the scope of public expenditures and
some of the characteristics of local government relevant to the analysis of public services. This includes per capita expenditures, intergovernmental relations, fragmentation, decision-making opportunities
and constraints, and the lack of quantitative measures for public
services. An analysis of public goals and externalities is presented.
Urban political processes are examined, with respect to how well
they reflect consumer preferences, and some political economy models
are discussed. The author concludes that the economic model of
choice as applied to public services is the optimal way to determine
consumer demand. The technique for achieving this is benefit-cost
analysis, which has been used extensively in water supply and urban
transportation, but is being extended to a much wider range of urban
public services.

Merget, Astrid E. "Equalizing Municipal Services: Issues for Policy Analysis."
POLICY STUDIES JOURNAL 4 (Spring 1976): 297-306.

In 1971, the U.S. Court of Appeals found that black residents of
Shaw, Mississippi were being discriminated against in the provision
of basic municipal services. Six major issues emerge for local officials from this historic case: the standard of equity in service
provision, the production of equitable services both in qualitative
and quantitative terms, the measurement of service conditions against
an equity standard, the collection of data to document actual service conditions, the interpretation of the data, and the reform of
inequitable service conditions.

Murphy, Thomas P., and Rehfuss, John. URBAN POLITICS IN THE SUBURBAN
ERA. Homewood, Ill.: Dorsey Press, 1976. 285 p.

An examination of metropolitics from a suburban viewpoint. Political, social, and economic data are integrated in an interdisciplinary
approach to urban, suburban, and metropolitan decision making.
There is substantial treatment of federal and state policy impact and
chapter 6 deals specifically with delivery of services.

Orden, Susan R. "The Impact of Community Action Programs on Private Social
Service Agencies." SOCIAL PROBLEMS 20 (Winter 1973): 364-81.

This is a study of the effectiveness of community action programs
based upon twenty-two variables measuring change in private social
service agencies. Questionnaires were administered to the directors
of three private social service agencies in each of fifty cities. The
community action program can be credited with exerting a modern
influence on change in the proportion of services delivered to the

poor and a strong influence on change in the levels of interaction between social service agencies and the poor residents in the neighborhood. Social service agencies funded by the Community Action Agency are more likely than nonfunded agencies to credit the community action program with influencing desired change in general service and service to the poor.

Piven, Frances Fox. "Cutting Up the City Pie: Who Gets What?" NEW REPUBLIC 166 (5 February 1972): 17-22.

The inability of city governments to administer and finance city services is attributed to the collapse of traditional political relations, especially those involving the distribution of goods and services through the bureaucracies. The author discusses the political uses of municipal services, the changing nature of urban politics, black demands for more and better services, and the impact of influence in city politics. Attention is also focused on federal programs which provide services to low-income communities and the inability of urban mayors to govern their political jurisdictions.

_____. "Slicing the Big Apple." LIBERATION 19 (Spring 1976): 9-18.

Strong resistance is needed to halt the cutbacks planned for welfare, education, and other services in New York City. Protest demonstrations, wildcat strikes, disruptions, and work slowdowns, coupled with a public education campaign could highlight the false assumptions on which these cutbacks are being justified. Resistance will be hard to organize because unions and other groups have become competitive and fear supporting one another. Patronage has become individual, ethnic, and neighborhood-oriented. Municipal workers in general are maligned but the individual groups are not. City workers will have to band together to protect each other and to educate the public about the crisis of service delivery.

Protess, David L. "Banfield's Chicago Revisited: The Conditions for the Social Policy Implications of the Transformation of a Political Machine." SOCIAL SERVICES REVIEW 48 (June 1974): 184-202.

This article is a rebuttal to Banfield's prediction that the Chicago political machine would slowly disintegrate due to reform politics and the changing nature of social policy. To understand the implications of social programs, the author feels you must understand the local political environment. It is at this level that social programs are delivered and implemented. The author challenges several traditional notions about local politics and concludes with a redefinition of machine politics which includes an analysis of the consequences for social policy implementation should the machine be dismantled.

Pruger, Robert. "Competition and the Public Social Services." PUBLIC WELFARE

31 (Fall 1973): 16-25.

> Competition in the provision of social services is not espoused as a
> panacea. Rather, arguments for and against competitive social ser-
> vice delivery are examined. Most of the arguments are gleaned
> from the social welfare literature and focus on the following sub-
> jects: the meaning of competitive social service delivery, the limits
> of this approach, and the most useful applications. The concept of
> competition is examined as applied to the organization of a public
> social service agency. Questions are raised about the structure and
> function of such an agency once the political decision was made to
> deliver social services in a competitive rather than a monopolistic
> manner. Obstacles to establishing perfect competition in social ser-
> vice delivery systems are also examined.

Rutledge, Philip J. "Three Uncommon Approaches to Services Integration."
HUMAN NEEDS 1 (July 1972): 14-19.

> Three different approaches to integrating social services are discussed.
> They are: the East Cleveland Community Human Services Center in
> Ohio, which matches people to the programs and agencies they need;
> the Anacostia Project in Washington, D.C., which uses a vocational
> rehabilitation model; and the Comprehensive Human Services Center,
> Devil Lakes, North Dakota, whose objective is to centrally locate
> all social service programs. The three programs are presented as
> models to ensure better social service delivery for clients. This is
> accomplished by coordinating responsibility, eliminating barriers that
> divide services, and freeing professionals from administrative chores.

Savas, E.S. "Municipal Monopoly." HARPERS MAGAZINE 243 (December
1971): 55-66.

> The current problems of the cities are attributed to the monopoly
> arrangements in urban service delivery. Lack of competition in the
> delivery of services leads to inefficiency, public frustration, inferior
> products, and a vulnerability to strikes and slowdowns. Case studies
> are provided of New York City's sanitation department, police de-
> partment, mass transit agency, and educational bureaucracy. Many
> of the problems are attributed to the civil service system which,
> instead of providing security and freedom from outside influences,
> has made the bureaucracy unresponsive to the changing needs of the
> people. Strategies for improving urban service delivery are: increase
> the number of agencies providing services, decrease the demand for
> services by decreasing the number of clients, and decentralize much
> of the government structure.

Schuman, Howard, and Gruenberg, Barry. "Dissatisfaction With City Services:
Is Race an Important Factor?" In PEOPLE AND POLITICS IN URBAN SOCIETY,
edited by Harlan Hahn, pp. 369-92. Beverly Hills, Calif.: Sage Publications,
1972.

This article examines urban service delivery by using random sample data from citizens concerning their satisfaction with four key city services: public education, parks and playgrounds for children, police protection, and garbage collection. Over 5,000 black and white citizens in fifteen American cities responded to the survey. For each service, blacks are more dissatisfied than whites though the level of dissatisfaction varies markedly from city to city. The degree of neighborhood "whiteness" is a definite source of satisfaction levels for both whites and blacks. As educational levels of the respondents increase, so does their dissatisfaction with the schools. It is difficult to determine if neighborhood differences in satisfaction levels are due primarily to discriminatory treatment by city officials or to racial composition.

Sonnenblum, Sidney; Kirlin, John J.; and Ries, John C. PROVIDING MUNICIPAL SERVICES: THE EFFECTS OF ALTERNATIVE STRUCTURES. Cambridge, Mass.: Ballinger, 1976. 226 p.

The authors state that the effort to improve the delivery of city services has forced local governments to turn toward new organizational structures and technological advances. City departments which historically have provided local services are being replaced in some cases by intergovernmental organizations and private sector institutions. Using California as a case study, the authors offer a definition of appropriate service delivery structures. They examine the California experience with alternative structures by discussing the frequency of adoption, reception by local officials, and the advantages and disadvantages of the structures chosen.

Sugarman, Jule M. "Why Change is Necessary." PUBLIC WELFARE 30 (Fall 1972): 26-29.

Examines the complex nature of delivering social services in New York City. The author suggests developing new methods of operation which would induce change and create new roles and approaches for the staff of the city's Department of Social Services. New plans are discussed which include: installation of a computer system to handle public assistance, encouraging greater community involvement in social services, and the initiation of three pilot projects financed by revenue-sharing funds.

Weise, R. Eric. "Municipal Government and Public Service." NATIONAL CIVIC REVIEW 63 (September 1974): 416-20.

Focuses on citizen attitudes toward local politicians and local programs with particular emphasis on essential services. Citizens have been rejecting pleas for increased taxes that accompany the provision of additional services except where they fear that the consequences of their actions might be worse than increased taxes. Citizens cannot understand why the cost of local services is so high.

Overcoming this problem requires educating the public about local government programs and the costs involved in implementing them. The author feels that citizens are anxious to learn about service delivery systems and their costs, but this will require locally elected officials to use television as an educational medium and to be more open and honest with the public.

White, Orion, Jr., and Gates, Bruce L. "Statistical Theory and Equity in the Delivery of Social Services." PUBLIC ADMINISTRATION REVIEW 34 (January-February 1974): 43-51.

Public organizations must alter their structure, their processes, and their concept of social equity if inequities in public services are to be reduced in the future. To achieve true equity in public programs, public organizations will have to develop decision-making techniques that are more open-ended and participative than currently exist. The authors suggest that future administrators will have to be trained to understand an open method of collaborative analysis and action which is built upon participation. One approach is the Bayesian view of statistical theory which permits data to be interpreted by all possible hypotheses and reality situations, thus providing a much more open-ended process to decision making.

Williams, Alan. "The Optimal Provision of Public Goods in a System of Local Government." JOURNAL OF POLITICAL ECONOMY 74 (February-December 1966): 18-33.

Focusing on public and private goods, the author examines two communities trying to cope with the problems of spillovers. A social optimum is discussed and ways of attaining social optimum in terms of intercommunity distribution of purchasing power are analyzed. If community boundaries are taken as constant and not as variable, it is easier to deal with inter- or intracommunity spillovers. This eliminates the need for the country or the state to decide how public goods should be allocated and leaves the decision making on the local level.

Yates, Douglas. "Service Delivery and the Urban Political Order." In IMPROVING URBAN MANAGEMENT, edited by Willis D. Hawley and David Rogers, pp. 147-74. Beverly Hills, Calif.: Sage Publications, 1974.

Government officials and analysts have come to realize that the delivery of urban services is the key issue and major problem facing urban decision makers today. It represents a less radical approach than the call for community control heard in the late 1960s. Service delivery problems reflect much deeper structural problems in the urban political system. Fragmentation means that often the urban mayor is unable to control his administration. It also means that citizen needs and demands are rarely aggregated with their full intensity felt by decision makers. The author traces the evolution of the urban political system from colonial times to the present, highlighting the issues of fragmentation and service delivery. The author offers several solutions to the problems examined, including policy planning to monitor the activities of service bureaucracies, policy coordination, meaningful citizen participation, and the formation of block associations.

Yates, Douglas, and Yin, Robert [K.]. "Street Level Governments: Lessons For Tomorrow." NATION'S CITIES 12 (November 1974): 33-49.

Contending that decentralized street-level governments are the most equitable and efficient manner in which to run local government, the authors examine the decentralized delivery of urban social services. The authors base their findings on 215 case studies of decentralization involving various types of social service delivery systems. Conceding that many problems still need to be worked out in the areas of staff development, expenditures, and policy implementation, the authors conclude that street-level governments have great potential for a more equitable and efficient delivery and use of social services.

Young, Dennis R. "Institutional Change and the Delivery of Urban Public Services." POLICY SCIENCES 2 (December 1971): 425-38.

A control systems framework is applied to the evaluation of the delivery of urban public services. Three reform strategies are presented as techniques for improving delivery system performance. These are: evaluation, decentralization, and market competition. The reform strategies are applied to sanitation and correctional services.

B. AGENCY-CLIENT RELATIONS

Arnstein, Sherry. "Maximum Feasible Manipulation." CITY 4 (October-November 1970): 30-38.

This is a case study of a Model Cities program in Philadelphia that generated so much conflict that the courts were eventually asked to resolve the problem. The community activists have documented in chronological order their conflict with city hall over funding and participation in a program which was designed to improve their community. The article includes a statement on the lessons learned by the citizens in dealing with public agencies on all levels of government. The second part of the article is a chronological rebuttal written by city hall officials in Philadelphia who present their interpretations of the conflicts that arose in the development and the implementation of this program.

Auerbach, Arnold J. "Confrontation and Administrative Response." PUBLIC ADMINISTRATION REVIEW 29 (November-December 1969): 639-46.

As confrontation and violence increase, public sector administrators are finding it more difficult to carry out their responsibilities in a rational and efficient manner. Citizen and student militancy has been directed toward a number of public institutions. The demands made by these groups are often unreasonable and impractical but they permit little room for negotiation or compromise. With pressure from both militants for change and sections of the public, the administrator finds it very difficult to consistently respond professionally and rationally. Sociological and psychological effects of organizational conflicts are discussed and several guidelines are suggested for professional response by public administrators.

Austin, David M. "Social Services and Dependency: The Critical Dilemma for Social Work." URBAN AND SOCIAL CHANGE REVIEW 5 (Spring 1972): 50-54.

Examines the historic link of minimum social welfare programs with social services and the proposed program of separating payments from services in the context of labor market forces. Views are presented which examine social case work as a form of harassment of welfare recipients designed to enforce eligibility regulations. The technique for reducing dependency by rehabilitating clients on a case basis is also discussed.

Bayley, David H., and Mendelsohn, Harold. MINORITIES AND THE POLICE: CONFRONTATION IN AMERICA. New York: Free Press, 1969. 225 p.

This is a study of police-community relations in Denver. The authors collected data in four surveys to examine the attitudes and behavior that exist in the relationship between the police and minority groups. The four surveys were conducted with police officers, the opinion-making elite, a cross-section of the community, and members of the black and Spanish-speaking community. Topics discussed include: socioeconomic status of the police, the amount of respect for the police, the degree of reliance on police assistance, attitudes toward violence, and police attitudes toward minority groups. The authors draw conclusions which suggest ways for improving police-community relations in Denver. Many of these suggestions are applicable to other cities.

Beck, Bertram M. "Community Control: A Distraction, Not an Answer." SOCIAL WORK 14 (October 1969): 14-20.

Making institutions more responsive usually requires altering the power relationships between bureaucrats and clients. Bureaucrats control behavior by being able to punish and reward clients. If bureaucrats and clients accept these roles, little conflict will surface. When clients rebel against repressive measures in the bureaucracy, they usually demand community control or greater client participation in decision making. Often community leaders were placed

on advisory boards, but this was not an answer to the problem.
The author suggests that bureaucratic power exercised by professionals in service delivery be reduced or eliminated until a system
is devised which penalizes bureaucrats for this action.

Bent, Alan Edward. THE POLITICS OF LAW ENFORCEMENT. Lexington,
Mass.: D.C. Heath, 1974. 203 p.

An analysis of how and why police obtain power individually and
collectively by solidifying their positions in the police bureaucracy
and through the use of discretionary authority. The struggle for
power is viewed as a conflict between the police bureaucracy and
other bureaus and agencies. Police behavior is examined in terms
of the screening, selection, and socialization processes. The impact
of police actions is related to community relations on the street
level in three cities. Antidemocratic practices are analyzed in the
discretion accountability problem which accounts for much of the
tension and conflict in police-community relations as well as with
other departments, public officials, and political actors.

Berkley, George E. THE DEMOCRATIC POLICEMAN. Boston: Beacon Press,
1969. 232 p.

In contemporary urban society the police are seen as undemocratic.
Policemen do not interact with citizens on an equal basis because
of the weapons they carry and the authority at their disposal.
Many children grow up with misconceptions about the police, ranging from fear to incompetence. Many of these images are wrong
and need to be changed if the police are to be effective in the
community. One solution proposed is the introduction of civilian
auxiliary units to work with the police department as well as the
use of more female police officers. Another suggestion is to reward policemen for continuing their education. This program can
be initiated at community colleges and will also bring the policemen into contact with other members of the community.

Better, Shirley. "The Black Social Worker in the Black Community." PUBLIC
WELFARE 30 (Fall 1972): 2-7.

The author believes that the community development model developed
under the Model Cities program is a form of racism since white local
officials determine the nature and scope of black communities and
services. Suggestions are made for black social workers to reject
present treatment techniques in community planning and organizing
and re-educate themselves in the effective use of political and
economic power. Social change can be achieved more effectively
through an analysis and a change of environmental constraints concerning black community problems than through continuous or increased interpersonal case work in these areas.

Bordua, David J., and Tifft, Larry L. "Citizen Interviews, Organizational Feedback, and Police-Community Relations Decisions." LAW AND SOCIETY REVIEW 6 (November 1971): 155-82.

Police-community relations programs have been criticized in the past for trying to raise the image of the police in the community or for trying to establish the value system of the power structure in the ghetto. This paper is based upon observations of the police in their everyday activities and on interviews with citizens who come into contact with the police. It focuses on the effects of different types of police contact and handling on the attitudes of citizens toward the police. Sources of citizen hostility are related to specific police practices. Police departments should continuously re-evaluate their operations using some system of feedback interviews.

Chakerian, Richard. "Police Professionalism and Citizen Evaluations: A Preliminary Look." PUBLIC ADMINISTRATION REVIEW 34 (March-April 1974): 141-48.

Professionalization of police forces is one way to improve citizen evaluation of law enforcement functions. This article tests this assumption as well as two others: professionalism is associated with effectiveness and restraint in the use of force, and effectiveness and restraint are positively valued by the public. The data in the study come from two sources: a survey of citizens in five central cities in metropolitan counties, and an evaluation of the police departments of four central cities and the sheriff's departments of their respective counties. The conclusions indicate that citizens are rather impressed with law enforcement services. Professionalism has a negative correlation to positive evaluation of the police. Citizens are positive in their evaluation of police when police are effective but exercise restraint.

Chackerian, Richard, and Barrett, Richard F. "Police Professionalism and Citizen Evaluation." URBAN AFFAIRS QUARTERLY 8 (March 1973): 345-49.

A brief discussion of police professionalism, police effectiveness, and citizen evaluation is presented. The authors hypothesize that the citizen's evaluation of a law enforcement agency would depend on its effectiveness in preventing crime and apprehending suspects and that the police would be more favorably evaluated if they showed restraint and equity in the application of the law. Conclusions indicate that a high arrest rate is a sign of effectiveness, while the definition of law enforcement problems is not likely to center on questions of fairness, due process, and equity.

Eimicke, William B. "Professionalism and Participation: Compatible Means to Improve Social Services?" PUBLIC ADMINISTRATION REVIEW 34 (July-August 1974): 409-14.

The debate over welfare policy in the United States can be reduced to the problem of whether or not the wealthy want to share their resources with the poor. Employees of welfare agencies find themselves in the middle of the conflict between welfare recipients and politicians and some citizens who believe welfare payments lead to permanent dependency. Several studies are reviewed which deal with bureaucratic dominance, professionalism, and citizen participation. A questionnaire was administered to workers in public and private welfare agencies in Onandaga County (Syracuse, New York). Based upon 167 responses, the author concludes that workers with masters degrees in social work are much more receptive to clients' needs and employees who lived in the area a long time were more negative toward clients.

Eisenberg, Terry; Fosen, Robert H.; and Glickman, Albert S. POLICE-COMMUNITY ACTION: A PROGRAM FOR CHANGE IN POLICE-COMMUNITY BEHAVIOR PATTERNS. New York: Praeger, 1973. 214 p.

Reports on a two-year (1968-70), police-community relations program in San Francisco which was based upon previous research and experience with American troops overseas and their relationships with the community. The program had three basic components. First, in order to avoid problems of past programs, a review of the literature was conducted and a series of attitude surveys was designed to assess resident attitudes toward police and police attitudes toward residents. Second, educational materials were developed based on the findings of the attitudinal surveys. Third, several individual and group action programs were developed and administered. Conclusions suggest that police-community relations programs cannot be effectively administered by law enforcement agencies. Success in this type of program usually includes: research, problem identification, skill training, minority recruitment, citizens' complaint mechanism, and a civilian education program.

Eisinger, Peter K. "The Patterns of Citizen Contacts With Urban Officials." In PEOPLE AND POLITICS IN URBAN SOCIETY, edited by Harlan Hahn, pp. 43-69. Beverly Hills, Calif.: Sage Publications, 1972.

Direct contacts initiated by citizens toward people in government agencies are one way individuals express their policy preferences. These citizen efforts are often difficult and frustrating. Blacks and whites were surveyed in Milwaukee in 1970 to ascertain the basic patterns of contact. Five dimensions of contact are identified: the nature of the contact, the content of the contact, the referent for whom the contact is made, the level of government at which the contact is made, and the target at whom the contact is directed. Contactors provide public officials with one indication of what activist citizens are thinking. Individuals who use contacts as a form of representation are likely to be middle-class whites, active in politics.

Fainstein, Norman, and Fainstein, Susan. "Innovation in Urban Bureaucracies." AMERICAN BEHAVIORAL SCIENTIST 15 (March-April 1972): 511-31.

Institutions such as the schools, welfare system, and health agencies have become centers of much controversy. No longer are the street-level bureaucrats accepted by their clients. Rather, they are the object of both verbal and physical abuse. Using a public school as a case study, the authors conclude that increased citizen aware-ness and action require that bureaucrats begin to change their mode of behavior. Specific mechanisms that inhibit innovation in public service bureaucracies, recruitment of civil service personnel with high-risk avoidance, and socialization of new recruits by agents with little interest in change are discussed.

Goldstein, Herman. "Police Response to Urban Crisis." PUBLIC ADMINISTRA-TION REVIEW 28 (September-October 1968): 417-23.

Police departments which have traditionally concerned themselves with controlling crime are now being asked to deal with civil disorders and community conflict. A conflict arises over which approach to take with these new functions. Some argue that the police should become more sensitive to the needs of the community while others suggest treating these activities with increased force. Police officers function in two worlds: crime prevention and abate-ment, and processing criminals who violate the law. Most of their time is spent in the former. The author discusses the changing de-mands and relationships of police work and reviews several recent surveys. The response of local police departments in several cities is discussed. Police administrators will have to broaden their out-look on the changes needed and in terms of not just new programs, but new recruitment, training, and reward systems.

Goudy, Willis J., and Richards, Robert O. "Citizens, Bureaucrats, and Legiti-mate Authority: Some Unanticipated Consequences Within the Administration of Social Action Programs." MIDWEST REVIEW OF PUBLIC ADMINISTRATION 8 (July 1974): 191-202.

An investigation of a social action program, the Model Cities pro-gram, identified three administrative variables as crucial between citizen boards and professional staff. These were: evaluation of the success of the program; actual and ideal power relationships, and the degree to which each group represents the public interests of the community. Data collected indicate that disagreement is evident in attitudes reflecting the legitimation of authority through the relative degree to which citizens' boards and professional staff represent the public interest. Citizen participation therefore is a new and important variable in social action programs.

Hoshino, George. "Separating Maintenance From Social Service." PUBLIC WELFARE 30 (Spring 1972): 54-61.

Discussion focuses on separating financial aid from social services and the related problem of claimants completing declarations of eligibility for assistance. The major issues discussed are: ideological, legal, political, economic, organizational, and administrative. Questions of agency programs and policies are discussed as are the policy implications of separating financial aid from services. Resistance to organizational change will be strong and some workers will find their positions downgraded. However, separating finances from social services can prove to be an important step toward achieving the goal of a workable public welfare system.

Kovak, Richard M. "Urban Renewal Controversies." PUBLIC ADMINISTRATION REVIEW 32 (May-June 1972): 359-72.

By identifying a single relationship in most urban renewal projects, the author isolates those factors leading to success or failure of protest groups and offers some suggestions to help alleviate the conflict in urban renewal. The major actors involved in urban renewal protests are the city government, the local renewal agency, and the protest groups. The integration capabilities of the administrative agency and dissent emanating from the lower-income classes are tantamount to political protest in urban renewal projects. After reviewing many studies of urban renewal programs by analyzing community organizational structure, community identity, community leadership, informational deficiencies, impact of the political environment, and class values, the author concludes much more research must be done on local renewal agencies and the value orientation of the community.

Lipsky, Michael. "Street-Level Bureaucracy and the Analysis of Urban Reform." URBAN AFFAIRS QUARTERLY 6 (June 1971): 391-409.

Policemen, teachers, and welfare workers are being criticized by clients for their insensitivity, incompetence, and their racist attitudes. Bureaucrats deny these charges, arguing for more resources with which to perform their jobs. The author views this as a major problem in urban political life and believes there is some validity to both arguments. Many of the conflicts between citizens and bureaucrats are the result of inadequate resources, challenges to authority, and contradictory or ambiguous job expectations. Several implications for public policy emerge from the analysis of street-level bureaucrats' reactions to specific work conditions. Many of these relate to more and better training, greater awareness of client problems, and more decentralization.

_____. "Toward a Theory of Street-Level Bureaucracy." In THEORETICAL PERSPECTIVES ON URBAN POLITICS, edited by Willis D. Hawley et al., pp. 196-213. Englewood Cliffs, N.J.: Prentice-Hall, 1975.

Street-level bureaucrats are public employees who in their face-to-face interactions with citizens represent the government to the people. This article attempts to develop a theory of the political behavior of street-level bureaucrats by examining the aspects or organizational life common to various urban bureaucracies. Street-level bureaucrats are teachers, policemen, welfare workers, and lower-court judges. Certain conditions are discussed which are salient among street-level bureaucrats. These are inadequate resources, threats and challenges to their authority, and ambiguous or contradictory expectations about job performance. Street-level bureaucrats develop mechanisms to cope with the three problems examined. Stereotypes of both street-level bureaucrats and their clientele help to exacerbate urban conflict. Under these conditions it may be impossible for street-level bureaucracies as currently organized, to respond to the demands for improved and more sympathetic service for their clients.

Litwak, Eugene. "An Approach to Linkage in 'Grass Roots' Community Organization." In STRATEGIES OF COMMUNITY ORGANIZATION: A BOOK OF READINGS, edited by Fred M. Cox et al., pp. 126-38. Itasca, Ill.: F.E. Peacock, 1970.

Outlines a theory of relationships between professionals and community groups and indicates how the theory might be used to guide social work practice. Grass roots organizations are families, neighbors, and informed groups of clients who are related to professionals in public service organizations. Three bodies of literature are reviewed. They are: what can client groups and bureaucratic organizations best do; what linkage mechanisms exist to connect these groups; and what organizational structures limit the kinds of linkages which can operate out of a social service agency? Three theories of social work depicting relationships between clients and professionals are discussed: office-bound, community-bound, and balanced. Several tables depicting different client types, linking mechanisms, and organizational structure are offered.

Main, Eleanor C.; Bowman, Lewis; and Peters, B. Guy. "Model Cities Workers' Perceptions of Clients." URBAN AFFAIRS QUARTERLY 7 (March 1972): 309-13.

Most social service agencies depend upon their employees' perceptions of their clients to determine whether to accept them and to ascertain what types of services should be provided to them. This study analyzes the correlation of social service workers' perceptions of their clients. The findings indicate that private agency employees, nonprofessionals, and blacks are more likely to describe their clients in terms of positive attitudinal characteristics. Public agency employees, professionals, and whites are more likely to emphasize demographic terms and negative attitudinal characteristics. The study is based on over 200 interviews in 24 social service agencies funded by the Atlanta Model Cities Program.

Piven, Frances Fox, and Cloward, Richard A. "Reaffirming the Regulation of the Poor." SOCIAL SERVICE REVIEW 48 (June 1974): 147-69.

The authors reaffirm their belief in the need for a humanitarian approach in relief agencies. The expansion of relief policies is designed to quell urban civil disorders, while restrictive rules and regulations help to reinforce work norms. The expansion of the relief roles is a response to economic, demographic, and political changes in society and is not attributable to the work of organizers and agitators. Public officials respond to the plight of the poor because they wish to maintain a stable social order and retain their own power.

_____. "Rent Strike: Disrupting the Slum System." NEW REPUBLIC 157 (2 December 1967): 11-15.

Rent strikes are viewed as a new strategy for breaking up the collusion that exists between agencies of government and slum lords. Successful rent strikes pressure agencies into enforcing housing code violations. If a landlord fails to correct the violations in the allotted time, the city agency would be forced to take over his/her building. Legislation coupled with resources should permit either the landlord or the city agency to manage the property and still make a profit. Tax benefits, low-cost loans, and rent supplements are some of the resources available from the federal government to help improve housing facilities. If cities decline to operate these buildings, it may be necessary to establish nationwide corporations to do so.

Reiss, Albert J., Jr. "Servers and Served in Service." In FINANCING THE METROPOLIS: PUBLIC POLICY IN URBAN ECONOMIES, edited by John P. Crecine, pp. 561-76. Beverly Hills, Calif.: Sage Publications, 1970.

The big issue in the 1970s in urban America will revolve around citizen or bureaucratic control of programs. In other words, who is going to provide the services and can the providers meet the needs of those to be served? Local communities will become the major areas of conflict and they in turn will find many conflicting interests within their boundaries. Citizen groups are becoming increasingly concerned about how their demands for services are recognized, how resources are allocated to them, and the types of services they receive. The ability of bureaucrats to control these decisions is called "discretionary justice." The author examines some of these major issues: citizen demands for service, client-centered systems, civic accountability of public employees, external accountability of public agencies, and internal accountability. The closest system in use today to satisfy and resolve these conflicts is the office of ombudsman.

Salber, Eva. "Community Participation in Neighborhood Health Centers." NEW

ENGLAND JOURNAL OF MEDICINE 283 (3 September 1970): 515-18.

There was very little agreement on what maximum-feasible-participation of the poor would mean. The civil rights movement and the growing discontent with welfare policy provided the impetus for community involvement in programs. Health programs have been slow to acknowledge the importance of citizen involvement and usually have tried to establish citizen advisory boards that were far removed from the actual needs of the community. The goal should be informed residents and concerned professionals sharing power and decision making. Developing this partnership involves many problems including a lack of communication between professionals and consumers and traditional hostilities and frustrations. First steps will have to include meeting of all interested parties to establish procedures for grievances, hiring, firing, policy, service, and training in the health centers.

Schmidt, Stuart M., and Kochan, Thomas A. "An Application of a 'Political Economy' Approach to Effectiveness." ADMINISTRATION AND SOCIETY 7 (February 1976): 455-73.

This article uses a political economy effectiveness model for analyzing the relationships between public sector agencies and their clients. Agency effectiveness is the dependent variable, the delivery agency characteristics are the intervening variable, and public policy is the independent variable. The delivery agencies analyzed are the state district offices of the U.S. Training and Employment Service. The author presents the model and then discusses it with respect to manpower policy, goal orientation, district office effectiveness, district office power and tactics, client factors, and environmental factors. Employers appear to interact with the employment service only when it is in their self-interest or when the district office can compel them to do so. Changing agency goals and internal structure will not change the motivation of external actors to comply with these changes.

Taebel, Delbert A. "Strategies To Make Bureaucrats Responsive." SOCIAL WORK 17 (November 1972): 38-43.

Political activity has been increasing steadily since the early 1960s. Citizen groups are now seeking an active role in decision making and no longer want the governmental agencies to monopolize policy making. The increased political and social awareness of citizens has placed a great deal of pressure on the bureaucracy. Taebel states the strategies used by many of our bureaucrats are unworkable and offers some alternative strategies to cope with the increased activism in American society. These new strategies will alter the political system but they also recognize the needs of organizations within the system.

Thompson, Frank J. "Sources of Responsiveness By a Government Monopoly: The Case of a People Processor." ADMINISTRATION AND SOCIETY 7 (February 1976): 387-418.

Many observers have concluded that government agencies which are essential monopolies have captive outlets for their product and provide a service which is critical to the well-being of the clients. These agencies tend to concern themselves with the interests of their own employees and are not very responsive to clients. This article analyzes the Oakland, California civil service office and draws generalizations about people processors which are essential monopolies in three areas: the conditions under which these agencies try to be responsive to clients, how attempts to please clients can backfire, and how client assertiveness can impact responsiveness to market units. The author suggests that under certain circumstances people processors which are essential monopolies try to be responsive to their clients. However, it is important to distinguish between responsiveness attempts and responsiveness.

C. SPECIFIC SERVICES

Berry, Brian. RACE AND HOUSING: THE CHICAGO EXPERIENCE 1960-1975. Cambridge, Mass.: Ballinger, 1976. 448 p.

This book focuses on a series of HUD-financed, experimental, fair housing programs in Chicago between 1967 and 1972. Each of the programs is outlined as well as the reasons for the program's inability to reach its stated goals. The author examines both black and white attitudes toward integration and considers questions relating to the operation of the metropolitan housing market. These issues are then analyzed in light of social-psychological and community issues and the dilemmas of open housing experiments.

Bingham, Richard D., and Kirkpatrick, Samuel A. "Providing Social Services to the Urban Poor: An Analysis of Public Housing Authorities in Large American Cities." SOCIAL SERVICE REVIEW 49 (March 1975): 64-78.

Social science research has been focusing on the total social environment of the poor. Public housing officials, however, have paid attention mainly to development, rent collection, and management efficiency. A questionnaire was mailed to seventy community service directors of all public housing authorities in cities having more than 2,000 public housing units in November 1971. The returns indicate that medical, legal, and financial counseling are regularly provided as are a wide variety of recreational and social activities. However, most cultural and fine arts activities are limited as are necessary transportation facilities.

Bloch, Peter B. EQUALITY OF DISTRIBUTION OF POLICE SERVICES: A CASE

STUDY OF WASHINGTON, D.C. Washington, D.C.: Urban Institute, 1974. 27 p.

> This study compares the equality of police services in two areas of Washington, D.C. The study was prompted by a lawsuit filed by a black community in Washington alleging an inequality in the distribution of police services. The author concludes the allegation cannot be supported either on the amount of police services or their effectiveness in dealing with crime. The comparative measures include property crime rates and trends, violent crime rates, citizen satisfaction, service calls per officer, police per 100 robberies, average police per 10,000 residents, number of service requests per police car, and daily average police per square mile. This study can be implemented in other cities.

Brouillette, John R. "The Department of Public Works: Adaptation to Disaster Demands." AMERICAN BEHAVIORAL SCIENTIST 13 (January-February 1970): 369-79.

> This article begins with a description of the public works departments in large cities, pointing out several common characteristics: large bureaucracy, abundance of resources, highly trained personnel, and a well-developed communications system. The major tasks of the public works department are listed and those which place special demands on the department during a crisis are discussed. These include: keeping the streets open, insuring the distribution of water to the community, and maintaining the sewer system in working order. There are four types of emergencies which might produce demands for changes in either the tasks or structure of public works organizations. They are: normal periods, anticipated periodic emergencies, unanticipated disasters, and unanticipated disasters of a serious magnitude.

Cervantes, Robert A. "The Failure of Comprehensive Health Services to the Urban Chicano." HEALTH SERVICES REPORTS 87 (December 1972): 932-40.

> Public health services are not effectively reaching Chicanos because public health officials view the Chicano community as a homogeneous rural minority instead of a complex and diverse group of people. Most of the Chicanos requiring health services live in our urban areas. Stereotyped thinking about Chicanos on the part of white public officials is one of the major problems. To increase the effectiveness of the public health programs, health agencies should employ bilingual, bicultural community health workers and advertise services in two languages. Services should be delivered in churches, shopping centers, and mobile units and should be available on weekends and in the evenings. Additional tax dollars are less important than a change in attitudes on the part of health officials.

Clawson, Calvin. "A Theoretical Approach to the Allocation of Police Preventive Control." POLICE CHIEF 60 (July 1973): 53-59.

Demonstrates the possibility of applying concepts of operations research to the complex problems involved in law enforcement. The
technique presented focuses on the problem of allocating patrol resources of a police agency for the suppression of crime. Obtaining
the optimum level of crime prevention is the goal of the allocation
technique. A graphic presentation outlines the characteristics of
the goal. The suggested solution is arrived at mathematically by
determining the optimum allocation of patrol forces by time and by
geographical area.

COMMUNITY HEALTH SERVICES FOR NEW YORK CITY: REPORT AND STAFF
STUDIES OF THE COMMISSION ON THE DELIVERY OF PERSONAL HEALTH
SERVICES. New York: Frederick A. Praeger, 1969. 696 p.

This is a report resulting from an investigation of health services in
New York City. It includes an analysis of services rendered by
public agencies and services delivered through voluntary and private
institutions. It also presents a model of the application of systems
analysis to problems of health services in a metropolitan area.
Topics covered are: population characteristics and potential of
municipal hospitals; medical manpower problems; the impact of
city, state, and federal funding; and the functions and roles of
city executive agencies in relation to health care services. Existing resources are reviewed and related to sources of new funds and
technological advances in the medical and data-processing field.
Recommendations are offered and can be utilized by other cities in
analyzing their own health care programs.

Davis, James V. "Decentralization, Citizen Participation and Ghetto Health
Care." AMERICAN BEHAVIORAL SCIENTIST 15 (September-October 1971):
94-107.

Medical care available to ghetto residents is much worse than that
available to middle-income communities. Suggestions are made for
decentralizing health care facilities and greater citizen participation
in the planning and administration of these facilities. These suggestions are seen as temporary since health care quality is related to
socioeconomic status. The problems of decentralization in health
care are viewed as higher costs, separate and unequal practices,
and the shortage of doctors in ghetto areas. The movement for increased participation by citizens is seen as superficial and confusing
because of a lack of precision in understanding the term.

Dirasian, Henry A. "Water Quality: The State of the Art." URBAN AFFAIRS
QUARTERLY 6 (December 1970): 199-212.

Focuses on the problem of treating liquid and solid wastes. Describes the conventional processes of eliminating these wastes from
our waterways as well as some recent technological advances. Local
jurisdictions are urged to recognize the seriousness of the problem

and particularly the archaic means by which they are dealing with the problem. Waterway treatment is not a technological problem. Rather, it is one of reordering priorities to meet needs. Strong federal leadership is required or else it will be difficult to overcome the fragmented efforts historically associated with environmental issues.

Duhl, Leonard J. "A New Look at the Health Issue." In METROPOLITANIZATION AND PUBLIC SERVICES, edited by Lowdon Wingo, pp. 43-55. Baltimore: Johns Hopkins University Press, 1972.

There is a growing movement in the country to reform the health services delivery system and eliminate much of the fragmentation and disorganization that exists. The source of the discontent is in most cases the neighborhood health clinics. The author believes a new multilevel delivery system will emerge in which neighborhoods, cities, and metropolitan areas will be organized to better deliver services. The lowest level will be the neighborhood comprised of volunteers who will send representatives to the next level, the city. The third level will be a metropolitan authority. Federal funding will be directed to each level which will have jurisdiction over program implementation congruent with federal guidelines and regulations. The article concludes with a discussion of the operation of the mental health program in California.

Fisk, Donald M., and Lancer, Cynthia A. EQUALITY OF DISTRIBUTION OF RECREATION SERVICES: A CASE STUDY OF WASHINGTON, D.C. Washington, D.C.: Urban Institute, 1974. 46 p.

Focusing on a lawsuit charging discrimination against blacks in one section of Washington, the authors seek to determine if predominantly black communities are receiving inferior public recreation services. The technique developed can be used to measure inequality in recreation services in other communities. The study advances several measurement criteria including capital expenditures, operating expenditures, quantity and quality of opportunities, and utilization. The authors conclude that in Washington, D.C., the determination of equity in distribution of recreation services depends upon the measures chosen for comparison.

Gittell, Marilyn. "Professionalism and Public Participation in Education Policy-Making: New York City, a Case Study." In URBAN POLITICS AND PUBLIC POLICY: THE CITY IN CRISIS, edited by Stephen M. David and Paul E. Peterson, pp. 197-217. New York: Praeger, 1973.

The New York City school system is an independent unit without independent taxing power. In 1964, a study by the state legislature concluded that over the past two decades the educational policy-making process had become insulated from public controls.

The contributing factors were found to be bureaucratization and professionalism. Professionalism has been accepted as the major concept in making competent decisions about educational policy. The mayor had taken a position of noninvolvement. The result has been narrow or closed participation in many areas of decision making. Only three or four issues show evidence of any outside influence on educational policy.

Hahn, Harlan. "Local Variations in Urban Law Enforcement." In RACE, CHANGE AND URBAN SOCIETY, edited by Peter Orleans and William Russell Ellis, Jr., pp. 373-400. Beverly Hills, Calif.: Sage Publications, 1971.

Decentralization has become a fundamental issue in the field of urban affairs. Disparities in the law and in the administration of law have created unequal standards as well as enforcement strategies across the country. The author examines the impact of community differences upon the performance of four basic police functions: protection, order, authority, and service. He also discusses inter-city and intracity differences in police operations. Variations in local police departments are found in recruitment practices, the socialization process, discretionary authority, absence of detailed guidelines, relations between police executives and civilian politi-cal leadership, and the movement toward police professionalism. The author concludes that there is a need for increased public sup-port of the police, equalization of police practices, and a resolu-tion of the inherent conflict between the policies of professionaliza-tion and decentralization.

Hillman, Bruce, and Charney, Evan. "A Neighborhood Health Center: What the Patients Know and Think of Its Operation." MEDICAL CARE 10 (July-August 1972): 336-44.

This is a study of an OEO-funded neighborhood health center in Rochester, New York. Examined are the patterns of development of the center and the general attitudes of the patients. The data supports the idea that a significant majority of the patients are very enthusiastic about the services offered in the center. The most important issues in determining patient satisfaction appear to be availability of quality health care and a positive and friendly atti-tude on the part of the health center staff. The question of com-munity control is not as important in determining satisfaction with neighborhood health centers.

Holtman, A.G.; Tabasz, T.; and Kruse, W. "The Demand for Local Public Services, Spillovers and Urban Decay: The Case of Public Libraries." PUBLIC FINANCE QUARTERLY 4 (January 1976): 97-113.

The problems of public libraries are examined in several middle-size urban areas in New York State. Evidence indicates that the burden placed upon central city libraries by nonresidents is substantial. Many educated people who have moved to suburbia no longer pay taxes to support the central city libraries but they continue to make extensive use of them. The projection is for this demand to increase while the central city ability to support the libraries will decrease. Changes will have to be made in current library financing techniques and public officials will have to begin promoting the consolidation of library districts.

Isler, Morton; Sadacca, Robert; and Drury, Margaret. KEYS TO SUCCESSFUL HOUSING MANAGEMENT. Washington, D.C.: Urban Institute, 1974. 70 p.

Research has established that the type of ownership is not the major variable in the quality of management. In each type of multifamily housing--cooperative, nonprofit, and limited-dividend projects-- there are project high-, low-, and medium-performance categories. Certain variables are identified which are related to successful housing management. These variables are: maintenance of physical conditions, tenant satisfaction with services and management, and reasonable costs of maintenance. Where tenant concern and responsiveness by management are found together, successful management often follows. The data are drawn from surveys and analyses of sixty multifamily projects.

Kirby, Ronald F., and Bhatt, Kiran U. GUIDELINES ON THE OPERATION OF SUBSCRIPTION BUS SERVICES. Washington, D.C.: Urban Institute, 1975. 76 p.

This study examines the planning, organization, and administration of subscription bus services which serve urban riders who agree to use the service on a regular basis. Using ten case studies, the authors develop guidelines for identifying and informing potential riders; buying vehicles; hiring drivers; meeting regulatory requirements; establishing fares, routes, and schedules; and arranging for express lanes and close-in parking. Also analyzed is the impact of the subscription bus service on congestion, pollution, fuel consumption, and residential location decisions.

Lett, Monica. RENT CONTROL: CONCEPTS, REALITIES AND MECHANISMS. New Brunswick, N.J.: Center for Urban Policy Research, 1976. 300 p.

The author presents an analysis of the conceptual issues, historical background, advantages and disadvantages, and economic consequence of rent control legislation. The question of rent control is examined from the standpoint of housing shortages, inflationary impact, and methods of regulation applicable to different local housing conditions. Data is presented from Boston, New York, and Fort Lee, New Jersey as well as data from one hundred other jurisdictions to give the reader a comprehensive view of rent control mechanisms. Also included is a discussion of the problems encountered in implementing legislation and administering a rent control program.

Lyday, James M. "An Advocate's Process Outline for Policy Analysis: The Case of Welfare Reform." URBAN AFFAIRS QUARTERLY 7 (June 1972): 385-402.

A guide for policy analysis which consists of nine steps through which policy outcomes might be improved. The outline focuses on the problem of welfare reform. The steps recommended are: specify the social performance sought; examine relevant statistical data; project the costs and benefits of existing and alternative policies several years into the future; improve the data base and experiment with program alternatives; draft legislation; design the rules of administration; assess the results of alternatives; evaluate program effectiveness; and modify legislation based on evaluation. Problems inherent in the model are also discussed.

Miller, Alfred E. "Remodeling the Municipal Health Services For a Unified System of Ambulatory Medical Care in the Central City." MEDICAL CARE 10 (September-October 1972): 395-401.

The problems of health care delivery in inner-city poverty areas are examined in order to develop a new model of municipal health services. History of the present health care system is presented. The new model of an integrated municipal health services delivery system requires the following action: assess existing health care facilities, upgrade preventive clinics to full adequate treatment clinics, improve relationship with the target population by judicious use of community health workers, and decentralize facilities to distribute the patient load widely. The system becomes unified with the establishment of a professional and effective management system.

Miller, Walter B. "Ideology and Criminal Justice Policy: Some Current Issues." JOURNAL OF CRIMINAL LAW AND CRIMINOLOGY 64 (June 1973): 141-62.

The author reviews ideological positions of the left and the right with respect to crime; assuming that ideologies influence the policies and procedures of the criminal justice personnel. The positions of the left and the right are distributed along an ideological scale and examined in the following areas: sources of crime, methods of dealing with crime with respect to offenders and with respect to criminal justice agencies. Ideological positions of academic criminologists, police, legal and judicial professionals, and correction employees are characterized and the consequences of such ideologies are analyzed.

Ostrom, Elinor, et al. "Community Organization and the Provision of Police Services." SAGE PROFESSIONAL PAPERS. Beverly Hills, Calif.: Sage Publications, 1973. 95 p.

The study seeks to determine if smaller community police departments provide police services in a more effective manner than larger police departments. Three neighborhoods in Indianapolis and three adjacent neighborhoods outside the city limits were used in the study. The study focuses on the general relationship between community organization and output of police departments in the areas of victimization, assistance, evaluation of promptness, crime trends, potential for bribetaking, police-citizen relations, and a general evaluation of the job being done. The authors conclude there is a higher level of output in the smaller, suburban communities than in the neighborhoods within the Indianapolis police department's jurisdiction. The study refutes the belief that an increase in the size of jurisdiction will correspond with an increase in service levels and a decrease in per capita expenditures.

Peart, Leo E. "Management By Objectives: The Palo Alto Team Management/ Team Policing Concept." THE POLICE CHIEF 38 (April 1971): 54-56.

This new team policing concept denotes a complete break from the traditional chain of command organization. Three teams operate on eight-hour shifts. Operations and line personnel are divided among teams based upon crime and service call needs. This technique lends itself toward selective enforcement and gives officers a broad range of responsibilities. The system is based on the concept that all personnel have contributions to make in the policy-making and operational process. Team policing has improved morale, communication, and cooperation. There has been some resistance to change, a lack of role definition, and inadequate coordination between teams.

Quarantelli, E.L. "The Community General Hospital: Its Immediate Problems in Disasters." AMERICAN BEHAVIORAL SCIENTIST 13 (January-February 1970): 380-91.

The author presents an overview of general hospitals including the major functions they perform in treatment, rehabilitation, and prevention of illness and injury. Major disasters often do not impair the ability of the community hospital to function but they do increase the demands placed upon hospitals in both a quantitative and a qualitative sense. Disaster plans are developed by many public hospitals to cope with a range of potential emergency situations. These plans range from voluminous documents to one-page outlines and are frequently incomplete or too specific on the topics covered. The key factors in public hospitals being able to meet demands placed upon them in emergencies are categorized under mobilization, information processing, task assignment, decision making, and interorganizational relationships.

Shreiber, Chanoch, and Sirousse, Tabriztchi. "Rent Control in New York City: A Proposal to Improve Resource Allocation." URBAN AFFAIRS QUARTERLY 11 (June 1976): 511-22.

Abolition of rent control would force those tenants whose subjective rental value is less than the current market value to vacate their apartments. This would help solve the efficiency problem by utilizing available resources more productively, but it would also change the distribution of wealth by enriching landlords at the expense of the current and future tenants. One possible solution would be to make the right of statutory tenants marketable by having tenants with low rents sell their rights to others. Another option would be to allow tenants to sell at any time with the proceeds being divided between the tenant and the landlord and granting the landlord the right to outbid any market offer.

Stone, Clarence M. ECONOMIC GROWTH AND NEIGHBORHOOD DISCONTENT: SYSTEM BIAS IN THE URBAN RENEWAL PROGRAM OF ATLANTA. Chapel Hill: University of North Carolina Press, 1976. 256 p.

This is a twenty-year study of urban renewal politics in Atlanta which analyzes the growth and development of the central business district to the exclusion of low-income neighborhoods and residential areas. The major political actors involved in the conflict are low-income neighborhood groups, the business community, and the top public officials. The author argues that because the business leaders exercised a great deal of political influence, a certain amount of bias existed in the system, which prevented the community groups from winning any of the major political confrontations. He concludes that the alliance between business leaders and public officials weakens the preconceived notions we have of pluralist theory in a democratic society.

Veeder, Nancy W. "Health Services Utilization Models for Human Services Planning." JOURNAL OF THE AMERICAN INSTITUTE OF PLANNERS 41 (March 1975): 101-9.

Planners of urban service delivery systems have relied heavily on mathematical models to predict the behavior of potential clients for these services. The most widely used example of this in planning has been the transportation model. Models of health services utilization currently are sensitive to psychological states, social pressures, motivations, and institutional barriers to service utilization. Health services utilization models could be extended to services such as housing, recreation, employment, and education. Social science modeling may help planners expand their understanding in a wide range of human service delivery systems.

Warheit, George J. "Fire Departments During Major Community Emergencies." AMERICAN BEHAVIORAL SCIENTIST 13 (January-February 1970): 362-68.

Fire departments are among the oldest emergency organizations in urban areas, dating back to 1736. There are four major types of fire departments in operation today: departments with only paid employees, departments with most employees paid, departments with a majority of volunteers, and departments with all volunteers. Fire departments are organized, equipped, and manned to respond, to events which jeopardize human life and property. How well they perform during disasters depends upon the nature of the precipitating event, the magnitude and duration of the emergency, the departmental resources, and the availability of other community and extracommunity resources. The major problems encountered by fire departments in responding to disaster are classified as interorganizational, intraorganizational, and supraorganizational.

Webb, Walter L., and Anderson, Eric A. "Unified Public Safety Operations." In MANAGEMENT INFORMATION SERVICES. Washington, D.C.: International City Management Association, April 1972. 16 p.

Increased costs of police and fire protection coupled with growing crime and fire rates have encouraged local governments to experiment with new ideas in public safety. Approaches range from full-scale consolidation of police and fire functions to limited coordination. Urban managers thinking about consolidation are urged to analyze their communities with attention to geographic, political, and socioeconomic characteristics affecting these services as well as the attitudes and opinions of police officers, firemen, and the public. The experiences of several cities are reviewed as are the factors of effective leadership and adequate training in successful consolidation programs. A model ordinance is also presented.

Wilson, James Q. VARIETIES OF POLICE BEHAVIOR: THE MANAGEMENT OF LAW AND ORDER IN EIGHT COMMUNITIES. Cambridge, Mass.: Harvard University Press, 1968. 309 p.

Examines eight randomly selected communities and analyzes how police behave with respect to the most frequently applied laws, problems facing the police administrator, different performance levels of policemen in different cities, and how much the differences are accounted for by explicit community decisions. Police administrators are engaged in maintaining order, enforcing laws, and providing service functions. Administrators are caught in a bind between legitimate complaints of citizens and the application of disciplinary action where no clear standards exist. The author identifies three styles of police operation: the watchman style which stresses order maintenance, the legalistic style which emphasizes law enforcement, and the service style which responds to both of the above but makes fewer arrests. Policemen appear able to cope with problems but cannot solve them.

Chapter 7

BUDGETING AND FINANCIAL MANAGEMENT

Bahl, Roy, and Vogt, Walter. FISCAL CENTRALIZATION AND TAX BURDENS: STATE AND REGIONAL FINANCE OF CITY SERVICES. Cambridge, Mass.: Ballinger, 1975. 192 p.

Using data from the Urban Observatory Project, the authors examine the equity consequences of having city government functions financed at the state and regional levels. The cities studied are Atlanta, Boston, Denver, Baltimore, San Diego, Nashville, Milwaukee, and both Kansas cities. The study indicates what would happen to individual tax expenditures of central city residents if state or regional governments began financing city services. The authors doubt that tax systems will become both progressive at higher levels and suggest that, depending upon the type of tax used for financing city services, the shift to state and regional financing might increase the regressive nature of the tax structure.

David, Miriam E. "Professionalism and Participation in School Budgeting in the USA." JOURNAL OF SOCIAL POLICY 5 (April 1976): 151-66.

School committees are responsible for deciding on elementary and secondary education: curricula, staffing, supplies and equipment, hiring, and salaries. Since the funds for the school system come from local government revenue, the system would appear to lend itself to citizen control. Research has shown the hegemony of educators in the determination of school decisions. This article is a study of two towns and two cities in Massachusetts. The author finds little evidence of citizen involvement. Budget changes were made primarily by the professional educators; the superintendent exerted control over the operating budget; and the teacher associations dominated the salary negotiations.

Gerard, Karen. "The Locally Inspired Fiscal Crisis." SOCIETY 13 (June 1976): 33-35.

The financial problems of New York City are exacerbated by both its sizeable commitment to municipal services in education, hospitals, and mass transit and by its high level of welfare. New York's spending is nearly three times the per capita average for the ten largest cities and is eight times larger than comparable outlays for all U.S. cities. In the past five years, New York has been severely hit by a loss of both population and jobs. This change was not anticipated and consequently it has had a dramatic impact on the city's revenue-raising capacity. In order to change this picture, the author recommends long-term financial restructuring and a closer examination of the support of municipal services.

Greene, Kenneth V.; Neenan, William B.; and Scott, Claudia D. FISCAL INTERACTIONS IN A METROPOLITAN AREA. Lexington, Mass.: Lexington Books, 1974. 256 p.

In any given metropolitan area, residents of one jurisdiction receive benefits not only from their own local governments but also from local governments that provide places to work, shop, or relax. The authors examine both benefit and tax flows to assess the net fiscal flows on central cities and suburbs. Using the Washington metropolitan area as a test case, the authors define the political problems of dealing with multiple jurisdictions and establish measurements and benefits for service costs. An alternative benefit measurement system is proposed which weighs indirect benefits to residents of a political jurisdiction.

Hirsch, Werner Z. URBAN ECONOMIC ANALYSIS. New York: McGraw-Hill, 1973. 450 p.

This book presents several new economic techniques for making decisions in cities. As a study in urban economics, Hirsch describes new analytical tools and shows how they can be applied to problems confronting urban administrators. The author uses techniques such as microeconomics and macroeconomics and public services economics and applies these to problems of land use, transportation, labor markets, reduced federal government spending in a city, fire and police protection, parks, culture, and the arts. Hirsch differentiates the traditional regional and national economic studies from those now required in urban areas. The final chapter on finance, regulation, and control focuses on pollution and public service unions by examining how a city can control these problem areas.

Jernberg, James E. "Financial Administration." In MANAGING THE MODERN CITY, edited by James M. Banovetz, pp. 347-76. Washington, D.C.: International City Management Association, 1971.

Financial administration in city government has undergone vast changes in the past few decades. Today the areas of purchasing, auditing, and accounting are under the direct control of professionals in the field. Local government administrators in assessing the public service needs of their constituents must also consider the

intergovernmental and metropolitan factors affecting their decisions.
The major focus of the chapter is on budget. Capital and operating
budgets are discussed in terms of planning, procedures, financing,
and decision making. PPBS and techniques for administering the
budget are examined. Financial administration is no longer concerned solely with accounting and auditing, but rather with budget
decision making and how the decisions can be implemented effectively.

Kimmel, Wayne A.; Dougan, William R.; and Hall, John R. MUNICIPAL
MANAGEMENT AND BUDGET METHODS: AN EVALUATION OF POLICY
RELATED RESEARCH. Washington, D.C.: Urban Institute, 1974. 150 p.

Local governments frequently adopt new management and budget
methods such as planning-programming-budgeting-systems (PPBS),
management by objectives, program and policy analysis, program
evaluation, and performance budgeting. The authors believe many
claims for these programs are exaggerated and the literature on
these subjects is descriptive, theoretical, anecdotal, or promotional.
Much of the literature is uncritical and little or no attempt is made
to assess the impact of some of these innovations. The authors reviewed over 1,000 documents on these management and budget practices and find very little writing on the application of these practices in local government. The report includes recommended readings, references, and bibliographies which local officials might want
to review before implementing any of these new techniques.

Liebert, Roland J. "Municipal Functions, Structure and Expenditures: A Re-
analysis of Recent Research." SOCIAL SCIENCE QUARTERLY 54 (March 1974):
765-78.

The author analyzes the literature relating public policy consequences
of different urban political systems and focuses on one major conse-
quence--municipal expenditures. Much literature has compared
urban expenditure outputs that were not comparable. This resulted
from failure to recognize differences in the assignment of governmental functions. The author calls this the functional scope of
city governments. This problem in intercity variance is illustrated
by using education and welfare examples to show that different
cities have different responsibilities in each of the two functional
areas. Municipal expenditures becomes a two-component variable
affected both by the degree of functional inclusiveness and the
level of municipal performance in providing service.

Masotti, Louis H. "Private/Public Partnerships: The Only Game in Town."
NATIONAL CIVIC REVIEW 64 (December 1975): 568-71.

Decentralization of traditional urban functions to suburbia and the
lessening of federal government attention to local problems has
placed a great strain on many local governments. Local govern-

ment tax bases and the economy have been adversely affected by the loss of industry and jobs. A positive response is seen in the coordinated efforts being mounted by state governments, minority leaders, business leaders, and local administrators to reverse the trend of urban core areas which are becoming unattractive and noncompetitive. New efforts undertaken include: larger lot size, large capital investment, enclosed malls, and multifunctional projects.

Meltsner, Arnold J. "Local Revenue: A Political Problem." In FINANCING THE METROPOLIS: PUBLIC POLICY IN URBAN ECONOMICS, edited by John P. Crecine, pp. 103-35. Beverly Hills, Calif.: Sage Publications, 1970.

Local officials believe they have insufficient resources to meet their problems. They are wary of increasing taxes on a hostile public and consequently look to the federal government for additional funds. The author accepts the fiscal crisis as a reality but views it more as a political problem than an economic one. To solve the fiscal crisis will require long-run redistributive policies by the federal government and short-term realistic policies by state and local governments. Assessing the public environment accurately is essential to building tax coalitions. One suggestion is to deliver services to citizens and have them pay for them as user charges. Some services will not lend themselves to this. Local governments should begin giving away those services it performs out of habit or for which there is not a great citizen demand. Several approaches are offered for maximizing local government revenues.

_____. THE POLITICS OF CITY REVENUE. Berkeley and Los Angeles: University of California Press, 1971. 320 p.

Focuses on the politics of city revenue in Oakland, California and the current dilemma of how a city should raise revenue. The cities suffer from a lack of political and economical leadership as much as from a lack of revenues. The city of Oakland is turning its taxing responsibility over to the state which produces consequences such as fewer and fewer resources available to the city. The author examines the behavior and orientation of the city manager, the council, and the departmental officials. While the manager and the council are concerned with revenues, the department heads are concerned with expenditures. Several suggestions are presented for city officials seeking to increase tax revenues but little will happen until there is strong leadership in city hall.

Mills, Edwin S. STUDIES IN THE STRUCTURE OF THE URBAN ECONOMY. Baltimore: Johns Hopkins Press, 1972. 151 p.

Cities have higher population densities than their surrounding jurisdictions. The size of cities is often determined by public and private decisions consisting of a trade off between low transportation and exchange costs on the one hand and diminishing returns to the ratio of nonland inputs to land inputs on the other. Several models are discussed showing how market forces affect employment and housing, forecasting growth, and the effects of zoning, taxation, and other public policies. A model is presented showing the effects of urban transportation costs on location decisions. Improvements in transportation may increase central-business-district employment slightly, and this, in turn, will reduce the urban area's density.

Scott, Claudia D. FORECASTING LOCAL GOVERNMENT SPENDING. Washington, D.C.: Urban Institute, 1972. 142 p.

Not many local governments make long-range budget forecasts that would predict gross fluctuations in revenues and expenditures. The author proposes a comprehensive technique for estimating expenditures which was tested in New Haven, Connecticut and proved more successful than existing methods. The model projects personnel and nonpersonnel expenditures of city departments for a five-year period and emphasizes spending estimates rather than revenue estimates. The model helps forecast expenditures under a variety of conditions including salary, services, and changing population levels. It offers local officials flexibility in forecasting while increasing the options available to decision makers.

Slavet, Joseph; Bradbury, Katharine L.; and Moss, Philip. FINANCING STATE-LOCAL SERVICES: A NEW STRATEGY FOR GREATER EQUITY. Lexington, Mass.: Lexington Books, 1975. 176 p.

Increasing urbanization has been characterized by greater urban fiscal problems and debates over tax disparities among long governments. The authors suggest these problems can be eased by having the state assume the administration and financing of certain urban services. Using Boston for their data, the authors select transportation, county courts, corrections, health and hospital services, air pollution services, and other services for transfer to state responsibility. Using four criteria, the authors analyze cost, quantity, and quality of public services to cities and assess the impact on state government of shifting these services to them.

Weicher, John C. "The Effect of Metropolitan Political Fragmentation on Central City Budgets." In MODELS OF URBAN STRUCTURE, edited by David C. Sweet, pp. 177-203. Lexington, Mass.: Lexington Books, 1973.

A model is presented which investigates the effect of suburbanization and metropolitan fragmentation on the fiscal capacities of local governments within the metropolitan area. The model assumes that citizens and business organizations require different services from government and this affects the amount spent on these services. Cities appear to spend more on manufacturing business than they receive in revenues, but the reverse is true for retail stores. Cities also appear to exploit suburbanites. The conclusions are that fragmentation, suburbanization, and a loss of manufacturing businesses have not negatively affected central cities.

Weiss, Edmond H. "The Fallacy of Appellation in Government Budgeting." PUBLIC ADMINISTRATION REVIEW 34 (July–August 1974): 377–79.

Recent innovations in budgeting--program budgeting, cost-benefit analysis, and management by objectives--have pointed up a major problem in budgeting which might impede budgetary deliberation. By naming line item "expenditures" we allocate dollars for agency goals and programs. However, too often there is no distinction made between the name of a budget account and the scope and quantity of activities in the community. Dollars allocated for a service do not comprise the total activities for that service and, conversely, the allocation of funds is no guarantee that services will be performed well. If the goal of several new budgeting techniques is to open up the public debate over budget, then public officials must become mindful of the problems inherent in the naming of budget line-items.

Whitelaw, W. Ed. "The City, City Hall, and the Municipal Budget." In FINANCING THE METROPOLIS: PUBLIC POLICY IN URBAN ECONOMIES, edited by John P. Crecine, pp. 219–43. Beverly Hills, Calif.: Sage Publications, 1970.

The author begins with a review of major analytical descriptions of the municipal budgetary process that have appeared in the past twenty years. Federal-local relationships and developments are traced, highlighting some of the problems which have resulted. Also discussed are the constraints imposed by the federal government on local public officials as well as some of the intragovernmental constraints at the local level. Several concepts of the municipal budgetary process are in use which help provide a step toward a theory of municipal finance. Included are discussions of ability and/or willingness to pay for municipal services, capital outlays, current outlays, property tax revenues, and general policy.

Chapter 8

INTERGOVERNMENTAL IMPACTS

ON URBAN MANAGEMENT

Beaumont, Enid. "The New York Case from a Public Administration Perspective." BUREAUCRAT 5 (April 1976): 101-12.

Since World War II over two million middle-income residents have departed from New York City and have been replaced by people paying less in taxes and requiring more in services. Many federal programs encouraged this migration. Other programs funded by state and federal grants were supplemented by local funding which often continued after state and federal funding ceased. The state legislature approved city programs that should have been cut back or eliminated. Union pressure resulted in rapidly increasing wages. The Emergency Financial Control Board must lead the way to a balanced budget by fiscal year 1978, reduce short-term borrowing, remove operating expense items from the capital budget, and control spending growth.

Benson, George C.S. THE POLITICS OF URBANISM: THE NEW FEDERALISM. Woodbury, N.Y.: Barron's, 1972. 132 p.

Instead of increasing funds to cities to help solve urban problems, a new approach for channeling money should be implemented. States and cities often have been bypassed in federal policy making. Citizens have to be involved in decisions affecting their communities. States should create bureaus of urban affairs to help develop and coordinate statewide programs that affect cities. Local governments have to learn how to use federal money better and develop better administrative structures. Many functions that are currently the responsibility of cities will be augmented by block grants and revenue sharing. Coordination of program planning on all three levels will be essential to combatting poverty.

Browne, Edmond, Jr., and Rehfuss, John. "Policy Evaluation, Citizen Participation, and Revenue Sharing in Aurora, Illinois." PUBLIC ADMINISTRATION REVIEW 35 (March–April 1975): 150-57.

Federal programs often cause unintended or unanticipated consequences in local government. This article examines the impact of the revenue-sharing program on the application of policy analysis and new or additional forms of citizen participation. Aurora created a revenue-sharing committee shortly after the passage of the act. The political conflict surrounding its inception and the procedures it uses are discussed. The committee has opened up access to decision making, increased cooperation between the local government and community agencies, and increased expenditures for social services and health programs. The policy evaluation program has been strengthened because there is increased accountability, more useful information, improved information, and management control systems, and a better-informed citizenry and public service as to the value of policy evaluation.

Bryce, Herrington J. "Problems of Policy Management and Implementation by Local Government: A Minority Perspective." PUBLIC ADMINISTRATION REVIEW 35 (December 1975): 812-18.

The federal government has played a major role in how state and local governments deal with their citizens, particularly minority groups. It is even more important now for the federal government to remain involved because power is being devolved to local governments which have been hostile to minority interests, unemployment, affirmative action, and inflation. This requires national supervision for equity, and disenchantment with public institutions is particularly acute in the willingness of local governments to deliver services to minorities. The author reviews the socioeconomic situation of different black communities and discusses factors such as: size, location, infra-structure, human resources, economic base, availability of data, expectations, and regional and intergovernmental cooperation. Recommendations are offered for each of the issues discussed.

Burgess, Philip M. "Capacity Building and the Elements of Public Management." PUBLIC ADMINISTRATION REVIEW 35 (December 1975): 705-16.

Recent shifts in intergovernmental relations have been caused by New Federalism programs such as revenue sharing, block grants, federal reorganization, decentralization, regionalism, and the simplification of the federal administrative role. An important component of these programs is capacity building at the local level so these governments can successfully manage the new programs. Three components of public management are isolated-policy management, resource management, and program management. Policy management involves the strategic functions of guidance and leadership. Resource management is the capacity to carry out support functions and routine management tasks. Program management concerns the tactical functions of executing policies. Three examples are used to illustrate the concept of capacity building. They are: developmental, analytical, and empirical.

Capoccia, Victor A. "Chief Executive Review and Comment: A Preview of New Federalism in Rochester, New York." PUBLIC ADMINISTRATION REVIEW 34 (September-October 1974): 462-70.

> This is a case study of one aspect of New Federalism, Chief Executive Review and Comment (CERC), which was implemented in Rochester, New York in 1972. The author discusses and analyzes the structural and procedural components of the program such as the Office of Federal Program Review, the staff review process, the citizen participation mechanism, and the intergovernmental task force. Relationships with the state and the Federal Regional Councils are also discussed. The author draws several generalizations from the Rochester experience concerning the relationship between formal and informal procedures, CERC as a true test of New Federalism, and the need for better planning in the transition period between categorical and noncategorical aid.

Caputo, David A., and Cole, Richard L. "General Revenue Sharing Expenditure Decisions in Cities Over 50,000." PUBLIC ADMINISTRATION REVIEW 35 (March-April 1975): 136-42.

> This study summarizes the findings of a questionnaire sent to the chief administrative officers in all cities over 50,000. The purpose of the survey was to determine what types of decisions were made about general revenue sharing and what opinions and attitudes these decision makers held about the program. This data was supplemented by other published reports. The findings indicate that revenue-sharing funds are being spent most in the areas of law enforcement, fire protection, environmental protection, street and road repair, and recreation and parks. Existing programs are receiving revenue-sharing funds as opposed to new programs. Few cities are designating specialized staff personnel to administer revenue-sharing programs. Other conclusions drawn indicate social service programs have not received a high percentage of revenue-sharing funds, tax rates have not been greatly affected by the program, and local officials appear to be very supportive of the program.

_____. URBAN POLITICS AND DECENTRALIZATION. Lexington, Mass.: Lexington Books, 1974. 180 p.

> Examines the fiscal, legal, social, and political impact of the revenue-sharing bill passed in 1972. Data was collected in January 1973 and 1974 from chief executive officers in cities with populations over 50,000. The history of revenue sharing as well as some policy questions are examined. Few cities show significant changes in their allocation patterns as a result of revenue sharing. Most revenue-sharing funds are spent on ongoing city programs. Revenue-sharing funds have reduced or prevented increases in property tax levels. Suggestions for altering the program are advanced. Large central cities should be the recipients of additional funds based upon need. While not a panacea for urban problems, the authors

feel revenue sharing has stimulated interest in local politics and
increased the amount of citizen participation in urban decision
making.

Carroll, Michael A. "The Impact of General Revenue Sharing on the Urban
Planning Process--An Initial Assessment." PUBLIC ADMINISTRATION REVIEW
35 (March-April 1975): 143-50.

This is an assessment of the impact of the general revenue-sharing
program on the planning process in local government. The New
Federalism program was designed to decentralize responsibility and
authority to state and local governments by consolidating programs
through joint funding, increasing planning and management capabilities of local governments, and increasing local decision making
and accountability. Several reasons are cited, explaining why the
planning function in local government has not been greatly affected
by the revenue-sharing program. The author suggests how local
planning and management capacity can be improved to make better
use of revenue sharing and what changes are needed to be made in the
revenue-sharing programs in order to strengthen the role of urban
planning.

Colman, William G. "Recipient Unit Eligibility Criteria under a Federal Assistance Program to Strengthen State and Local Policy Management Capability."
PUBLIC ADMINISTRATION REVIEW 35 (December 1975): 798-803.

Presents an assessment of the major issues to be resolved in formulating and developing a federal assistance program for improving
policy and management capabilities of state and local governments.
The focus is on the eligibility to participate in such a program and
not on criteria for allocating funds. Seven eligibility issues are
discussed: type of local government, population size, range of
services provided, structure of government, tax base mix, fiscal
capacity and modernization, and management improvement progress.
The author concludes that there is a great deal of overlap in the
discussion of these issues and suggests that the federal government
might develop requirements that were tough, moderate, or soft, and
possibly combine criteria from all three.

Del Guidice, Dominic. "The City as a Full Partner." PUBLIC ADMINISTRA-
TION REVIEW 30 (May-June 1970): 287-93.

This study was conducted by the National Academy of Public Administration for the Department of Housing and Urban Development.
It assesses those factors which help and hinder the decision making
and administrative process in four HUD-financed programs affecting
local governments. The programs are: open-space grants, water
and sewer facilities grants, nonprofit housing, and turnkey housing
programs in Atlanta, Durham, Kansas City, Milwaukee, Seattle,
and Philadelphia. Recommendations were developed to improve

performance. Factors such as demography, intergovernmental relations, regional planning, finances, and private-sector involvement
were applied to the specific projects in formulating the recommendations.

Farkas, Suzanne. "The Federal Role in Urban Decentralization." AMERICAN
BEHAVIORAL SCIENTIST 15 (September–October 1971): 15–35.

Defines the term "urban decentralization" and shows how it is linked
to federal urban policy. Changes in local governmental structure
are not apt to occur unless there are corresponding changes in federal government policy making and organization. Simple panaceas
advocated for local government change will be impossible, since
these changes involve the shared powers and functions of many
actors on the federal, state, regional, metropolitan, urban, and
neighborhood levels.

Fox, Daniel M. "Federal Standards and Regulations for Participation." In
CITIZEN PARTICIPATION: EFFECTING COMMUNITY CHANGE, edited by
Edgar S. Cahn and Barry A. Passett, pp. 129–42. New York: Praeger, 1971.

Citizen participation can be traced back to the founding of this
country in the concept of the New England town meetings and the
writings of many of our early political philosophers. It is difficult
for the federal government to reach consensus on a particular set
of standards to regulate the process of citizen participation. Even
when this is accomplished, it is difficult to measure the impact of
this intervention because of many variables at the local level which
are likely to impact upon the process. The author discusses the
major assumptions which guided federal decisions to implement citizen
participation policies in the 1960s. These were: decentralization,
engineered consent, therapy, equal protection, employment, redistribution of power and resources, and constituency development.
The political climate had a major impact on the formulation of
participation policy. This was particularly true with respect to the
civil disorders in our cities. Once standards are developed there
is no guarantee that they will be implemented or implemented in
the manner suggested.

Frieden, Bernard J., and Kaplan, Marshall. THE POLITICS OF NEGLECT:
URBAN AID FROM MODEL CITIES TO REVENUE SHARING. Cambridge, Mass.:
M.I.T. Press, 1975. 281 p.

This book analyzes the development, administration, and eventual
decline of the Model Cities program. The authors suggest that the
failure of this program is not attributable to any one group, but
rather that it was the structure of the federal government agencies
which seriously impeded the coordinator role envisioned for the program. Failure to reorganize the involved federal agencies and consequently their relationships with city officials made the program

almost impossible to implement. The political struggles surrounding
the program and the necessary organizational reforms are discussed
as well as the congressional reaction to federal money flowing into
cities to be used at the discretion of mayors. The authors review
special and general revenue sharing which have replaced Model
Cities programs, but conclude that these programs are unlikely to
fill the gap created by the demise of the Model Cities program.
They conclude with suggestions for making better use of revenue
sharing.

Goetze, Rolf. BUILDING NEIGHBORHOOD CONFIDENCE: A HUMANISTIC
STRATEGY FOR URBAN HOUSING. Cambridge, Mass.: Ballinger, 1976.
128 p.

The reduction in federal subsidies has forced many cities to reevalu-
ate their policies toward neighborhoods. This book develops new
approaches for revitalizing neighborhoods and evaluates these strategies as they were applied in Boston. Focusing on neighborhood
dynamics, the author suggests that public officials who understand
how neighborhoods regenerate can often make use of the valuable
resources therein. The book shows expanded opportunities that are
available under the new community development block grants. This
study illustrates the pragmatic approach tried in Boston of building
neighborhood confidence rather than just rehabilitating buildings.

Harrison, Bennett. "Ghetto Employment and the Model Cities Program." JOUR-
NAL OF POLITICAL ECONOMY 32 (March-April 1974): 353-71.

During the 1960s, many programs were initiated by the federal
government to help the poor living in urban ghettos. This article
focuses on two major aspects of these programs: the type of services delivered, and the extent to which the poor--recipients of
these services--participated in the design and administration of the
programs. The author examines the Model Cities program--one of
the largest manpower programs operating in the urban areas--and
concludes that it failed because it did not achieve its major goal
of employing ghetto residents but rather it became a haven for
middle-class outsiders. Harrison concludes that future attempts at
decentralization may be just as unsuccessful as the Model Cities
program.

James, Judson L. "Federalism and the Model Cities Experiment." PUBLIUS 2
(Spring 1972): 69-94.

The Model Cities program was designed to improve the delivery of
government programs to the cities, increase decentralization and
citizen participation at the same time that it maintained national
goals and coordinated grant-in-aid programs. Several factors have
inhibited the achievement of these goals. Outside consultants,
inadequate staff communications, and competition from other orga-

nizations seeking grants have helped to stifle innovation. The goals of coordination and decentralization have not been achieved. Changing priorities, budget cutting, and a lack of enthusiasm on the part of Congress have contributed to a declining interest. Many new programs have abandoned the requirements for citizen participation and involvement by the poor.

Kasarda, John D. "The Impact of Suburban Population Growth on Central City Service Functions." AMERICAN JOURNAL OF SOCIOLOGY 77 (May 1972): 1111-24.

This is a study of the relationship between suburban population growth and service functions performed by central cities in 168 metropolitan areas. The analysis indicates that suburban populations have a large impact on central-city retail trade, wholesale trade, business and repair services, and public services provided by central-city governments. Suburban commuters exert a strong affect on police, fire, highway, sanitation, recreation, and general administrative functions of local government. The impact on central-city governments remains strong even when controls for central-city size, annexation, per capita income of central-city residents, and percent of nonwhite central-city population are used.

Kepler, Edwin C. "The Push to Give Municipal Officials Maximum Control Over Human Services." URBAN AND SOCIAL CHANGE REVIEW 9 (Winter 1976): 9-17.

General revenue sharing, according to the author, has failed as an effective way to allocate funds on state and local levels of government. Researchers who monitored revenue-sharing programs indicate that increased public participation and efficient use of funds for Human Service programs have not been met. In addition it is claimed that revenue sharing has increased federal control over state and local funding. Despite these findings, the federal government is expanding revenue-sharing programs. The author suggests a counter movement to reverse these trends before they become fixed.

Lindley, Christopher. "Changing Policy Management Responsibilities of Local Legislative Bodies." PUBLIC ADMINISTRATION REVIEW 35 (December 1975): 794-97.

The guidelines established by federal government programs allocating resources to state and local governments usually have a more important impact on power and administrative arrangements than legal documents such as charters and laws. This essay examines the implications of current changes as they affect the functions of local government and the policy management role of local legislative bodies. One major impact has been to dilute the authority of locally elected officials while enhancing the administrative responsibilities of department heads. However, this also absolved locally elected officials from taking blame for ineffective programs. New Federalism has shifted the responsibility back to local officials in many programs and consequently is making them more accountable to local residents. The federal government should become more aware and concerned about expanding its programs to include local legislative bodies in the definition of policy management needs.

Lugar, Richard G. "UNIGOV: Finding the Boundaries of the Real City." URBAN REVIEW 6 (1973): 32-34.

Urban systems and governments based on the unrealistic political, geographical, and economical boundary lines of most cities are likely to fail. State and federal agencies continue to subsidize and encourage these inefficient and divisive political structures, particularly through the grant-in-aid system. This system is supported both by congressional subcommittees and local government department heads who have become dependent on it. Indianapolis and Marion County have been consolidated into one governmental unit with a mayor and a council. This alternative governmental structure is one way of developing new policies, strengthening the urban system, and encouraging new patterns of communication and cooperation in the complex intergovernmental system.

Marris, Peter, and Rein, Martin. DILEMMAS OF SOCIAL REFORM: POVERTY AND COMMUNITY ACTION IN THE UNITED STATES. 2d ed. Chicago: Aldine, 1973. 309 p.

Examines the origins and development of community action programs from the initial efforts funded by the Ford Foundation through the rise and decline of the poverty and Model Cities programs. The authors believe that large-scale programs are too complex to have anything but minimal success. Some of the obstacles to success are: the conservatism of the bureaucracy, the rivalries among political and administrative jurisdictions, and the apathy of the poor. Some of these obstacles can be overcome through imaginative leadership, greater participation, and more carefully conducted research. An epilogue includes a narrative history of the major community action programs undertaken during the 1960s.

"Municipal Bootstraps: How Cities Could Help Themselves." NATION'S CITIES 10 (February 1972): 9-39.

This report is the result of a roundtable conference sponsored by the National League of Cities, U.S. Conference of Mayors, Council of State Governments, National Governors Conference, ICMA, and the National Association of Counties. Twenty-one major reasons are listed detailing why cities are having difficulty solving their problems. Lack of federal funding is the major reason cited but state governments are criticized for failing to devolve additional power and authority to cities for more self-government and greater flexibility in taxing powers.

Murphy, John C. "General Revenue Sharing's Impact on County Government." PUBLIC ADMINISTRATION REVIEW 35 (March-April 1975): 131-35.

A National Association of Counties survey indicates that general revenue sharing is allowing counties to at least maintain and in some cases increase the level of services they provide, while at the same time offering property tax relief to homeowners. Citing surveys taken by the National Association of Counties, the General Accounting Office, and the House Intergovernmental Relations Subcommittee, the study points out that in the first year a majority of funds went for capital expenditures. Other categories receiving funding allocations were: public safety, health and hospital programs, and social services. Directly and indirectly these funds are also being used to stabilize or reduce property taxes. Counties in general are very favorably disposed to the revenue-sharing program and will work to get the program extended when it expires.

Piven, Frances Fox, and Cloward, Richard A. REGULATING THE POOR: THE FUNCTIONS OF PUBLIC WELFARE. New York: Pantheon, 1971. 389 p.

The authors focus their study on an analysis of the large-scale economic and political forces which underlie the expansion of relief for the poor. The study shows that the welfare explosion occurred during the height of the urban disorders and with the development of grass roots organizations designed to eliminate some of the welfare restrictions. The increase in the welfare rolls also coincided with the enactment of a series of ghetto-placating federal programs such as the War on Poverty. These programs, among other things, provided jobs for thousands of poor people, social workers, and lawyers who encouraged people to apply for relief programs. Once the disorders are ended, the relief systems begin their task of regulating the poor by assisting the ablebodied to take menial and dead-end jobs in order to escape the stigma of welfare.

Pressman, Jeffrey L. FEDERAL PROGRAMS AND CITY POLITICS: THE DYNAMICS OF THE AID PROCESS IN OAKLAND. Berkeley and Los Angeles: University of California Press, 1975. 159 p.

This book is part of the Oakland Project and examines city politics in Oakland, the impact of federal aid programs in the city, the perceptions of federal and local officials, and the aid-giving process as viewed by donors and recipients. The lack of political groups, organized parties, and contested elections are keys to the behavior of local political leaders. Local leadership is weak because there are no strong groups supporting the mayor. Federal aid is seen as external to city hall. Only by developing local programs that are administered through city hall will participation increase and more power be exercised by the mayor. The author suggests that future programs be framed with the intention of increasing the capacity and responsiveness of political institutions.

Rondinelli, Dennis A. "Revenue Sharing and American Cities: Analysis of the Federal Experiment in Local Assistance." JOURNAL OF THE AMERICAN INSTITUTE OF PLANNERS 41 (September 1975): 319-33.

An evaluation of initial revenue-sharing decisions suggests some implications for new policy development. General revenue-sharing payments have been allocated primarily for the operation and maintenance of existing programs, services, and facilities in larger cities and for capital investments in smaller cities. Relatively small amounts of these funds were allocated for social services to low-income, minority or disadvantaged groups. The program serves mainly as a federal income supplement to local taxing powers and as a redistributive device to help local governments expand limited revenue bases. The author suggests redesigning the program to make it an unrestricted grant of federal funds to state and local governments.

Sadacca, Robert; Isler, Morton; and DeWitt, Joan. THE DEVELOPMENT OF A PROTOTYPE EQUATION FOR PUBLIC HOUSING OPERATING EXPENSES. Washington, D.C.: Urban Institute, 1975. 111 p.

HUD now spends about a half-billion dollars in federal subsidies for public housing operating subsidies. This study explains the development of a prototype equation which is an essential component of a performance funding system designed to determine effective management policies in local housing authorities. The prototype is directed to high-performance authorities and discusses the annual inflation factor which helps in updating the allowable expense level of housing authorities receiving operating subsidies.

Scott, Paul, and Macdonald, Robert J. "Local Policy Management Needs: The Federal Response." PUBLIC ADMINISTRATION REVIEW 35 (December 1975): 786-94.

For many years the federal government has assumed that governments are managed by strong mayors or city managers who wield a great deal of power. In practice, local chief executives often resolve conflict and allocate resources, carefully reacting to local pressure. Local governmental powers are limited, fragmented, and often exaggerated. Many federal programs have been enacted which had as their goal improving the capacity of local government to deliver services. However, most of these programs were fragmented and uncoordinated at the federal level and only increased the chaos at the local level. The authors recommend a coordinated federal program with adequate resources to deliver urban programs. The federal program would: require all grant programs to have a fixed percentage allocated to centralized planning and management in local government, provide technical assistance coupled with responsibility to a single federal agency and eliminate duplication of effort, and conduct adequate field tests on interagency delivery structures before implementing programs nationally.

Wright, J. Ward. "Building the Capacities of Municipal Governments." PUBLIC ADMINISTRATION REVIEW 35 (December 1975): 748-54.

> American cities are not governed effectively because of governmental resources and institutions and the process of governance. The policy-making process in local government has remained the same in the past twenty years while the nature and scope of urban problems have changed dramatically. In assessing the policy-management process, the author discusses the steps in the policy-management process, resource management, municipal output, and state-local relationships. He concludes the federal government should reduce the risks involved in trying innovative approaches at the local level by supporting demonstration projects, which if successful could be transferred to other cities. He recommends that this be an ongoing commitment of the federal government.

Wright, James Lee, Jr. "Community Development." MUNICIPAL SOUTH 20 (September 1973): 12-13.

> Changes in federal program administration and guidelines are going to alter the way urban programs are developed and delivered. Cities are going to have to develop new delivery mechanisms if current programs are to continue uninterrupted. The new delivery systems will require flexibility and community acceptance if cities are to continue receiving federal funds. Community development approaches are the feedback mechanisms through which all diverse program activities are integrated, controlled, and directed. Congress and HUD give every indication of requiring community development systems for all new urban programs.

Chapter 9

METROPOLITAN GOVERNANCE:

ORGANIZATION AND SERVICES

Adrian, Charles R. "Governing Megacentropolis: The Politics." PUBLIC AD-MINISTRATION REVIEW 30 (September-October 1970): 497-505.

America's largest cities are more highly politicized than smaller cities because these cities have become centers of political broker-age. This brokerage function is heightened because of the unique relationship that exists between these cities and their state govern-ments. The author discusses problems of representation, councils, access, decentralization, and the role of the mayor. Several sug-gestions are offered for the electoral process, size of city councils, field offices for councilmen, and an ombudsman. The author con-cludes that the neighborhood concept is not likely to be a very effective mechanism in dealing with expensive programs but may encourage the development of a feeling of community.

Aron, Joan B. "Decision Making in Energy Supply at the Metropolitan Level: A Study of the New York Area." PUBLIC ADMINISTRATION REVIEW 35 (July-August 1975): 340-45.

Most new institutional arrangements for decision making in the field of energy have focused on the national level. Little attention has been paid by either scholars or practitioners to the energy decision-making processes at the urban and metropolitan level. Consequently, we have little information about the major actors, their influence, the issues, and the decisions. Using two time periods, the author examines the actors and the issues before and after 1965. In the earlier period Consolidated Edison Company of New York dominated the process because of their discretionary power and the limited number of issues that emerged. In the post-1965 period many new public and private actors became involved in energy policy. New federal legislation, expanding energy facilities, and increased costs have heightened the interest in energy. The policy process has be-come more open and visible, but despite these changes the process remains relatively unchanged with local governments playing a minor and reactive role.

_____. "Regional Governance for the New York Metropolitan Region: A Reappraisal." PUBLIC ADMINISTRATION REVIEW 34 (May-June 1974): 260-64.

The New York metropolitan region has been the subject of numerous scholarly studies exploring the performance of functional services in the area. Recommendations have included new structural mechanisms which are multipurpose, areawide, and representative. More recently a commission study has suggested leaving the existing structure intact and not creating a regional government. The author reviews many of the proposals for a regional government and finds that many of the proposed benefits never materialized in the quality of life, reduced tax rates, more equitable services, and citizen involvement.

Baldinger, Stanley. "Governing the Metropolis." AMERICAN COUNTY 36 (March 1971): 16-23.

Concentrating on the Minneapolis-St. Paul experiment, the author analyzes the concept of the Metropolitan Council as a unique fifteen-member policy- and decision-making body. The original idea and the development of the council are traced, examining the extreme fragmentation of the Twin Cities area. As the ability of local government to deliver municipal services lessened, more people began developing ideas to combat the cause of the problem-- fragmentation of local government. Out of this crisis there was developed a plan for the Metropolitan Council.

Beeler, Park L. "The Merger Urgers of Jacksonville are Winning a Quiet Revolution." URBAN REVIEW 6, nos. 5 and 6 (1973): 57-61.

The governments of Jacksonville and Duval County, Florida were consolidated in 1967. Since then, there has been continued economic, social, cultural, and environmental growth and the property tax rates have decreased for five consecutive years. Law enforcement activities have been centralized and streamlined with a resulting decrease in crime. Transportation programs have been developed and new powers were delegated to the transportation authority to control bridges, tolls, and automobiles, with public transit receiving additional funding. New industry has moved into the area and the education system has shown marked improvement over preconsolidation levels of achievement.

Bernstein, Samuel J.; Mellon, W. Giles; and Handelman, Sigmund. "Regional Stabilization: A Model for Policy Decision." POLICY SCIENCES 4 (September 1973): 309-25.

A model is presented to show different ways of reversing the continuing concentration of poor minorities in the core of central cities. Using the Newark, New Jersey metropolitan area, the authors developed a series of eight equations describing changes in middle- and lower-income classes, white and minority group members, central city and suburban residents and housing, employment, education, migration, and discrimination factors. Data were used to describe the conditions in Newark over the past ten years and then simulations were created for assumptions of no change for the next fifteen years and a large increase in allocated funds to the city. The model can be utilized by local public officials who are willing to authorize collection of necessary data on basic location equations and the effect of increased outlays on residence location-determining indicators.

Bish, Robert L., and Ostrom, Vincent. UNDERSTANDING URBAN GOVERNMENT: METROPOLITAN REFORM RECONSIDERED. Washington, D.C.: American Enterprise Institute for Public Policy Research, 1973. 111 p.

Many academics and practitioners have recommended eliminating fragmentation and duplication in metropolitan areas by substituting a metropolitan government. The authors offer a new approach using a public choice methodology which begins with individuals and examines the nature of public goods and services and how they satisfy individual preferences. People-to-people services, such as police, fire, and education, are analyzed as being sensitive to individual demands and therefore unlikely services for delivery at the metropolitan level. Intergovernmental relations are particularly important because of tax competition, service contracts, fiscal transfers, and coordination. The study concludes with some practical problems to be solved in the future and suggestions for further research.

Bollens, John C. "Overlapping Governments." In GOVERNING URBAN AMERICA IN THE 1970S, edited by Werner Z. Hirsch and Sidney Sonnenblum pp. 85-96. New York: Praeger, 1973.

The growing number of overlapping political jurisdictions created during the era of suburban expansion has resulted in a disparity between service needs and financial resources within political units. This fragmentation has reduced public control and accountability, weakened efforts at coordination, and increased racial and ethnic polarization. Movements for consolidation and federation would increase coordination and responsibility for services and distribute resources more equitably. Opponents fear a loss of local control, access for citizens, and increased taxes. It is likely that major changes in metropolitan area political and administrative structures will have to be brought about by state governments.

Canty, Donald. "Metropolity." CITY 6 (March-April 1972): 29-44.

The author traces the historical development of the current metropolitan pattern which has contributed to the establishment of racial and class boundaries. An urban growth strategy is evaluated including rural development, new towns, federal assumption of welfare costs, and revenue sharing. An areawide elected metropolitan development agency is proposed as a way of increasing housing and employment. Areawide governmental structures such as metropolitan states, city-county consolidations, and federations of existing local governments are discussed.

Caputo, David A., and Cole, Richard L. "Dimension of Elite Opposition to Metropolitan Consolidation." PUBLIUS 2 (Fall 1972): 107-18.

Public officials and civic leaders who opposed the consolidation of Indianapolis and Marion County were interviewed to determine the reasons for their opposition. Previous studies have attributed this opposition to emotionalism or self-interest. General disagreement with the consolidation centered on the emphasis on efficiency as opposed to human needs and the increase in the number of appointed positions. Other reasons for the opposition were fear of higher tax rates, destruction of suburban identity and property values, dilution of black voting strength, lack of information about the proposal, and the lack of a referendum on the issue. Other factors were concern for job security and the threat to party power.

Carver, Joan. "Responsiveness and Consolidation." URBAN AFFAIRS QUARTERLY 9 (December 1973): 211-50.

Acknowledging that city-county consolidation is one of the most drastic reforms taken by local governments in a metropolitan area, the author uses a case study of Jacksonville, Florida to analyze the responsiveness of the new government and which groups it has been responding to. New metropolitan governments which have increased their problem-solving abilities may find it difficult to solve some of the social problems in the area. This results from a lack of understanding of the needs of minority members of the community and is compounded by the fact that these people have a limited involvement in political life.

Cronin, Thomas E. "Metropolity Models and City Hall." JOURNAL OF THE AMERICAN INSTITUTE OF PLANNERS 36 (May 1970): 189-97.

Examines the views of metropolitan area mayors and city councilmen toward governmental reorganization. The views of these officials are thought to be important in determining the structural approach to dealing with metropolitan problems. Several reorganization proposals have been defeated because proponents failed to take into account the views of locally elected city officials. Three alternative models are discussed: localist, regionalist, and intergovernmentalist. Survey data is presented from the San Francisco Bay area where data was collected from over 400 mayors and councilmen in 88 cities. The results indicate that 28 percent of the sample favors the localist model, 13 percent favor the regionalist model, and 19 percent favor the intergovernmentalist approach. The remaining 40 percent support some variation of the intergovernmentalist or regionalist approach.

Downs, Anthony. OPENING UP THE SUBURBS: AN URBAN STRATEGY FOR
AMERICA. New Haven, Conn.: Yale University Press, 1974. 219 p.

> The author examines the question of whether the suburbs can or
> should be opened up to house the poor. By estimating the future
> deterioration of cities if they permit ghettos to grow, Downs argues
> that the suburbs must begin integrating the poor into their communi-
> ties if the rapid decline of the cities is to be arrested. By per-
> mitting small numbers of poor to live in suburban areas, the middle-
> class character of these communities would not be changed markedly.
> On the other hand, diluting urban poverty by spreading it to many
> more communities might make it easier to cope with. At the same
> time, we would be reducing the tension and crisis atmosphere that
> pervades many ghettos today. The same actors who have been re-
> sponsible for the growth and the development of suburban areas are
> ultimately the ones who will have to decide whether or not to open
> these areas to a limited number of poor people.

Erie, Steven P.; Kirlin, John J.; and Rabinovitz, Francine F. "Can Something
Be Done? Propositions on the Performance of Metropolitan Institutions." In
REFORM OF METROPOLITAN GOVERNMENTS, edited by Lowdon Wingo, Jr.,
pp. 7-41. Baltimore: Johns Hopkins University Press, 1972.

> The authors examine the effects of various institutional changes
> that involve cooperation among or consolidation of governmental
> units in metropolitan areas. The structural changes include city-
> county consolidations, federation, special districts, urban counties,
> inter-local agreements, contracting, and councils of governments.
> An analysis of process effects and goals include: efficiency, econ-
> omy, professionalization of decision making, spillovers, externalities,
> and the incorporation of previously excluded groups. The authors
> also examine the costs, distribution, and levels of service and con-
> clude metropolitan reform has changed little primarily because not
> much has been attempted.

Frisken, Frances. "The Metropolis and the Central City: Can One Government
Unite Them?" URBAN AFFAIRS QUARTERLY 8 (June 1973): 395-422.

> Surveys recent proposals to stimulate metropolitanwide policy making.
> Discusses whether metropolitan government is a viable means of re-
> conciling central city priorities and needs with those of outlying
> areas. Earliest metropolitan movements were put forth as a cure
> for local fragmentation and the problems of inefficiency and dupli-
> cation of services. More recently studies have begun to examine
> the political feasibilities of metropolitan proposals. Political feasi-
> bility engenders questions of suspicion and distrust between central
> city and suburban politicians. Proponents have focused on federa-
> tion and cooperation, using a two-tiered system with divided re-
> sponsibilities or the council of governments approach. A case study
> is presented to illustrate the problems involved in cooperative metro-
> politan efforts.

Haefele, Edwin T., and Kneese, Allen V. "Residuals Management and Metropolitan Governance." In METROPOLITANIZATION AND PUBLIC SERVICES, edited by Lowdon Wingo, Jr., pp. 57-69. Baltimore: Johns Hopkins University Press, 1972.

> Residuals management concentrates on the desire and the capacity of local government to effectively deal with the results of our enormous production and consumption activities. Citizens at all levels of government are concerned about residuals but few are worried about our past inability to manage this continuing problem. The authors suggest the most feasible solution depends upon collective action by a regional, general-purpose government. Economies of scale and common property problems help dictate this choice. Left open are questions of the size of the region, the type of executive branch needed, and the authority of the legislative branch elected from single-member, equal-population districts.

Harris, Charles W. "Blacks and Regionalism: Councils of Governments." NATIONAL CIVIC REVIEW 62 (May 1973): 254-58.

> As blacks gain power in all aspects of the political process their position on metropolitan forms of government has changed dramatically. Blacks who have achieved some degree of power in our larger urban areas are apprehensive of those who seek metropolitan and/or regional decision-making arrangements. The Councils of Governments movement is an extension of existing power relationships and black input and influence is likely to be minimal under this mechanism. The author concludes that the difficult social and political problems of the central cities are unlikely to be solved by metropolitan approaches, such as Councils of Governments.

Hawley, Willis D. "On Understanding Metropolitan Political Integration." In THEORETICAL PERSPECTIVES ON URBAN POLITICS, edited by Willis D. Hawley et al., pp. 100-145. Englewood Cliffs, N.J.: Prentice-Hall, 1975.

> Metropolitan reform in this country has a fairly consistent record of failure, while, at the same time, there has been an acceleration in the number and types of interjurisdictional arrangements designed to solve the major problems facing urban areas. The author seeks to identify the variables leading to empirical research which will give us a comprehensive theory of metropolitan political integration. The study focuses on the need for political jurisdictions to engage in collective action, the perceived desire to act collectively, and the difficulties in achieving such action. Metropolitan political integration is defined and four types of integration are outlined. Political administrative, economic, and social factors are related to the possibilities of collective action. State and federal governments could enhance the possibilities for collective action by taking steps to reduce the costs involved.

Kirp, David L., and Cohen, David K. "Education and Metropolitanism." In METROPOLITANIZATION AND PUBLIC SERVICES, edited by Lowdon Wingo, Jr., pp. 29-42. Baltimore: Johns Hopkins University Press, 1972.

The authors examine the major arguments for delivering educational services on a metropolitan level and conclude that consolidation of these services will no longer solve our educational problems. Fiscal disparities between urban and suburban schools are dismissed on the grounds that these disparities are part of the overall fiscal problem confronting metropolitan areas. Consolidation arguments on the grounds of efficiency and integration are countered by the rising demands for neighborhood preservation and community control. The authors recommend a Metropolitan Education Authority that would issue tuition vouchers. This authority would also serve to monitor and evaluate educational quality. This new plan requires the concurrence of existing school districts and a resolution of the problem of state aid to parochial schools.

Kolderie, Ted. "Reconciling Metropolis and Neighborhood: The Twin Cities." NATIONAL CIVIC REVIEW 62 (April 1973): 184-88.

The Twin Cities--Minneapolis-St. Paul--are used as a case study to discuss the two-tier concept of government in a metropolitan area. The upper tier or metropolitan level is a new intermediate level between the state and the local units of government. The upper tier is a policy-making level and examples are given of policies in sewer programs, transit, and the redistribution of low- and moderate-income housing. The lower tier is difficult to define. The role of communities or neighborhood organizations is examined. General observations on both the upper and lower tiers are presented.

Leiken, Lawrence S. "Governmental Schemes for the Metropolis and the Implementation of Metropolitan Change." JOURNAL OF URBAN LAW 49 (May 1972): 667-87.

Examines and evaluates some of the existing institutions of local government and some alternative structures in terms of efficiency in solving urban problems. Emphasis is placed on metropolitan federation. The political obstacles to change from the present structures to alternative forms are discussed in the context of reform struggles using several case studies as examples. A strategy which maximizes the chances for change is presented and legal obstacles to implementation of governmental reform are discussed.

Marando, Vincent L. "An Overview of the Political Feasibility of Local Governmental Reorganization." In ORGANIZING PUBLIC SERVICES IN METROPOLITAN AMERICA, edited by Thomas P. Murphy and Charles R. Warren, pp. 17-51. Lexington, Mass.: Lexington Books, 1974.

Reorganizing local governmental structure is often suggested as one way of solving our urban problems. Yet between 1949 and 1972 voters in affected areas rejected twenty-six out of thirty-six plans to reorganize their local governments. This chapter assesses the factors that were important in deciding reorganization efforts and evaluating those factors that influence voter reactions to reorganization proposals. Also examined are the problems that led to the reform proposal, initiation of the proposal, public awareness of reform, voter turnout, support for reorganization, and the types of campaigns conducted. Some of the major factors discussed are city versus county vote, race, political and administrative realignments, and economic factors. State legislative action is seen as the only way reorganization plans will be successful in large metropolitan areas. A table is presented summarizing the factors related to reorganization support.

———. "The Politics of City-County Consolidation." NATIONAL CIVIC REVIEW 64 (February 1975): 78-84.

City-county consolidations are viewed as one of the major forms of local governmental reorganization. Viewing metropolitan reorganization in political terms, the author suggests that political nonfeasibility is the major problem confronting the proponents' of consolidation today. Reviewing a list of forty-nine consolidation efforts which failed, the author cites several reasons for this tendency, most of which are political. Consolidation efforts appear to be political strategies which benefit only certain groups in the area, particularly those concerned with rising tax rates. Better political organizing is needed if city-county consolidations are to become political realities in metropolitan America.

Marando, Vincent L., and Whitley, Carl. "City-County Consolidation: An Overview of Voter Response." URBAN AFFAIRS QUARTERLY 8 (December 1972): 181-203.

Examines the factors which affect voter reaction to city-county consolidation referenda. Voter approval is almost always a requirement in the process. The League of Women Voters and the Chamber of Commerce often lead the way in establishing a charter commission to draft the consolidation plan. City-county consolidation efforts have not been very successful for a number of reasons. Plans are too abstract and too long in range to capture voter interest. Voters often are not reached by the proponents of the consolidation and the movement is usually not a grass roots effort. Consolidation efforts are often characterized by low voter turnout and opposition of county residents.

Mathewson, Kent. "Governing Megacentropolis: The Leader." PUBLIC ADMINISTRATION REVIEW 30 (September-October 1970): 506-12.

The author states that any discussion of urban leadership must recognize

the mounting pressure for regional governance mechanisms and view
the leadership role in that context. Four alternatives are proposed
for possible leadership in the metropolitan area: central-city mayor,
county chairman, governor, and regional federation chairman.
After evaluating the advantages and disadvantages of each form,
the author concludes that the most promising alternative is to invest
leadership responsibility in an executive from a regional federation.
To make this alternative a political reality, operational powers will
have to be given to the federation and a new electoral mechanism
will have to be implemented.

Moffitt, William, and Schiltz, Timothy. "Inner-City/Outer-City Relationships
in Metropolitan Areas." URBAN AFFAIRS QUARTERLY 7 (September 1971):
75-108.

The authors summarize many recent studies in the fields of political
science, economics, sociology, and law as they relate to the subject of inner-city/outer-city relationships. The article is divided
into four major sections: inner-city/outer-city disparities, governmental fragmentation--causes and effects, responses to governmental
fragmentation, and urban development. Each of the sections is
subdivided to help organize the material. An extensive bibliography is included at the end of the article.

Mogulof, Melvin B. "Federally Encouraged Multijurisdictional Agencies."
URBAN AFFAIRS QUARTERLY 9 (September 1973): 113-32.

All local governments are facing problems which are beyond the
capacities of these governments to solve. The author believes
multijurisdictional agencies might be the solution to some of the
problems metropolitan areas are confronting. These agencies could
be viewed as administrative mechanisms for certain functions which
have been designated as areawide by federal legislation or administrative guidelines. Recent federal legislation and policy guidelines
have encouraged the creation of multicounty agencies in many parts
of the country. We need more clarity in determining where, how,
and why multijurisdictional agencies will fit into the intergovernmental system.

_____. FIVE METROPOLITAN GOVERNMENTS. Washington, D.C.: Urban
Institute, 1972. 145 p.

This is a study of the governance of metropolitan areas, using comparative data drawn from five different forms of metropolitan government. The five governments are: the consolidated government of
Jacksonville, Florida; the urban county in Dade County, Florida;
the federated two-tiered structure in Toronto, Canada; the multi-
function special-purpose district in Portland, Oregon; and the planning and policy unit of the Minneapolis-St. Paul area. The history
of each reorganization effort is traced. An analysis is presented of

the policy-making structure, the financing arrangements, and the allocation of services to different levels. The author also discusses questions of efficiency, effectiveness, conflict-producing issues, the role of dominant cities, the role of blacks, and state and federal government. He concludes that the metropolitan arrangements discussed in this study work at least as well as the existing arrangements and often better.

_____. GOVERNING METROPOLITAN AREAS: A CRITICAL REVIEW OF COUNCILS OF GOVERNMENT AND THE FEDERAL ROLE. Washington, D.C.: Urban Institute, 1971. 127 p.

The council of government movement in this country has expanded rapidly in response to federal requirements for metropolitan clearinghouses so local governments can qualify for federal grants. This study analyzes and evaluates the council activities in trying to comply with federal guidelines set down for them. The authors observed the operations of seven councils over a four-month period by examining their structures, their relationship with other levels of government, and the nature of regional decision making. The author concludes that councils of governments are associations and not governments themselves. Federal pressure should be increased to insure a more critical review of local government grant proposals. The council of government movement may be a step toward two-tier government.

_____. "Metropolitan Councils of Government and the Federal Government." URBAN AFFAIRS QUARTERLY 7 (June 1972): 489-507.

The author begins by asserting that each of the nation's 223 standard metropolitan statistical areas has developed some type of regional council. These are usually councils of governments, economic development districts, or regional planning councils. Mogulof does not view councils of governments as regional governing bodies but rather as clearinghouses which act on regional plans and policies. Councils of governments are intricately linked to new federal policies on regional governance. The article concludes with questions for further study on the structure, the participants, and the decision-making process in councils of governments.

Murphy, Thomas P., and Florestano, Patricia [S.]. "Allocation of Urban Governmental Functions." In ORGANIZING PUBLIC SERVICES IN METROPOLITAN AMERICA, edited by Thomas P. Murphy and Charles R. Warren, pp. 85-105. Lexington, Mass.: Lexington Books, 1974.

Assumptions are stated about the allocation of urban functions in metropolitan areas. The most realistic approach combines features of centralization and decentralization, allowing larger units of government to take advantage of economies of scale while permitting smaller units to exercise local control over local matters. A model for the assignment of functions to different levels might be based

upon the following criteria: the nature of the activity, the scope
of the problem, costs, economies of scale, and the government environment. The authors discuss a study done by the Advisory Commission on Intergovernmental Relations in which they delineate economic and political criteria for the allocation of services. Thirteen
services are reviewed to determine how local governmental reorganizations allocated each of the services.

_____. "The New Criteria." In ORGANIZING PUBLIC SERVICES IN METRO-
POLITAN AMERICA, edited by Thomas P. Murphy and Charles R. Warren,
pp. 191-210. Lexington, Mass.: Lexington Books, 1974.

The complex web of the metropolitan area has made it extremely
difficult to allocate functional responsibility by governmental level.
Efforts in this direction require an analysis of subfunctions by governmental jurisdiction since many levels of government are involved
in providing most functions. Traditional criteria of economy and
efficiency are no longer sufficient to determine how to organize
to meet public needs. The entire governmental structure must be
considered. Allocation decisions are often made on the basis of
tradition, political compromise, or accepted fact. Several functional issues are discussed in terms of these criteria. Major functional areas are broken down into subfunctions and tested against
a set of criteria to determine if the subfunction should be performed
on an areawide or local level. The authors conclude that a two-
tier form of government offers many advantages in meeting the
criteria for service allocation.

_____. "Unimplemented Metropolitan Reorganizations." In ORGANIZING
PUBLIC SERVICES IN METROPOLITAN AMERICA, edited by Thomas P. Murphy
and Charles R. Warren, pp. 71-81. Lexington, Mass.: Lexington Books, 1974.

This chapter examines unsuccessful metropolitan governmental reorganizations, primarily city-county consolidations, two-tier and multipurpose district models. The primary focus is on how the various
reorganization plans allocated public functions among the governments involved. A table is presented depicting a matrix of fifteen
cities that attempted reorganizations and how they allocated responsibility for thirteen different public services. Thirteen American
cities, London and Ontario are discussed. Most of the data presented is taken from the reorganization plans and proposed charters
of the cities studied.

Ostrom, Elinor; Parks, Roger B.; and Whitaker, Gordon P. "Do We Really Want
to Consolidate Urban Police Forces? A Reappraisal of Some Old Assertions."
PUBLIC ADMINISTRATION REVIEW 33 (September-October 1973): 423-32.

This study tests two basic assumptions about the organization and
provision of police services in a metropolitan area. First, it is
necessary to have large police forces in order to specialize and

professionalize. Second, larger agencies are able to provide more efficient services at the same or lower costs than smaller departments. The assumptions were tested in three neighborhoods in Indianapolis and in three adjoining independent communities. Output was measured from results of a survey of citizens in the six neighborhoods. The satisfaction level in the smaller communities was higher than in the large city. The measures used were: responsiveness of police, impressions of the crime rate, perceptions of police-citizen relations, and the overall rating given the police based upon performance. Allocation of police expenditures were also studied. The authors conclude that more research should be done on the division of services being provided between small- and large-scale police organizations.

RESHAPING GOVERNMENT IN METROPOLITAN AREAS. New York: Committee For Economic Development, 1970. 83 p. Paperbound.

The committee report examines the structure of governments in metropolitan areas and the problems facing these governments in crime control, education, transportation, welfare, and environmental protection. The committee finds that the present system is too fragmented to work effectively and smaller local governmental units resist attempts at consolidation. To overcome these problems, the states and the federal government must modify the present tax system and better coordinate the grants-in-aid program. The states must encourage more metropolitan planning units and develop legislation for increasing consolidation and cooperation.

The objective of two-tier government is to centralize certain functions such as education, welfare, planning, and transportation. At the same time, other functions are to be decentralized so that local communities can retain control over activities that directly affect them. Area governments would set general guidelines, leaving the final decisions on implementation to the local communities. The final section of the book is a report on the two-tier system of government in Toronto, Canada, showing how the system functions with particular respect to education, housing, crime control, transportation, and environmental problems.

Ross, Stephen B. "The Metropolitan Impact on Fiscal and Governmental Reforms." URBAN LAWYER 2 (Fall 1970): 495-517.

A sizeable percentage of the U.S. population now lives in standard metropolitan statistical areas. Population increases have created financial, governmental, and service delivery problems which can be solved only by state and federal action. Analyzing the various types of reform proposals--fiscal, governmental, taxing, and consolidation--the author concludes no one policy provides the optimum solution of equitably supporting the local service needs for the metropolitan area as a whole. A mixture of several alternatives appears most likely to succeed.

Shalala, Donna E., and Merget, Astrid E. "Transition Problems and Models."
In ORGANIZING PUBLIC SERVICES IN METROPOLITAN AMERICA, edited by
Thomas P. Murphy and Charles R. Warren, pp. 179-87. Lexington, Mass.:
Lexington Books, 1974.

> Little has been written on the transition period of local government
> reorganization with all of its political and administrative uncertainty.
> The reorganization of London local government highlighted four tran-
> sitional issues that might assist local governments in the United States.
> The four issues are: staffing, ad hoc administrative mechanisms,
> financial assistance, and service standards. Staffing presents a
> problem because traditional functions must be continued while new
> staff arrangements are implemented. Special administrative arrange-
> ments were necessary to effect the changeover in London. In some
> communities, the transition imposes extreme financial burdens and
> special assistance is needed. Reorganization may also affect the
> level of services. Several conclusions are suggested for reformers
> about to initiate reorganization proposals.

Silverman, Jane, and Whitaker, Constance. "Regional Government: Its Problems and Potential in Relation to the Solution of Urban Problems." JOURNAL
OF HOUSING 30 (January 1973): 23-30.

> Starting with a brief history of regional government in America,
> the authors suggest that more and more people see this alternative
> as a way to help solve urban problems. Using three case studies
> in Minneapolis-St. Paul, Washington, D.C., and San Antonio,
> councils of governments are shown to be helpful in both regional
> planning and supplying technical assistance to local governments.
> Housing is one area where councils of governments have been useful
> in allocating subsidized housing on a regional basis. There are both
> proponents and opponents of the regional approach, but the future
> seems to indicate a movement in this direction.

Warren, Charles R. "Developing Alternative Models for Servicing Metropolitan
America." In ORGANIZING PUBLIC SERVICES IN METROPOLITAN AMERICA,
edited by Thomas P. Murphy and Charles R. Warren, pp. 3-14. Lexington,
Mass.: Lexington Books, 1974.

> A system of governance for a metropolitan area should involve con-
> sideration of four main values: equity, economy-efficiency, citizen
> access and control, and legitimacy. Three distinct approaches to
> metropolitan governance are identified--polycentricity, consolidation,
> and federation. Several alternative approaches are also discussed.
> These are: urban counties, multipurpose authorities, metropolitan
> councils, traditional federation, consolidation-decentralization, and
> the two-tier model. Each of these models contains elements of
> centralization and decentralization and, as a result, each espouses
> an idea of how functions, powers, and activities should be distributed
> throughout the newly created metropolitan governmental system.

Weiler, Conrad. "Metropolitan Federation Reconsidered." URBAN AFFAIRS QUARTERLY 6 (June 1971): 411-20.

A short synopsis of the various alternatives to a centralized metropolitan government is offered. The review includes metropolitan federation as well as community-oriented solutions such as those proposed by Milton Kotler and Alan Altshuler. The author believes in a compromise between the proponents of decentralization on the one hand and those favoring centralization on the other. Suggestion is made for a two-fold application of the principle of federation within large cities in the form of neighborhood governments while at the same time establishing a metrofederation throughout the SMSA.

Wilken, William H. "The Impact of Centralization on Access and Equity." In ORGANIZING PUBLIC SERVICES IN METROPOLITAN AMERICA, edited by Thomas P. Murphy and Charles R. Warren, pp. 127-37. Lexington, Mass.: Lexington Books, 1974.

Efficiency and effectiveness of metropolitan government is sought by proponents of centralized service delivery in the metropolitan area. However, many residents in metropolitan areas want local government to be accessible, equitable, and fair. Using numerous case studies as examples, the author analyzes the relationship of centralization and access. The variables discussed are the number of governments, the type of government, the number and selection of officials, the method of official selection, and the access of minority groups. Also discussed is the relationship between centralization and equity. Several limitations of service centralization are presented. The author believes that successful service delivery will only come about with effective regional planning, adequate authority for service delivery units, legitimacy in the eyes of the residents, elimination of fiscal disparities between jurisdictions, and strong executive leadership.

_____. "The Impact of Centralization on Effectiveness, Economy and Efficiency." In ORGANIZING PUBLIC SERVICES IN METROPOLITAN AMERICA, edited by Thomas P. Murphy and Charles R. Warren, pp. 107-25. Lexington, Mass.: Lexington Books, 1974.

Centralization of metropolitan services has been promoted primarily on the grounds that it would increase functional effectiveness, efficiency, and economy. The author examines what impact this centralization has had on the use of personnel, the realization of technical economies, and the satisfaction of public wants. This analysis is conducted for Toronto, Miami, Nashville, Jacksonville, Indianapolis, Minneapolis, and Los Angeles County. The author concludes that centralizing service delivery makes metropolitan government more effective than efficient or economical. These gains appear to be in personnel quality and utilization. Satisfaction of public wants increases and duplication and overlap decrease under a metropolitan service delivery arrangement. However, centralization of services in each case studied resulted in substantial increases in public outlays.

Wofford, John G. "Transportation and Metropolitan Governance." In METRO-POLITANIZATION AND PUBLIC SERVICES, edited by Lowdon Wingo, Jr., pp. 7-27. Baltimore: Johns Hopkins University Press, 1972.

Transportation facilities are essential physical structures in the metropolis. Therefore, transportation problems are part of the metropolitan governance problem. Four major aspects of metropolitan transportation are discussed. First is the importance of transportation in defining the scope of the area. Second are the major problems encountered. Third are alternatives to changing governmental structure that could help solve some of the problems. And fourth are some of the changes necessary to help solve these problems. Recommendations include a strong secretary of transportation to promote efficiency and participatory planning with questions of equity being resolved by the governor. Increased citizen and local government participation, independent hearings, and greater accountability resting with the governor are suggested as ways of legitimatizing the process.

Zimmerman, Joseph F. "Metropolitan Reform in the U.S.: An Overview." PUBLIC ADMINISTRATION REVIEW 30 (September-October 1970): 531-43.

Fragmented local governments in a metropolitan area have not moved toward consolidation because of political inertia, strong citizen opposition to reorganization, and the failure of federal and state governments to promote reorganizations. The author reviews the history of consolidation in the country and discusses the factors which are common to each area or to each reorganization. The factors examined are the number of political units in the area, degree of competition in the political system, racial overtones, and the degree of consolidation attempted. Failure to move towards consolidation will produce alternative arrangements such as authorities, interstate compacts, and more direct state and federal intervention.

Appendix A
URBAN PUBLIC INTEREST AND
PROFESSIONAL ASSOCIATIONS

Urban managers often belong to professional associations or organizations which provide them with services and occasionally present their members' views before city, state, and federal legislative and administrative bodies. The majority of these organizations represent functional specialists in the public sector although some of them represent political jurisdictions as well as individuals. Interested persons seeking additional information--membership, activities, publications, or officers--about a specific association concerned with urban management should contact the association directly.

American Institute of Planners
1776 Massachusetts Avenue, N.W.
Washington, D.C. 20036

American Public Health Association
1015 18th Street, N.W., 7th Floor
Washington, D.C. 20036

American Public Transit Association
1100 17th Street, N.W.
Washington, D.C. 20036

American Public Welfare Association
1155 16th Street, N.W., Suite 201
Washington, D.C. 20036

American Public Works Association
1313 East 60th Street
Chicago, Ill. 60637

   Washington Office
   1776 Massachusetts Avenue
   Washington, D.C. 20036

American Society for Public Administration
1225 Connecticut Avenue, N.W.,
Room 300
Washington, D.C. 20036

American Society of Planning Officials
1313 East 60th Street
Chicago, Ill. 60637

Council for International Urban Liaison
1612 K Street, N.W., Room 904
Washington, D.C. 20036

Council of State Community Affairs
   Agencies
1612 K Street, N.W., Room 906
Washington, D.C. 20006

Council of State Governments
Iron Works Pike, P.O. Box 11910
Lexington, Ky. 40511

   Washington Office
   444 North Capitol Street
   2nd Floor
   Washington, D.C. 20001

223

International Association of Chiefs
of Police
11 Firstfield Road
Gaithersburg, Md.   20760

International Association of Fire Chiefs
1329 18th Street, N.W.
Washington, D.C.   20036

International City Management
Association
1140 Connecticut Avenue
Washington, D.C.   20036

International Personnel Management
Association
1313 East 60th Street
Chicago, Ill.   60637

Washington Office
1776 Massachusetts Avenue
Washington, D.C.   20036

Labor-Management Relations
Service of Conference of Mayors
1620 Eye Street, N.W., Room 616
Washington, D.C.   20036

Municipal Finance Officers
Association of U.S. and Canada
180 North Michigan Avenue
Chicago, Ill.   60601

Washington Office
1730 Rhode Island Avenue
Suite 512
Washington, D.C.   20036

National Academy of Public
Administration
1225 Connecticut Avenue, Room 300
Washington, D.C.   20036

National Association for Community
Development
1424 16th Street, N.W.
Washington, D.C.   20036

National Association of Counties
1735 New York Avenue, N.W.
Washington, D.C.   20036

National Association of Housing and
Redevelopment Officials
2600 Virginia Avenue, N.W.,
Room 404
Washington, D.C.   20037

National Association of Regional
Councils
1700 K Street, N.W., Room 1306
Washington, D.C.   20036

The National Civil Service League
917 15th Street, N.W.
Washington, D.C.   20005

National Conference of State
Legislatures
1405 Curtis Street
Denver, Colo.   80202

Washington Office
444 North Capitol Street, N.W.
Washington, D.C.   20001

National Governors' Association
444 North Capitol Street, 2d Floor
Washington, D.C.   20001

National League of Cities
1620 Eye Street, N.W., 4th Floor
Washington, D.C.   20006

National Municipal League
47 East 68th Street
New York, N.Y.   10021

National Recreation and Park Association
1601 North Kent Street
Arlington, Va.   22209

National Training and Development Service
for State and Local Government
5028 Wisconsin Avenue, N.W.
Washington, D.C.   20016

Public Administration Service
1313 East 60th Street
Chicago, Ill. 60637

   Washington Office
   1776 Massachusetts Avenue, N.W.
   Washington, D.C. 20036

Public Technology, Inc.
1140 Connecticut Avenue
Washington, D.C. 20036

United States Conference of Mayors
1620 Eye Street, N.W.
Washington, D.C. 20006

Appendix B

PERIODICALS WITH CONTENT RELEVANT
TO URBAN MANAGEMENT

There are many academic and professional periodicals publishing materials on urban management. The most significant and readily accessible are listed below. The best guides for ascertaining the contents of these journals are the Public Affairs Information Service, the Social Service Index, and Urban Affairs Abstracts.

ADMINISTRATION AND SOCIETY. Beverly Hills, Calif.: Sage Publications, 1969-- . Quarterly. (Formerly JOURNAL OF COMPARATIVE ADMINISTRA-TION.).

ADMINISTRATIVE SCIENCE QUARTERLY. Ithaca, N.Y.: Cornell University, 1956-- .

AMERICAN BEHAVIORAL SCIENTIST. Beverly Hills, Calif.: Sage Publications, 1957-- . Bimonthly.

AMERICAN JOURNAL OF POLITICAL SCIENCE. Detroit: Wayne State University Press, 1957-- . Quarterly.

AMERICAN JOURNAL OF PUBLIC HEALTH. Washington, D.C.: American Public Health Association, 1911-- . Monthly.

AMERICAN JOURNAL OF SOCIOLOGY. Chicago: University of Chicago Press, 1895-- . Bimonthly.

AMERICAN POLITICAL SCIENCE REVIEW. Menasha, Wis.: George Banta Co., 1906-- . Quarterly.

AMERICAN POLITICS QUARTERLY. Beverly Hills, Calif.: Sage Publications, 1973-- .

AMERICAN SOCIOLOGICAL REVIEW. Menasha, Wis.: American Sociological Association, 1936-- . Bimonthly.

ANNALS. Philadelphia: American Academy of Political and Social Science, 1890-- . Annually.

BUREAUCRAT. Beverly Hills, Calif.: Sage Publications, 1972-- . Quarterly.

CALIFORNIA MANAGEMENT REVIEW. Berkeley and Los Angeles: University of California, 1958-- . Quarterly.

CANADIAN PUBLIC ADMINISTRATION. Toronto: Institute of Public Administration of Canada, 1958-- . Quarterly.

COMMUNITY DEVELOPMENT JOURNAL. London: Oxford University Press, 1966-- . 3/year.

DAEDALUS.. Boston: American Academy of Arts and Sciences, 1958-- . Quarterly.

GOVERNMENTAL FINANCE. Chicago: Municipal Finance Officers Association, 1926-- . Quarterly. (Formerly MUNICIPAL FINANCE).

HARVARD BUSINESS REVIEW. Boston: Harvard University, 1922-- . Bimonthly.

HUMAN ORGANIZATION. Boulder: University of Colorado, Institute of Behavioral Science, 1941-- . Quarterly.

HUMAN RESOURCE MANAGEMENT. Ann Arbor: University of Michigan, 1961-- . Quarterly.

JOURNAL OF APPLIED BEHAVIORAL SCIENCE. Arlington, Va.: NTL Institute for Applied Behavioral Science, 1965-- . Quarterly.

JOURNAL OF BLACK STUDIES. Beverly Hills, Calif.: Sage Publications, 1970-- . Quarterly.

JOURNAL OF HOUSING. Washington, D.C.: National Association of Housing and Redevelopment Officials, 1944-- . Monthly.

JOURNAL OF POLICE SCIENCE AND ADMINISTRATION. Gaithersburg, Md.: International Association of Chiefs of Police, 1973-- . Quarterly.

JOURNAL OF POLITICAL ECONOMY. Chicago: University of Chicago Press, 1892-- . Bimonthly.

JOURNAL OF POLITICS. Gainesville, Fla.: Southern Political Science Association, 1939-- . Quarterly.

JOURNAL OF SOCIAL POLICY. New York: Social Administration Association, 1972-- . Quarterly.

JOURNAL OF THE AMERICAN INSTITUTE OF PLANNERS. Washington, D.C.: American Institute of Planners, 1935-- . Quarterly.

JOURNAL OF URBAN LAW. Detroit: University of Detroit, 1916-- . 5/year.

LAW AND SOCIETY REVIEW. Denver: Law and Society Association, 1966-- . Quarterly.

MANAGEMENT INFORMATION SERVICE REPORTS. Washington, D.C.: International City Management Association, 1946-- . Monthly.

MANAGEMENT SCIENCE. Providence, R.I.: Institute of Management Sciences, 1954-- . Monthly.

MEDICAL CARE. Philadelphia: American Public Health Association, 1967-- . Monthly.

MIDWEST REVIEW OF PUBLIC ADMINISTRATION. Parkville, Mo.: Park College, 1967-- . Quarterly.

MODERN GOVERNMENT AND NATIONAL DEVELOPMENT. Stamford, Conn.: Intercontinental Publications, 1960-- . 9/year.

NATIONAL CIVIC REVIEW. New York: National Municipal League, 1911-- . Monthly.

NATION'S CITIES. Washington, D.C.: National League of Cities, 1963-- . Monthly.

ORGANIZATIONAL DYNAMICS. New York: American Management Association, 1973-- . Quarterly.

PERSONNEL. New York: American Management Association, 1919-- . Bimonthly.

PERSONNEL ADMINISTRATION AND PUBLIC PERSONNEL REVIEW. Washington, D.C.: Society for Personnel Administration, 1972-- . Bimonthly.

THE POLICE CHIEF. Gaithersburg, Md.: International Association of Chiefs of Police, 1933-- . Monthly.

POLICY AND POLITICS. London: Sage Publications, 1972-- . Quarterly.

POLICY SCIENCES. New York: American Elsevier, 1970-- . Quarterly.

POLICY STUDIES JOURNAL. Urbana: University of Illinois, 1972-- . Quarterly.

POLITICAL SCIENCE QUARTERLY. New York: Academy of Political Science, Columbia University, 1886-- .

POLITY. Amherst: University of Massachusetts, 1968--. Quarterly.

PSYCHOLOGICAL BULLETIN. Washington, D.C.: American Psychological Association, 1904-- . Bimonthly.

PUBLIC ADMINISTRATION REVIEW. Washington, D.C.: American Society for Public Administration, 1940-- . Bimonthly.

PUBLIC FINANCE QUARTERLY. Beverly Hills, Calif.: Sage Publications, 1973-- .

THE PUBLIC INTEREST. New York: National Affairs, 1965-- . Quarterly.

PUBLIC MANAGEMENT. Washington, D.C.: International City Management Association, 1919-- . Monthly.

PUBLIC PERSONNEL MANAGEMENT. Chicago: International Personnel Management Association, 1940-- . Quarterly. (Formerly PUBLIC PERSONNEL REVIEW).

PUBLIC POLICY. Cambridge, Mass.: Harvard University Press, 1975-- . Quarterly.

PUBLIC WELFARE. Washington, D.C.: American Public Welfare Association, 1943-- . Quarterly.

PUBLIUS. Philadelphia: Center for the Study of Federalism, Temple University, 1971-- . Quarterly.

SOCIAL POLICY. New York: Social Policy Corporation, 1970-- . Bimonthly.

SOCIAL PROBLEMS. Notre Dame, Ind.: Society for the Study of Social Problems, 1953-- . 5/year.

SOCIAL SCIENCE QUARTERLY. Austin: Southwestern Social Science Quarterly, University of Texas, 1920-- . Quarterly.

SOCIAL SERVICE REVIEW. Chicago: University of Chicago Press, 1927-- . Quarterly.

SOCIAL WORK. New York: National Association of Social Workers, 1956-- . Bimonthly.

SOCIETY. New Brunswick, N.J.: Rutgers University, 1963-- . Monthly.

SOCIOLOGICAL INQUIRY. Toronto: Alpha Kappa Delta, 1930-- . Quarterly.

STUDIES IN COMPARATIVE LOCAL GOVERNMENT. The Hague, Netherlands: International Union of Local Authorities, 1967-- . Semiannual.

URBAN AFFAIRS QUARTERLY. Beverly Hills, Calif.: Sage Publications, 1965-- .

URBAN AND SOCIAL CHANGE REVIEW. Chestnut Hill, Mass.: Boston College, 1967-- . Semiannual.

URBAN DATA SERVICE REPORT. Washington, D.C.: International City Management Association, 1969-- . Monthly.

URBAN EDUCATION. Beverly Hills, Calif.: Sage Publications, 1966-- . Quarterly.

WESTERN POLITICAL QUARTERLY. Salt Lake City: Institute of Government, University of Utah, 1948-- .

Appendix C
BIBLIOGRAPHIES

The bibliographies listed below are a source of additional information in the field of urban management.

Bryfogle, Charles. CITIES IN PRINT. Tucson, Ariz.: Dawson and Company, 1975. 367 p.

Hoover, Dwight W. CITIES. New York: R.R. Bowker, 1976. 231 p.

Ross, Bernard H., and Fritschler, A. Lee. URBAN AFFAIRS BIBLIOGRAPHY: AN ANNOTATED GUIDE TO THE LITERATURE IN THE FIELD. Washington, D.C.: College of Public Affairs, American University, 1974. 85 p.

The most comprehensive list of bibliographies in print, on a variety of urban topics, is published by the Council of Planning Librarians. A complete listing of their publications can be obtained by writing to Post Office Box 229, Monticello, Illinois 61856.

Several of their bibliographies relevant to urban management are cited below.

"The Administration of Criminal Justice: An Exploratory Bibliography," by Lenwood G. Davis. 1975. 35 p.

"A Bibliography for a Program for Continuous Renewal of Our Cities and Metropolitan Regions: A Design for Improved Management, Decision-Making and Action," by Frank W. Osgood. 1971. 42 p.

"A Bibliography on Public Budgeting for State and Local Administrators," compiled by Blue Wooldridge with the assistance of Robert Murphy and Maureen Wilson. 1974. 26 p.

"Big-City Mayors Speak Out: A Selected Bibliography," by Anthony G. White. 1974. 7 p.

Bibliographies

"Citizen Participation: A Review of the Literature," by Judith V. May. 1971. 82 p.

"Citizen Participation in Mental Health: A Bibliography," by William R. Meyers and Robert A. Dorwart. 1974. 15 p.

"Citizen Participation in Planning: Selected Interdisciplinary Bibliography," by David E. Booher. 1975. 20 p.

"Citizen Participation in Urban and Regional Planning: A Comprehensive Bibliography," by John David Hulchanski. 1977. 61 p.

"Community Action Programs, An Annotated Bibliography," by Ruth E. Brown. 1972. 37 p.

"Community Development Corporations: An Annotated Bibliography," 4th ed., by Florence Contant. 1974. 42 p.

"Community Mental Health Centers: Planning, Systems Analysis, and Program Evaluation," by Morris E. Davis. 1973. 11 p.

"Consumer Participation in Comprehensive Health Planning," by William Boothe, Mary Alice Beetham, and Marvin Strauss. 1969. 7 p.

"Councils of Government," by Cynthia Stoots. 1968. 6 p.

"Councils of Governments in the 1970's: A Selective Annotated Bibliography," by Susan G. Weintraub. 1976. 19 p.

"Decentralization in Urban Government: An Annotated Bibliography," by Xenia W. Duisin. 1972. 24 p.

"Decentralization in Urban Government: An Annotated Bibliography with Special Reference to New York City (Revised)," by Xenia W. Duisin. 1975. 48 p.

"Ethics in Local Government: A Selected Bibliography," by Anthony G. White. 1977. 8 p.

"Fiscal Management and Planning for Local Governments: A Selected Bibliography of Recent Materials," by Nan C. Burg. 1973. 30 p.

"Guide to the Literature of Cities: Abstracts and Bibliography, Part VIII: Urban Government," by Morris Zeitlin. 1972. 20 p.

"Information Sources for Local Governmental Officials and Administrators: Selected Periodicals and Reference Material," by Don Levitan. 1974. 20 p.

"Local Government: Form and Reform, A Selected Bibliography," by Nan C. Burg. 1974. 71 p.

"Local Public Service Site Selection: A Bibliography," by Anthony G. White. 1975. 6 p.

"Management by Objectives and Goal Setting," by Gerald L. Musgrave and Richard S. Elster. 1974. 39 p.

"Management Information Systems," by Barbara Witt. 1974. 11 p.

"Management Information Systems, 1972-1975," by Patricia Bieber, Charles Townley, and Glenn R. Wittig. 1976. 43 p.

"Metropolitan Organization for Planning," by Cynthia F. Stoots. 1968. 5 p.

"Municipal Public Relations: A Selected Bibliography, 1960-1974," by Anthony G. White. 1977. 8 p.

"Neighborhoods and Neighborhood Planning, Selected Bibliography," by Donald F. Mazziotti. 1974. 20 p.

"Operations Management in Health Care Institutions--A Working Bibliography," by Carl W. Nelson. 1975. 23 p.

"Optimum City-Size and Municipal Efficiency: A Revised Version of Exchange Bibliography No. 52," by William A. Howard and James B. Kracht. 1971. 8 p.

"Participation in Decision-Making: A Selected Bibliography," by Milo C. Pierce. 1972. 15 p.

"PERT Program Evaluation and Review Technique, 1962-1974, An Annotated Bibliography," compiled by Dana Collier Rooks. 1976. 42 p.

"Planning--Programming--Budgeting Systems (A Supplement to Exchange Bibliography #121 of March 1970)," by Dean Tudor. 1971. 5 p.

"Planning--Programming--Budgeting Systems (PPBS): A Selective Bibliography, Supplement to CPL Exchange Bibliography #289, 1972," by Eric L. Swanick. 1975. 16 p.

"Political Structure, Urban Spatial Organization and the Delivery of Municipal Services," by J. Ross Barnett. 1973. 81 p.

"Public Participation in Environmental Decision-Making," by Dianne Draper. 1973. 28 p.

"Public Participation in Environmental Policy: An Annotated Bibliography," by Joseph Chisholm. 1976. 17 p.

"Readings in Municipal Finance for Local Government Officials, A Selected, Non-Technical Bibliography," by Nan C. Burg. 1976. 26 p.

"A Selected Bibliography for the Training of Citizen-Agents of Planned Community Change (revised edition of CPL Exchange Bibliography #125 of April 1970)," by Charles K. Bolton and Kenneth E. Corey. 1971. 31 p.

"A Selected Bibliography of Readings in Management Theory and Practice," by Milton M. Pressley. 1974. 38 p.

"State and Local Government Finance: A Selectively Annotated Bibliography," by James Jay Brown. 1975. 55 p.

"Towards a Scientific Study of Information and Communication Theory Relative to Groups and Organizations: A Bibliographic Essay," by Anthony G. White. 1974. 17 p.

"Urban Property Taxation: I--Administrative Aspects," by Anthony G. White. 1973. 13 p.

AUTHOR INDEX

This index includes all authors, editors, and other contributors to works cited in this text. It is alphabetized letter by letter.

Author Index

Bloch, Peter B. 63, 121, 179
Boettcher, Richard E. 160
Bollens, John C. 53, 209
Boone, Richard W. 132
Bordua, David J. 172
Bosselman, Fred B. 131
Botein, Bernard 25
Boyce, David E. 63
Boynton, Robert Paul 48, 54
Bradbury, Katharine 193
Brager, George 146
Bresnick, David 113
Brewer, Garry D. 26, 72
Bridgeland, William M. 147
Brieland, Donald 147
Brody, Stanley J. 132
Brooks, Wendy Goepel 132
Brouillette, John R. 13, 180
Brown, David S. 26
Brown, F. Gerald 1, 93
Browne, Edmond, Jr. 195
Bryce, Herrington J. 196
Buchannan, Bruce 26
Burby, Raymond J. 161
Burgess, Philip M. 196
Burke, Edmund M. 133
Burkhead, Jesse 112
Bushey, Harold T. 107

C

Cahn, Edgar S. 133
Cahn, Jean Camper 133
Campbell, John P. 13
Cantine, Robert R. 27, 45
Canty, Donald 209
Capoccia, Victor A. 197
Caputo, David A. 64, 197, 210
Caro, Robert A. 27
Carrell, Jeptha J. 54
Carroll, James D. 2
Carroll, Michael A. 198
Carter, Genevieve W. 64
Carter, Steven C. 49
Carvalho, Gerard F. 85
Carver, Joan 210
Cary, Lee J. 134
Catanese, Anthony James 72
Cervantes, Robert A. 180
Chakerian, Richard 172

Charles, Henry T. 55
Charney, Evan 183
Chetkow, B. Harold 86
Chitwood, Stephen R. 14, 107
Churchman, C. West 73
Clawson, Calvin 180
Cloward, Richard A. 203
Cohen, David K. 213
Cohen, Henry 27, 28
Cole, Richard C. 134, 210
Coleman, Charles 2
Coleman, Charles J. 94
Colman, William G. 198
Cookingham, L.P. 55
Costello, Timothy W. 28
Costikyan, Edward N. 121
Costner, Herbert L. 149
Crabtree, James S. 99
Crecine, John P. 73
Cronin, Thomas E. 210
Culbert, Samuel A. 14
Cummings, L.L. 103
Cunningham, James V. 48, 134
Cunningham, Luvern 28
Curry, Martha 140

D

David, Miriam E. 189
Davis, James V. 181
Davy, Thomas J. 73
De Ladurantey, Joseph C. 108
Del Guidice, Dominic 198
Derr, C. Brooklyn 29
Dewitt, Joan 204
Diamond, Ted 48
Diebold, John 74
Dinunzio, Michael 94
Dirasian, Henry A. 181
Doig, Jameson W. 29
Donabedian, Avedis 29
Dougan, William R. 191
Downs, Anthony 74, 211
Drucker, Meyer 29
Drucker, Peter F. 2, 86
Drury, Margaret 184
Dueker, Kenneth J. 75
Duel, Henry J. 75
Duhl, Leonard J. 182
Dunn, Diana R. 66

Author Index

Author Index

Author Index

TITLE INDEX

This index includes all titles of books which are cited in the text. Titles of articles, enclosed in quotation marks, are also included. This index is alphabetized letter by letter.

Title Index

Title Index

Title Index

SUBJECT INDEX

This index is alphabetized letter by letter.   Underlined page numbers refer to main areas within the subject.

Subject Index

Subject Index

Highways. See Streets and highways

Holyoke, Mass., neighborhood team policing in 121

Hospitals 40
disaster planning by 186
finance of 193
revenue sharing in 203
management of 3
potentials of 181
rates of innovation in 42
See also Medical and health services

Housing 55, 210
attitudes of blacks toward 163
case method approach to the study of 90
citizen concern with 148
effect of land development on 69
failure to solve problems of 26
federal government and 50, 177, 198, 200
formulation of policy for 31-32
in government reorganization and consolidation 218, 219
management of multi-family 184
models of 193, 209
need for statistics concerning 81
neighborhood boards and 131
patterns of in New York City 41
for the poor in the suburbs 211
racism and 25
redistribution of low- and moderate-income 213
rising cost of 4
systems and organizational analysis in policy setting for 90
See also Fair housing programs; Public housing

Houston, decentralization programs in 129

Hueristic programming 72

Humanism in management 3, 8, 9, 14, 19-20

Human resources. See Resources, human

I

Illinois, citizen mobilization in 147. See also Aurora, Ill.

Immigration 148
in solving urban problems 24

Incentive systems 93, 108, 111, 112
organizational development and 17
in police work 174
See also Motivation

Income
impact on local government 4
need for statistics concerning 81
public service activity and 160
social change and 44

Income maintenance plans 44

Indianapolis, Ind.
decentralization programs in 128
Model Cities Program in 152
neighborhood government in 157
police in 185-86, 218
politics and government in 202, 210
service delivery systems in 85, 220

Industrial humanism. See Humanism in management

Industry. See Business and industry

Inflation
hostility of local government of 196
public housing subsidies and 204

Information systems 71-85, 91
bibliography 235, 236
of labor markets 79
need to improve municipal 30
public administrators need for 27

Inner-city areas. See Central city areas

Innovation 93
administrative control and rates of 19, 42
federal government and 201, 205
need to develop a climate of 84
in productivity programs 110
in public service bureaucracies 174

Institutions 2
comparative studies of 42
failure of 148
need to create new 13
oppressive features of 126
racism of 25
in solving urban problems 35

270

Subject Index

Subject Index

Migration
  influence of urban environment on 4
  models of 7, 209
  as an urban problem 27
Mill, John Stuart 10
Milwaukee 173
  concept of community in 148
  intergovernmental relations in 198
  politics and government in 43
  public finance in 189
Minimum wage, in solving urban problems 24
Minneapolis, Minn.
  politics and government in 208, 213, 215, 219
  service delivery systems in 220
Minority groups
  bureaucratic response to 99, 123, 125
  citizen participation of 138, 139
  city manager government and 59
  civil service system and 116
  concentration of in central city areas 208-9
  decentralization programs and 116, 117
  employment of 32, 95, 97, 99
  government reorganization and 210, 220
  influence on machine politics 52
  intergovernmental relations and 196
  job training programs for 51
  neighborhood government and 158
  police and 102
  politics of 23
  service delivery systems and 163
  See also Blacks; Ethnic groups; Mexican-Americans
Model Cities Act (1966) 154
Model Cities Program 44, 64, 115, 116, 128, 131, 135, 136-37, 139, 142-43, 144, 152, 169, 171, 174, 176, 199-200, 200-201, 202
Models and modeling 8, 72, 75, 78
  in agency-client relations 5, 21, 178
  in communications 89-90
  in decision-making 12, 73

in disaster response 13
in government function allocation 216-17
in government reorganization and consolidation 217, 219
in health care 29, 181, 185, 187
in human resource development 18
in labor-management relations 18
in land use planning 73
in mayoral behavior 49
in municipal governance 9, 33-34, 210
in organizational behavior and development 12, 15-16, 22
in organizational responsibility 5
in participatory management 38
in personnel management 94
in police administration 79
in population migration 7, 209
in public finance 193-94
in public policy formation and evaluation 33-34, 64
in public welfare delivery 70
in racial conflict 50
in residential location 208-9
in service delivery 161, 162, 163, 164, 166
in social change 7, 44
in urban decentralization 119, 126-27, 128
in urban growth 73
in urban management quality 5
in urban planning 91
in urban renewal 26
See also Computers in management; Simulation methods; Systems theory and analysis
Monopolies, management of 3
Moonlighting 97
Moses, Robert 27
Motivation
  in civil service systems 98
  as an element of management 23, 45, 77, 96, 111, 112
  in nonbureaucratic organizations 6
  See also Incentive systems
Municipal government 27, 30, 32-33, 35, 37, 38, 40, 43, 207-21

Subject Index

Public health departments
  decentralization in 119-20
  power and control in 19
  See also Medical and health
    services
Public housing 179
  citizen participation in programs
    of 132, 139
  evaluation of management of 69
  operating subsidies in 204
  service delivery systems in 160
Public interest theory
  bureaucracy and 3
  management styles and 5
Public investment. See investment,
    public
Public officials 33
  accountability of local 202
  blacks as 39
  citizen attitudes toward 167-68
  decision-making by 26
  leadership of 42-43
  need to communicate with the
    ghetto 54
  protest politics and 146
  role of in policy formation 30
  in solving urban problems 91
  technological education of 84
  urban renewal and 187
  See also City managers; Mayors;
    Politics
Public opinion 85
Public planning 5, 27, 39-40, 48
  bibliography 234, 235
  citizen participation in 38, 131,
    136, 142, 221
  of city services 25
  effect of revenue sharing on 198
  as an element of management 23
  in government reorganization and
    consolidation 218
  as an indicator of bureaucratization
    24
  information systems in 81, 84
  as a means of controlling
    bureaucracies 169
  models of 91
  need for increased municipal 30
  need for in federal programs 204
  neighborhood government and 155,
    158

systems management in 90
  of transportation services 140, 221
  See also Decision-making; Goals
Public policy 25, 35, 43, 48, 56,
    205, 216
  analysis of 185
  bureaucrats in the formation of
    30-31
  citizen involvement in 64, 68,
    119, 124, 125, 131, 140,
    142, 144
  city managers and 55, 57-58, 61
  in education 124, 182-83
  in energy supply 207
  evaluation of 64, 67, 196
  in health care 136
  in housing 31-32
  influence of blacks on 39
  information systems in formation of
    81, 85
  mayors and 50-51
  models of formation of 33-34
  neighborhood government and 154,
    155
  school superintendents and 37
  urban indicators in formation of
    63-64
Public relations
  bibliography 235
  in municipal government 51, 85
Public safety 2, 188
  decentralization in 130
  effect of revenue sharing on 203
  See also Fire departments; Police
Public schools. See Education;
    Schools
Public welfare programs 42, 50,
    170, 174-76
  accountability and evaluation of
    45, 64, 70
  administration of 44
  budgeting and finance in 191
  case method approach to the study
    of 90
  decentralization of 124-25
  federal assumption of 209
  forces behind expansion of 203
  in government reorganization and
    consolidation 218
  paraprofessionals in 94-95

Subject Index